Management for Professionals

For further volumes:
http://www.springer.com/series/10101

Roger Gutbrod • Christian Wiele

The Software Dilemma

Balancing Creativity and Control
on the Path to Sustainable Software

 Springer

Dr. Roger Gutbrod
Sandhausen
Germany

Dr. Christian Wiele
Eppingen
Germany

ISSN 2192-8096   e-ISSN 2192-810X
ISBN 978-3-642-27235-6   e-ISBN 978-3-642-27236-3
DOI 10.1007/978-3-642-27236-3
Springer Heidelberg New York Dordrecht London

Library of Congress Control Number: 2012933774

Printed on acid-free paper

Springer is part of Springer Science+Business Media (www.springer.com)

To
my wife Vera
and my parents Lydia and Karl-Adam

To
Inga,
Lasse, Rasmus, and Kjell,
and
my parents

Foreword

By

Manfred Wolf, Senior Vice President, Head of Global Internal Audit
   Services (GIAS), SAP AG

Corporations today are increasingly focusing on what the concept of Corporate
Governance means for their operations and structures. The impact is felt throughout
the entire organization. This is true for all branches of industry, in particular for
modern sectors such as the software industry and other innovative high-tech fields,
including biochemistry, biotechnology, and energy research.

As a result, corporations have to be assessed and managed increasingly in terms
of risk, in order to ensure the Executive and Supervisory Boards' accountability to
their employees and third parties, incl. customers, business partners, public
authorities, markets, banks and other financial institutions, and to comply with
internal and external regulatory reporting requirements.

In practical terms, this means that compliance with corporate rules and
regulations is increasingly prevalent in each employee's daily work and is no longer
restricted to a few individuals. Consequently, all employees in the corporation are
obliged to act in accordance with the rules and regulations which constitute
Corporate Governance. The individual employee's obligation to adhere to the
documented corporate principles and guidelines applies to all lines of business in
the corporation. Needless to say, it is also relevant for all those creative and
innovative divisions, which (due to the very nature of their roles) have a strong
inclination towards individuality and autonomy. Here, it is important to ensure that
the principles and guidelines, embodied in the corporate value system, are not seen
as a restriction on the individual, but more as a frame of reference that must be
clearly defined for employees, so that the impact on everyday work is clear.
Appropriate communication and training must also take place. A control and
monitoring function ensures that this framework is implemented in practice. This
general "supervisory" obligation is put into action using a range of approaches,
including different audit objects (product/process) and various monitoring methods,

such as specific process controls or a cyclical audit engagement by the audit department.

In order to secure business success, the common goal of all audit activities must be to allow all employee and management levels to contribute freely and creatively to the value chain, while always operating within the prevailing Corporate Governance terms of reference.

The "Software Dilemma" looks at the resulting conflicting priorities facing an audit function, namely striking an appropriate balance between individualism and creativity on the one hand, and Corporate Governance compliance on the other. This work impressively illustrates this dilemma as concepts and tools for efficiency and effectiveness are presented:

As a background to the topic, Chap. 2 summarizes the challenges in software development and creates a general understanding of governance by citing specific examples from the business world which apply equally to the software industry. In Chap. 3, the authors outline the relevance of the topic for the three roles (CIO/CTO, software architect and auditor) and their common interests.

Chapter 4 concentrates on the toolset required for software audits and Chap. 5 focuses on how software audits fit into the governance environment. Since these chapters provide additional, optional content, depending on their own personal interests, readers may choose to continue directly to Chap. 6, which addresses the basic concept of Software Sustainability Audits. Chapter 7 develops the theme, introducing an additional governance concept as well as the methodology behind software sustainability audits.

Process and product audits (special variants of the software sustainability audits presented in Chaps. 6 and 7) feature in Chaps. 8 and 9 respectively and, along with instruments for software architects, provide a basis for putting theory into practice. Taking the example of software sustainability audits, Chap. 10 looks at risk assessment.

Chapters 11 and 12 can be read either as a self-contained unit, independently of the software audit concepts presented in Chaps. 4–10, or as supplementary information. The basics of effective control in software development are covered in Chap. 11, while the principle of control self-assessments in software development is explained in detail in Chap. 12. A recurring theme throughout "The Software Dilemma", the significance and impact of communication is examined in greater depth in Chap. 13.

This type of audit function, integrated in the software development division, acts as an operational monitoring function, which reports to the operational management level responsible, with the aim of optimizing processes in order to contribute efficiently to business results. This book is intended to (and surely will) encourage other divisions to build up a comparable function.

In addition, one of the responsibilities of the corporation's Internal Audit team, mandated by the CEO and Supervisory Board, is to monitor how these operational audit departments function. This can lead to a variety of cooperation models for joint audit activities. Internal Audit therefore welcomes the trend towards increased audit activities across the corporation and encourages their further development, as a means of collaborating for the overall benefit of the corporation and the assurance to the Executive Board, to jointly ensure compliance with the Corporate Governance framework, documented in duly defined processes and products.

We wish our colleagues the best of success for this book which we recognize as being the outcome of many hours of hard work and dedication. We hope that the readers will be inspired to innovate and that the authors will be motivated by stimulating feedback to work on the next edition.

Preface

What you hold in your hands is the result of many years of working on the development of business software. Our aim was and still is making software more sustainable. Software that focuses on customer needs, taking the operational and other related costs into account. We learned what works, and what does not work. And finally, we decided to share our experience with a larger audience by writing a book.

This book would not have been possible without the huge support and dedication of our wives. Many nights and weekends of work have been spent on this book. We know that this journey was not only painful for us.

In our endeavor to establish software audits at SAP, we have received valuable support from our colleagues Manfred Wolf, Markus Falk, and Matthias Ems of Global Internal Audit Services (GIAS). The discussion and concepts enabled us to set up a professional audit environment.

Communication is an essential ingredient to successful auditing. Communication concepts used in mediations sharpened our understanding of the different aspects of communication. We would like to thank Christian Bähner and Elke Schwertfeger from the institute Zweisicht at Freiburg for their stimulating training in mediation.

Furthermore, we could not have got this book out the door without the help of our colleagues and friends. Many fruitful discussions helped shape the content. The feedback we received affirmed our belief that the topic of this book is of utmost importance. The book got its final polish through the copy editing of our native speaking colleagues and friends. They ensured the readability of this work. In first-name alphabetic order we would like to thank Adam Thier, Andreas Gebauer, Christoph Mülleneisen, Christoph Welsch, Detlef Plümper, Elizabeth Winkler, Gordon Mühl, Guy Paladino, Horst Schnörer, Jochen Böder, Karol Bliznak, Markus Ament, Mathias Pöhling, Oliver Kling, Paul Abraham, Ron Silberstein, Serge

Thepaut, Tobias Stein, and Wolfram Kleis. We would like to thank Susanne Wilding for copy editing and fruitful discussions and hints on style and structure of the book. Finally, special thanks to Carl Lane who took the biggest part of copy editing without ever complaining.

Roger Gutbrod
Christian Wiele

Prolog

I still remember the first business application I developed. It was more than 20 years ago. Software, computer, Personal Computer (PC), were all new words, which sounded weird for most of the people at that time. Letters and documents were written with a typewriter. Nowadays, kids most likely have not seen or heard about typewriters.

One of my sisters wanted to buy a typewriter. She was starting studies to become a teacher and needed a typewriter to prepare the lessons she taught. I convinced her to buy a computer instead of a typewriter. "Your work will be much more efficient with a computer, and computers are the future", I said. A very strange opinion at that time! How can people work with such an odd machine, which I called computer?

At the same time, a friend of mine asked me for advice concerning his small business. He had heard about computers and wondered whether a PC could help him to run his business more efficiently. He asked me whether I knew of software that would help him to print orders, maintain materials which he needed for an order, and to calculate the prices. Actually, he specifically asked whether software is capable of handling all those tasks for his business. At this time, it was unknown to what extent software was able to perform tasks. After a short discussion, I promised to develop a computer program, which will do what he expected. I did not think about or consider technology. I had Turbo Pascal from Borland; it would enable me to develop software to meet my friend's business needs. "Any integration to any other application?" was not a question I was aware of. So, I developed a material management system and a small Customer Relationship Management (CRM) program – as it would be called today – without any boundary conditions, without any additional non-functional requirement. I only had to make sure that I could easily add further functions as requested to my software and that the program ran as expected. Yes, I thought about my own software architecture – a word not existing at that time.

Roger Gutbrod

More than 10 years ago I worked as an Information Technology (IT) consultant. One of my customers was a global company running a single huge Enterprise Resource Planning (ERP) system controlling their world-wide production and operations. My job was to assist in improving the software change management process for this ERP system. The company had many projects from different business units ongoing in their development systems and needed better control over the changes made to the code and configuration. Besides the simple 3-system landscape for development, test, and production, they had an additional 15–20 sandbox systems used for prototyping by the business units. One day, towards the end of my engagement, the IT manager approached me to get my opinion on a change he wanted to propose. I don't remember the exact conversation, but the conversation may have started like this: "You know we are facing a lot of pressure from our business units. They want to become agile and reduce the dependencies between projects. They have asked us to split the test landscape and provide an individual system for each unit. What do you think?" I guess this was my first time facing IT reality. Was this really meant seriously? Did they really ask me whether water was wet and could make you drown? Admittedly, coordinating all the projects in a single system landscape was quite a challenge. But to make it clear, this suggested change was their way to escape this by developing with all projects in a single development system, split the testing into different test systems, then consolidate the changes back into a single production system. I tried my best to explain my concerns and the risk of jeopardizing production through inconsistent software changes. But how successful could I be if they didn't see these obvious risks? Shortly after this discussion I left consulting, so I did not follow their adventure.

About 2 years later I met the IT manager on a different occasion. As he knew I was not consulting anymore, he asked me "Can you recommend a good colleague that can help us with our software change management? We are having trouble with our process now." Can you imagine how the little smart aleck in me cried 'Well guys, I told you . . .'? But the manager continued "We are so grateful you prevented us from splitting our test system. Otherwise, we would be dead in the water by now."

Christian Wiele

Contents

Introduction

The world of software has changed dramatically in the past decades. Today, software is pervasive in our daily life. Almost any technical item comprises a little computer with corresponding software. It's not only used to control nuclear power plants, aircrafts, or the traffic of big cities. You can find it in any modern car, heart rate monitor watches, our beloved smart phones, and even toys. The internet with its social networks – all based on software – has become a kind of backbone of our culture. But this did not come over night.

Software entered our life in several waves. In the early times only a few experts – mainly in research – were using computers and wrote corresponding code. With the advent of the personal computer and little later the home computer, software started entering our personal life. With the business process reengineering wave and the introduction of Enterprise Resource Planning (ERP) systems in the nineties the demand for IT experts grew considerably. The number of graduates from the traditional faculties – software engineers, mathematicians, physicists, etc. – was not sufficient to still the need for IT experts. Companies started hiring economists, historians, sociologist, or even philosophers and theologians and taught them how to develop software. The last wave – best characterized by the introduction and combination of the internet and mobile phones – has brought digital technology into the middle of our society. The young generation – coined *Generation Y* – has grown up with digital technology (and thus software) and its usage has become a natural thing.

Software Development Everywhere

With the *usage* of software also the *development* of software has become much more pervasive. To make software development accessible to a larger group of people development tools were improved over time. In the early days of punch cards and raw machine code only highly specialized people were able to program a computer. In several waves (reflected by 5 different generations of programming languages 1GL, 2GL, etc.) software development has become a widely adopted task. Today software development is taught in school as any other subject like mathematics or geography. Code often is generated automatically from models. A vast number of libraries are available (often as open source) that can be re-used for

R. Gutbrod and C. Wiele, *The Software Dilemma*, Management for Professionals,
DOI 10.1007/978-3-642-27236-3_1, © Springer-Verlag Berlin Heidelberg 2012

speeding up development. Not only do professional software developers write code today, business experts develop macros or scripts to perform special calculations in their spread sheets. Software has gained the notion that it can be developed by almost anyone. A rather negative side effect of today's ease of code generation is the appearance of so called script kiddies. Script kiddies use and assemble freely available code to exploit security vulnerabilities in software solutions. They are doing this without really knowing what the code is doing and what impact they are causing.

There is one thing we have to remember. The success of software has only become possible through the stunning development of the underlying hardware. Consider a state-of-the-art tablet computer used today by millions of people in their daily lives. Imagine – this tablet has the computing power in the range of the fastest available computer mid of the eighties. And that had the size of a washing machine [1]! Isn't that amazing? The computing power used 25 years ago to simulate earthquakes, compute a weather forecast, or simulate nuclear bombs today is at your disposal. This computing power comes in a box less than a piece of paper and thinner than 1 cm. And we are using it for surfing the internet, chatting with friends, writing mails, or playing games.

The miniaturization of hardware generated complete new industries and markets for servers, personal computers, mobile phones, and others. The software industry has grown with each new step. Over time the relation between hardware and software has changed. In the past the emphasis was on the hardware (just alone of its size and price) and software was just something to utilize this hardware. Hardware was often built and acquired for a specific purpose, for instance simulations in research institutes.

While this kind of business still exists, in wide ranges of the industry the perception has changed. Today hardware is merely seen as the enabler. The real value comes with the software. A new smart phone without a rich offering of applications is doomed the day it is launched to the market (or sometimes even before that). But the same holds true for business applications. The current rise of in-memory databases and computing technology allows searching and aggregating billions of data records in less than a second. But this technology is worth nothing without software supporting a company with compelling scenarios. The added value comes with software providing new insights not available in the past. It does not come with the raw computing power.

Creativity: The Driver Behind Software

This shift from hardware to software has a significant consequence – you need creativity for building software. New technologies like the touch screen allow doing things differently than in the past. But it is up to the software developer's creativity finding beneficial and thus successful solutions for the end user. We use creativity to solve known problems or requirement in a different way than in the past. For instance we provide new solutions for companies to do accounting, planning, or talent management. We also use creativity to generate new markets or demands. Examples are computer games and mobile business applications. Room for creativity is a key prerequisite for attracting talented software developers. These people want to shape solutions and drive ideas. There is no major software company without some kind of developer challenge where people can drive and present their own ideas. Creativity and the resulting innovation fuel the engine of the IT industry.

Complexity: The Challenge in Software Development

The continuing spread and adoption of software yields another inevitable trend – the complexity increases over time. More business processes are automated by software. Business data is stored in different specialized systems, optimized for dedicated use cases. This leads to an ever growing system landscape. But business demands that data from different sources like sales or production systems is integrated and consolidated to perform analytical or predictive tasks. The automation of processes is not limited to a single company. Data flow between businesses is increasingly automated. New clients like smart phones or other handheld computers are introduced. These clients come with their own software that has to communicate and integrate with software running in backend systems. New technologies and software versions arise but old ones continue to exist. User interface technologies are a good example. Browsers have to render web sites built in all the different technologies of the past 15–20 years. They cope with this issue by providing a plug-in concept to handle different rendering technologies. But the different plug-ins must not interfere with each other to keep the overall system stable.

The complexity increases also within a single software product. Imagine we develop and release a new version of a software product. Still, customers may stick to an older release with no intention to upgrade. Upgrades of business systems are expensive and need a business justification. As long as customers do not see added value in an upgrade they have the expectation to receive updates and patches for the old release they are operating. The result is an increased complexity for the software vendor. Besides developing and maintaining the latest release, the vendor also has to maintain a set of older versions.

There are also organizational aspects that we have to take into account when talking about complexity. Today's software development often requires a fine granular division of work. Some people work on a core engine, others on the application logic, again others focus on the integration with other systems or the user interface. The code is not necessarily developed and owned by a single company anymore. Software components from other vendors and suppliers are reused to speed up development. The use of open source components is a good example. Furthermore, it has become common that development teams are spread across the globe. Cooperation of teams has to be coordinated across remote locations. Still, at the end all pieces have to fit together.

Looking at Other Industries

The situation in software development is not unlike other industries. Take for instance the long-lasting history of aircrafts. Aviation started with the myth of Icarus. Icarus and his father built the first aircraft – a human body with wings made of feathers and wax. A simple construction built without any additional suppliers.

Unfortunately, it was not built for the given environment. The sun made the wax on Icarus' wings melt and he crashed. From that time we have seen an incredible increase in complexity in aviation. Modern aviation – starting with Otto Lilienthal – has seen a tremendous developed from simple flying objects (very similar to the idea of Icarus) to ever more complex ones. One of the most complex and advanced aircrafts, the Airbus A380, is built from thousands of parts. Many are produced by other companies. Alone 530 km of cable are built into an A380 with a complex cabin wiring of about 100.000 wires and 40.300 connectors. Despite some (in the aviation industry not untypical) delays the industry has learned to deal with increasing complexity. They divide and distribute work across suppliers and locations. All design, development, and production work has to be performed with extremely high quality. This is required to ensure reliability of the end product – the airplane. This is what we call an engineering culture.

So, what's the issue with software development? For an answer we need to take a closer look at what actually is required in software development. There is one important aspect we have not yet addressed. With complexity the risk of failure or of an incident with significant impact increases. Take the aircraft example. The aircraft (or rather flying machine) of Otto Lilienthal affected only a single person in case of an incident, the newest version of the A380 affects up to 900 people. Let us look at an example.

Dealing with complexity in software development we need to distinguish two different types. So far we described the natural increase in complexity due to the continuous spread and adoption of software. For instance, the business processes covered by software become more complex and higher integrated. This is what we want to call *inherent* complexity. On the other hand, software can be made unnecessarily complex, i.e. the additional degree of complexity does not add value and is not based on business requirements. This is what we call *excessive* complexity. An example of excessive complexity is the use of different technologies. Different programming languages, user interfaces, integration, or workflow technologies within in a single software solution unnecessarily increase the complexity. Such a solution will be harder to maintain, operate, and analyze.

Whether a certain aspect of a software product imposes excessive complexity might depend on the context of its use. A Java application deployed into an existing Java landscape might not increase complexity, but deployed into a NET environment it certainly does. An application might be perfectly fine for experts but unacceptable for casual users. Thus it is indispensible for understanding the context and environment the software product has to fit into. Excessive complexity negatively impacts costs of development and operations, supportability, and at the end the acceptance of the software.

Sustainable Software: Meeting Today's Requirements

The increased risk due to complexity has a consequence for the way software is developed. This is not different to other industries. While planning and developing a new software product we have (at least try) to anticipate the complete software lifetime and lifecycle. Small apps for smart phones might have a relatively small lifetime of few years, month or even just weeks. Business applications on the other hand have a much longer lifetime of even several decades. During its lifetime the software needs to be securely operated, patched, upgraded, extended, integrated with other systems, etc. Not to forget – the software still has to meet the functional requirements of customers and users.

Taking a broader perspective we have to ensure that the software is *sustainable*. Sustainability in our understanding (compared to a narrow focus on carbon emission) covers all aspects that potentially impact the use of any limited resource. Many things in software development, operation, and usage can be considered a limited resource. It can be the number and expertise of administrators, the time of end users getting used to software or fulfilling a certain task, the available hardware, the IT budget of a company, the number of security experts on the market, the bandwidth of a network, number of developers and support engineers, and so on. Sustainable software takes these constraints into account and balances them with the value added by the software.

For instance, I want to use a new technology to provide a certain feature. On the other hand this new technology increases the costs for the customers: administrators have to acquire knowledge and adapt the operational procedures, additional hardware is required, as well as more time for patching the overall solution, etc. These are only the direct costs associated the use of a software. Beyond these costs the lack of sustainability of software has a tremendous impact on the business of a company. The A380 yields an interesting example. The initial delivery of the A380 was delayed as Airbus had issues in the assembly of the cabin wiring. The delay cost billions of Dollars. One reason claimed for this delay concerns the use of different and *incompatible* versions of the same CAD software product used in different locations [2, 3].

The sustainability of a software product is largely defined by one important factor – its core architecture. We do not want to go into a detailed discussion what exactly architecture means. We know there are different opinions and perspectives. We currently assume a rather broad understanding of architecture. It comprises the conceptual ideas behind the product – the used technology and programming language, the componentization and interfaces, the granularity of objects, etc. The core architecture affects the sustainability in two ways. On one hand architecture determines important non-functional aspects like performance, supportability, operational costs, etc. On the other it is nearly impossible to change the core architecture after the product has been developed and delivered. It is like in construction. You perform do some minor improvements on a house or fix a broken pipe. But if the core architecture and concepts do not fit to your needs you have to tear it down and rebuild it.

We have to accept an additional risk for our software development projects – the risk of building non-sustainable software. Effectively addressing this risk requires transparency about our software development projects. And we need rules and guidelines to enforce sustainability. We have to put additional control to the software development processes – we need governance. Rules need to be defined for technology selection and architecture to make the software products fit to the company's strategy. We have to ensure meeting customer and market requirements with our development. We require new ways to enforce these rules and to create transparency for making educated decisions in management. Quality assurance has to be broadened to reflect not only classical bugs. We have to come to an engineering culture similar to other industries.

The Software Dilemma: Balance Governance and Empowerment

"So what? What's the difference to other industries? Where's the dilemma?" you might ask. For an answer we have to get back to another prerequisite of software development. We discusses that software development requires creativity and freedom to find adequate solutions to complex problems. We need an environment attracting talented people able to master the inherent complexity. Furthermore, development teams need empowerment to drive solutions and decide on the best approach. The dilemma lies in the requirement for creativity and freedom on one hand, and sustainability governance on the other hand. Both aspects need to be carefully balanced as both are antagonists.

Too much freedom and empowerment puts sustainability at risk. It leads to "organic" growth of the software. Tactical decisions not aligned with a central strategy dominate. On the other hand, too many restrictions through governance put a meaningful solution at risk. Developers love freedom and new technologies. Talented people like to work on the edge of technology following current trends and hypes. Being up-to-date on current trends increases their (perceived) market value. Sustainability on the other hand requires sticking to known and mature technologies rather than riding each new wave of technology trends.

Too strict and improper governance is counterproductive in a creative environment. You require the buy-in from key players in software development. Product owners, software architects, and developers want to understand why they have to follow certain rules. If these rules are not carefully explained or do not make sense to the affected people governance becomes easily ineffective. People ignore the rules or try finding a bypass. In the worst case talented people leave and seek other opportunities with more freedom and fewer restrictions. We have to face the fact that the market demand for talented software experts is higher than the supply.

There is an additional issue with software development. Delivering software is too easy. Software does not require a long production or assembly process like in other industries. Software can be locally compiled by a developer and sent out via mail or put on a web site. This alleged ease of delivery combined with high market dynamics and competition yields the risk of delivering software too early. This software is sarcastically coined bananaware – delivered green and ripens with the customers. Unfortunately, if the core architecture is delivered "green" it might not be possible to ripen it. So, through governance we have to ensure that at least the core architecture is sustainable before a product is delivered to the market.

How This Book Can Help

We have seen how the software market has evolved over time and how complexity increased. Software development faces the dilemma finding the right balance between creativity and empowerment on the one hand and governance (especially of the core architecture) on the other hand. We need new mechanisms to create transparency on the status of a software product. Transparency becomes ever harder with increasing complexity. But only transparency will allow for meaningful management decisions.

So, how can this book help? The aim of this book is to provide concepts and tools to efficiently and effectively address the software dilemma. This not only requires a relatively broad spectrum of topics as we will see. We also have to consider different points of view. We need alignment across different parts of the organization to develop sustainable software – executive management, software development, and governance.

To make this more tangible we have picked representatives from each group. Based on the roles of the Chief Information Officer (CIO)/Chief Technology Officer (CTO), a software architect, and an auditor we discuss the different views, needs, and expectations. The required balance of empowerment and governance is only be possible if a mutual understanding between these groups exists. Each chapter starts with a section "What's in for me?" guiding the different roles and emphasizing important aspects for each of the viewpoints. We don't want to limit the target audience to these three dedicated role. Rather view the three explicit roles as representatives of groups representing executive management, development, and governance.

The book starts with a closer look at the motivation for governance in software development. We look at different approaches, and analyze success factors. In our work in software development we have seen a typical pattern how governance can start: A software architects is asked by management to provide an assessment of some software product. This assessment acts as a basis for some management decision. Whatever the trigger for the assessment is – customer escalations, possible acquisitions, changes in ownership of a product, etc – architects are often not prepared for such a task. They have the technical expertise but might lack the procedural knowledge. We take the architect by the hand and give guidance on making the assessment a success. This kind of assessment does not require a formal governance framework but just some structured approach.

The pattern extends if such an assessment is seen as adding value. The results might have helped resolving a critical situation. Management might demand and request such a service on a regular basis. To this end we introduce the concept of *Software Sustainability Audits* as a standard means of addressing software development audits. Software Sustainability Audits provide a holistic approach to auditing software development processes and the resulting products. We introduce the required audit framework and details to set up a corresponding service.

We introduce governance as a response to the risk of delivering non-sustainable software. We complement the discussion on Software Sustainability Audits by a chapter about handling the question of risk. We outline how to identify and tackle risk in the context of the software development process.

The main theme of the book – balancing and reconciling governance and empowerment – is addressed by the concept of control self-assessment (CSA). This concept is known from auditing but we have adopted it for the specifics of software development. Simplified it can be viewed as a kind of guided and facilitated review process.

An essential and often underestimated part of governance in software development is the aspect of communication. Not only do facts matter but also the way they are communicated. Communication is important when performing interviews, but also when reporting findings in an audit report. Therefore we focus on this topic in a dedicated chapter. We also refer to communication whenever it is required.

This book is based on the experience of the authors with large scale standard software development and the corresponding governance and audit infrastructure. Furthermore it is based on the results of many technical due diligences conducted in the context of (potential) acquisitions covering software companies of almost any size.

Making Things Tangible: The Stories

We tried making the book livelier by enriching it with small stories from real life. Although made up they might remind you every here and there of situations in your own professional career in software business. The stories should help making the different aspects more tangible. We have invented three protagonists driving these little stories. CIO *Kai Salvish,* principle software architect *Gregory (Greg) Naizirk*, and auditor *Sam Tamies* all work in a growing software company. You will meet them every here and there trying to master their different challenges on the way to sustainable software.

References

1. John Markoff, The iPad in Your Hand: As Fast as a Supercomputer of Yore. http://bits.blogs. nytimes.com/2011/05/09/the-ipad-in-your-hand-as-fast-as-a-supercomputer-of-yore/.
2. Nicola Clark, The Airbus saga: Crossed wires and a multibillion-euro delay – Business – International Herald Tribune. http://www.nytimes.com/2006/12/11/business/worldbusiness/11iht-airbus.3860198.html.
3. Max Kingsley-Jones, Farnborough first news: The race to rewire the Airbus A380. http://www. flightglobal.com/news/articles/farnborough-first-news-the-race-to-rewire-the-airbus-207894/.

The World Has Changed

What's in It for Me?

Software and IT Governance is never in place from the beginning of a companies lifecycle. It evolves over time. This chapter takes inspiration from patterns observed in the world of economics and applies them in the software development world. Initial impact for the software development and the role of a software architect are discussed in this chapter.

CIO/CTO

If you are already keenly aware of the changes in software development in the past 20 years, we advise you skip Sect. 2.1 and select a single example from Sect. 2.2 to learn about a governance patterns in economics. Choose an example from 2.3 to understand the complexity observed in the software industry. Do your software architects still have all the required skills? The new software architect role in discussed in Sect. 2.4 will encourage you to think about further education for them. Before you start governance in development, Sect. 2.5 highlights limitations and restrictions which help you to balance your governance methods.

Software Architect

Software architects are often told that software development is different from other industries. Learn from Sects. 2.1 and 2.2 that the software industry is in fact not very different. At least you can recognize similar patterns as in economics. Section 2.3 will be very familiar to you. Section 2.4 could be your central take-away from this chapter. Are you aware of these – mostly unspoken – requirements of a software architect? Check, where you are with your training and discuss this opportunity for education with your manager.

(continued)

R. Gutbrod and C. Wiele, *The Software Dilemma*, Management for Professionals, DOI 10.1007/978-3-642-27236-3_2, © Springer-Verlag Berlin Heidelberg 2012

Section 2.5 could be your guide to consult management on a balanced
architecture governance approach.

Auditor
The economic patterns as described in Sects. 2.1 and 2.2 will be very familiar.
You may have discussed this and more patterns extensively with your
colleagues. These paragraphs serve as a warm-up to the more detailed
discussions later. Section 2.3 then takes you into the world of software
development with assimilate-able patterns. You may skip the second half
starting with Sect. 2.4. If you want to understand software architects and their
business, however, Sects. 2.4 and 2.5 can give you some deeper insights.

2.1   The Need for Orientation

The world of software development has changed; we are in the middle of a
transition. We have left the world where only few people practiced software
development, where few dependencies needed to be considered by programmers,
where software was easy to understand and code was easy to write. We have not
reached the next phase yet – a stage where software development has been adopted
as a mature engineering style or is a broadly established discipline. We are in
between an engineering discipline that was just born and one that is well
established. There are many indications that this is an industry that is nascent.
Look at the continuous discussion concerning waterfall and agile methodologies as
development approaches. The continuous emergence of new software technologies
and programming languages, or the discussions about deployment models like on
premise and on demand are all indicators of a changing industry.

On our path forward we need guidance and direction on what to do for next steps.
What do we need to master? How do we balance complexity and the requirements
of sustainable software with the need for creative freedom? Such a journey does not
come without many frustrations and detours. It is like in real life – growing up is
exciting and painful at the same time. We need the advice of our parents for overall
orientation, but need freedom to develop our own personality. Some children
develop faster while others lag behind. The same is true in software development.
There are software developers who understand the complexity surrounding their
software products. But we also see software developers ignoring complexity of
software development to move forward quickly, which can succeed short term, but
also have painful consequences long term. The awareness that requirements for
security in software development have significantly increased in recent years while
other topics like complexity, supportability, or other non-functional aspects still
lack this awareness.

Improving software industry practices can follow two approaches; the first is
learning from our failures. The other is learning from other industry failures.

A failure can help mastering complexity and a way to navigate through it. A crisis in software development projects is often a starting point for learning how to master dependencies and unspoken, unaddressed requirements. Security is such an example where the software industry had (and still continues) to learn from its mistakes the hard way. The phenomenon of hackers exploiting vulnerabilities in the code is unique to the software industry. Nevertheless, there are other areas where we can learn from other industries or even the whole industrial economy. The software industry is still young. We still have a long journey ahead before our industry becomes a grown up. Why don't we look at the economy as a whole, where we have progressed considerably over the last few centuries? Why should we not learn from the processes there?

There are many patterns in our economy, which can be simply tweaked and applied to the software business. And there is a very prominent lesson we have in mind, which deals with complexity or even is the result of economy's complexity. The economy has learned to live with crises and needs crises to learn. A common pattern is: Once there is a crisis, the world cries for governance.

2.2   Crisis: And the World Cries for Governance

2.2.1   A First Example from the Stock Market

Our tour through crisis and regulation rides along the curve of the stock market performance. Figure 2.1 shows crises in the national economy at the inflection points marked. We will look at some of these reversal points as examples to understand regulatory behavior in the economy. Before we start, let's have a look at a simple principle, the awareness of risk.

Risk Awareness Becomes Emphasized When the Stock Price Crashes
It is an almost symptomatic phenomenon in business. And though you do not recognize it, you are affected. When you notice it, it is often late, too late.

Risk is an important factor in business life. In many instances, you have to identify, regulate, and manage risk by enacting laws. Even if regulatory bodies or others do not have legal enforcement in place, a good businessperson is aware of the risks he takes. The measures vary and the prevalent business culture shapes the kind of risk treatment. In the end, everybody balances business opportunities with risks.

This is where the game starts. What is more important? The opportunity you currently see at your fingertips, or the risks which are unknown or ignored. Individuals tend to bounce between euphoria and fear. Apparently there is nothing in between. They either put all their eggs in one basket to take the ultimate chance, or they take "a bird in the hand is worth two in the bush" mentality to avoid any risk. You can see such a behavior in the stock market – as in all markets we participate in. If the share price of a stock rises, individuals first watch the upward trend, with everybody tending to hold and buy even more even if the peak is almost reached or

Fig. 2.1 Crises in economy – reflected by the performance of German share index DAX

passed. When the trend turns down, still invisible because of the known volatility of the share price, individuals are still optimistic, hoping the share price will climb further, i.e. wait and make more money. Then it is almost too late, the stock price goes into the red. You are better off selling rather than losing even more. But individuals still wait; even though it is too painful to watch losing their money. Better wait, the stock price will climb again – at some time. And at the time when it is really, really late to sell, they sell anyway, almost everyone sells. There are only a few people that can sense the forthcoming turning point. As the many individuals hysterically sell their last shares, there are a few people buying these low price shares shortly before the stock price starts to ascend again.

When these things happen, the balance between risk and opportunity is lost. It has been replaced by greed and fear. In the aftermath of such a crisis, the awareness of risks and how to treat risks properly returns or is emphasized.

The Fig. 2.1 above shows a typical share performance. It demonstrates the tracking of such behavior.

Now, let's turn to some examples where we show the treatment of risk in business with governance. Similar patterns seem to apply here as well, where a bouncing between zero and extensive governance is visible at each inflection point. Let us look at these examples.

2.2.2   SOX as Result from Corporate and Accounting Scandals

We all know companies have to report their business results. They need to compile a balance sheet. The Franciscan Friar Luca Pacioli described in his book "Summa de Arithmetica, Geometria, Proportioni et Proportionalità" in 1494, a first version of corporate accounting. At that time Venetia was the center of the global economy. Lunca Pacioli's accounting principles seem to have been used in trading in Italian states back then [1].

The generally accepted accounting principles (GAAP) today, are accounting principles that describe how to compile a balance sheet. The GAAP protects shareholders from incorrect information being reported. The principles provide certain insights into risks faced by companies' – to the extent risks can be derived from accounting data. Eventually, these accounting principles do indeed prevent losses for the shareholders.

Do we need further governance? The accounting process seems to be diligent. Besides, there are financial auditors who audit and sign-off on the balance sheet as watchdogs. So, what can go wrong? We have a simple and lean process in place consisting of a compilation of balance sheets and financial audits by auditing firms.

Yes, there was some debate in the past about the independence of auditing firms. Major auditing firms used to sell consulting and auditing services at the same time. There could potentially be a conflict of interest, when an auditing firm offers both financial auditing and consulting services. Audit firms had built a reputation as honest and respectable companies. They certainly would not endanger their business by allowing fraud in financial auditing. Apparently not!

Discussions concerning conflict of interest where not at the forefront of peoples' minds during the dot com bubble. Greed prevailed and fear faded away. During the dot com bubble all conservative valuations of companies' values receded. The balance between risk and revenue opportunity was broadly ignored. The more obtuse a company's idea was, the more its estimated value. A viable business case for emerging companies was not needed at all. There was no place for continuing the debate about the independence of auditing firms and necessary governance.

And then the bubble burst in 2000. This should have been an appropriate time to re-launch the discussion about accounting governance, but the public wished to nurse its wounds from the bust. The time was not yet right for corporate and accounting governance.

The public needed further scandals of companies like Enron, WorldCom and others to move to action. Credit rating agencies rated Enron as excellent even as late as 2001. Enron suddenly reported insolvency in late 2001. It had – creatively – falsified its balance sheets, which was not revealed by the auditing firm Arthur Andersen. After the burst of the dot-com bubble the next crisis happened. But this time the world cried for governance.

As a reaction to these famous corporate and accounting scandals the United States enacted a federal law called "Public Company Accounting Reform and Investor Protection Act". It is better known as Sarbanes–Oxley act or short form SOX, named for the co-sponsors of this act, Paul Sarbanes and Michael G. Oxley. The new "accounting governance" by SOX comprises aspects like.

- *Clear and new defined responsibilities*: e.g. section 302 defines principal officers (typically CEO and CFO), who have to approve the company's financial reporting,

- *Empowered governance institutions*: e.g. section 1101 enables the SEC, the U.S. Securities and Exchange Commission, to temporarily freeze unusual payments,
- *Enforcing governance processes*: e.g. the specific procedures for compliance audits are defined and the effectiveness of the internal control system has to be audited yearly.

While the Sarbanes–Oxley act responded to the failures and grievance of accounting and accounting auditing, there is plenty of criticism for the new law as well. The biggest issue is the tremendous cost to a publicly listed company that is associated with adhering to section 404. As reaction to the implementation of SOX foreign companies unlisted themselves. Other reports mention a decrease of the number of initial public offerings on the American Stock Exchange. An issue of the Wall St. Journal even stated "The new laws and regulations (. . .) damage entrepreneurship."

Summarized, a battery of governance rules has been initiated by SOX to protect investors. We are not sure how effective all these immediate activities are and we observe debates about the effectiveness of the sections of SOX. For instance, in 2009 the congress debated what measures are actually needed to avoid a repeat of situations like the Enron case.

A Pattern as Governance Evolves

The pattern we recognize that is unique for governance activities is as follows: *Risk is ignored; a crisis is needed to make the risk tangible and make the public demand oversight.* This particular event triggers countless other governance activities, all of which need to be consolidated, or will have been consolidated later. It takes time to find the most effective governance which can be further improved as time goes by. Figure 2.2 depicts such a pattern.

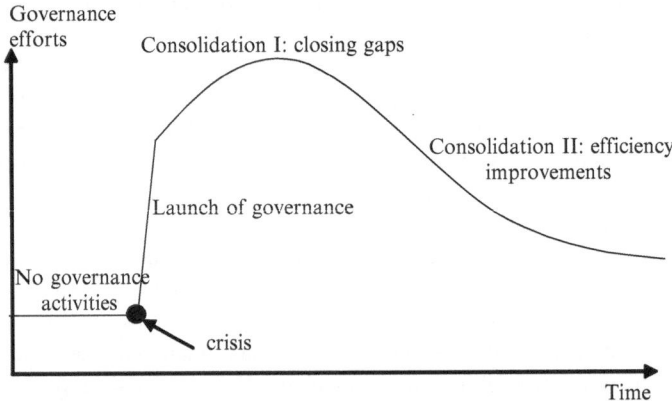

Fig. 2.2 Launch of governance due to crisis and governance evolution

2.2.3   Insolvency of Lehman Brothers

Another good example of calls for oversight follows the event of Lehman Brothers' insolvency, the impact this insolvency had on a series of banks, which ended as a world-wide economic crash. It started quite innocuously. Financial institutions have many opportunities to make good money, sometimes quick money. The risks associated with such business deals are well known and should have been regulated.

The first joint world-wide governance activities have started to cope with these risks. Basel II is the latest initiative to control these risks by balancing business opportunities with the associated risks. This is the basic idea of the Basel II initiative, an accord issued by the Basel Committee on Banking Supervision. Basel II creates a framework for recommendations on banking regulations. The concept was that banks need to put aside equity capital to insure against their credit, market and operational risks. The higher their risk exposure, the more capital adequacy they are supposed to reserve.

According to Basel II, "the fundamental objective [. . .] has been to develop a framework that would further strengthen the soundness and stability of the international banking system [. . .]" [2]. In other words, Basel II attempts to protect the international banking system from situations where one or more bank crashes, other are left untouched.

So, bank governance appeared to have started quite well. Potential risks had been identified, rules had been defined (pillar I of Basel II), and procedures aligned (pillar II and III of Basel II). And then tragedy struck. Europe has already implemented the accord, while the USA, initiator of this regulatory framework, requested a delay and postponement in 2005 [4]. Moreover, word has it that US governmental and financial institutions assessed its business as safe. US loan practices had already compensated its risks. Compared to other countries, much higher interest rates for high default risks should balance the banks' risks. US institutions planned a first parallel run (with Europe) of its regulation initiatives in 2008, the year that Lehmann Brothers crashed.

Governance Is as Good as at Its Weakest Implementation

When you bend a stick, it will break at its weakest point. And that is what happens in financial regulations as well. With Lehman Brothers, a bank crash started in a country, where the governance implementation was delayed, but the economic crisis spread all over the world. Debates about stiffer governance and regulation started again. As a consequence, Basel III, a new accord is now being discussed. The former Basel II was just a global framework for bank regulation. Local financial supervision did exist and had existed with all its local rules. Why did these local governance measures fail in the absence of a fully rolled out global regulation? Do we have a chance at all to govern locally in a complex and networked world? Effectiveness of global governance became drastically more important than local governance.

Basel III defines corrective measures as answers to the financial and economic crisis in 2007. One question still seems to be unanswered: What will happen with the weakness in regulation the next time a crises occurs? Remember, the next weakness point in governance could be at a different place. And you might continue asking: Which countries are not committed to Basel III?

A Pattern of Governance for Weak Points

There is a pattern we can derive for architecture governance. Whenever we try to govern a complex process distributed among several units, we tend to optimize process description and central processes. All this is important, but in addition, it is always good advice to verify the implementation of the parts. The weakest unit that fails can make the whole process fail. So, it would be a better idea to improve the implementation in one unit rather than trying to optimize the whole governance process.

2.2.4   Risk of Greece's Insolvency

Let's have a look at a third example. On January 1st in 1999, a new currency was introduced, the Euro. It started as an accounting unit. Notes and coins for trading were made available 3 years later. Currency stability was an important reason for the introduction of the Euro. Convergence criteria, also known as Maastricht criteria (from the European Treaty's original name, the Maastricht Treaty, signed in Maastricht, Netherlands), were defined to guarantee stability when a country introduces the Euro as a new currency. Some of these criteria still have to be fulfilled after the entry into the European Monetary Union. Punishments have been defined for countries which fail with their given commitments on the stability criteria. But what is the answer to the situation of a country totally deviating from the stability criteria? Actually several countries already violated the Maastricht criteria when they joined the Euro community. What happens if a country is faced with impending bankruptcy? There were many debates right from the beginning of the European Monetary Union on this issue. Some have requested that a stronger political union will have to follow a monetary union. Other aspects of the issues were discussed as well. These questions remained unanswered for a long time. With the sudden risk of Greece's insolvency, these discussions have started again. A European monetary fund has been created and Euro Bonds have been discussed. Credit aids for a financially suffering country have been introduced. A separation of the Euro currency into "North Euro" and "South Euro" could address the different economic structures of current Euro countries. And again, a demand for more regulation of the Euro currency and the current stability criteria followed the crisis. However, governance gaps are still being closed and a further consolidation process will need to take place.

We assume that it will take a long time to achieve a consolidated governance structure for the Euro currency and for the affected countries. We assume a series of

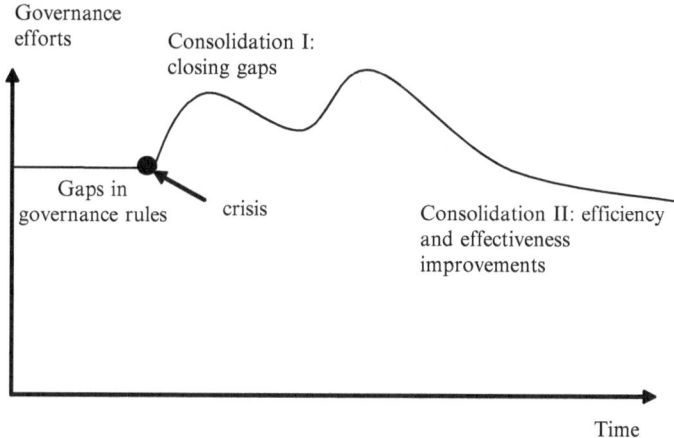

Fig. 2.3 Waves of consolidation of governance activities

governance consolidations steps, where each one will introduce new measures and refine existing ones. Figure 2.3 shows such a pattern of waves of consolidation.

2.3   Crises in Software Development

In the previous section we have learned from the economy examples, how a singular effect can have global impact. And we learned about behaviors that exist in global governance. We dare not say that a crisis in software development at a company can trigger a world-wide economic crisis, but we can take these examples and project them on an enterprise. We can see similar governance patterns in software development. To extend this premise we first need a crisis, before we talk about governance.

2.3.1   Security as a Global Responsibility

For quite some time security has been known as a topic to take seriously in the software industry. Hackers around the world have made us aware of the risks companies have with security gaps. Once in a while we read in the press news about another hacker attack. Most of the hackers were targeting prominent software preys. Individual hackers even formed hacker clubs. Many of the hackers had no criminal intent. They were trying to increase awareness of security or their prowess in circumventing software's security measures. Additionally, on a global scale, many people became aware of information systems security gaps through movies.

While for many companies security had been a rising topic, the attitude of software developers was different. "My software is so unknown that nobody will try to break into it." Or: "I do not have to implement anything special since there is a firewall which ensures the security of my software." Those and other ideas bounced around in the software development community for quite some time. In 2002, Bill Gates sent an e-mail to all Microsoft® employees to make them aware of the seriousness of security: "When we face a choice between adding features and resolving security issues, we need to choose security" [3]. This happened after a series of security problems, resulting in heavy complaints about security vulnerabilities, culminated in a Microsoft® security crisis. According to rumors, several measures were taken at Microsoft® to ensure a level of security quality for its products. The authors cannot judge whether those rumors were true or false, but 2 years later Microsoft® launched a new concept Security Development Lifecycle, to provide information about secure programming. This process was communicated both internally and to Microsoft® partners.

Is security solved with having a security governance process in place? Security is a tricky subject. You cannot apply a measurement to security like "99% of the software is secure". Such a key performance indicator (KPI) sounds great; unfortunately this type of measurement can't be applied. Hackers are constantly seeking weaknesses in your software. The part of your software with the weakest security is the determining factor for the level of security. A 1% weakness in your product is an open invitation for hackers to find this 1% of your code. Security is as good as its weakest software part. Governance is not completed with governance of 99%. Governance of security means governance of 100% of the code.

2.3.2   Manage Software Complexity

What has changed in the past 20 years? Twenty years ago software was just a growing industry. As a company you had few choices – if any – on available software for the tasks you want to automate. In most cases, larger companies entrusted consulting companies to develop appropriate software or there were in-house development teams to provide proper solutions for the most urgent needs.

Over time software packages have been bought and added to the home-grown software. Integration experts, mainly from consulting firms, ensured that all pieces were smoothly integrated. Requirements could be easily addressed to software providers to ensure a seamless process resulting in sound and easy handling of all software solutions within a company.

Later, the complexity of requirements continued to increase tremendously. With the diverse bunch of software, came even further complexity in usability, resulting in dissatisfaction from the users. The users asked for software that is easy or easier to use. In some countries, Workers Councils refused to approve the release of new software to the company's user community if the software was not perceived as easy to use. Legal authorities began to claim that certain criteria must be fulfilled before the software could be implemented or used. People with disabilities needing accessible software and protection of data privacy are examples of those legal requirements. Or take as example the simple request for smooth integration between software products. I have heard stories where the result from one application is printed and the print-outs are entered in another application. That is certainly a type of integration, but I would not consider that to be the smoothest.

This describes the situation software producers are facing: A diversity of available software in the market, requirements from different sources, new technologies emerging frequently, and their software must fit in this complex world. The software solutions are threatening to burst at the seams due to the complexities of addressing this manifold of requirements.

And what is the resolution? One option is to let software development ignore your risks. You are now in a reactionary mode of operation, solving problems as they arise, waiting for your crisis. Just like Europe has waited for Greece's insolvency, without mitigating the risk earlier, without defining rules and controls to prevent such a situation. In software development, you also can continue to develop the product to a point where changes are painful and expensive, and you have to replace parts of your software to comply with given rules.

Another option is to govern software development right from the beginning. You try to define a perfect infrastructure that will ensure compliance with all rules and accepted criteria. With this solution you find yourself hunting everywhere to capture all items within your governance model. This most likely will end as the situation of Basel II [2], where one unit is not able or not willing to implement the governance model and causes the whole software to break.

So, what can we use as a resolution? There are two tips we can share at the moment. First, don't wait for a crisis. Second, whatever governance model you define, ensure an appropriate consolidation of the model at the same time. Software Sustainability Audits, as we will introduce later, can be your first choice of all your options.

2.3.3   The Software's Patch Curse

Do you know any software system that cannot be patched? Well, with the exception of the software used in little toys there are hardly any examples. Smart phones, car electronics, personal computers, business software, and even software for satellites and space ships can be – and has to be – patched. Software is everywhere and applying patches is a natural thing. While patching is annoying for users, we in the software industry have gotten used it. The real story is not about patching software, but about t an attitude of "a patch can resolve everything later – even architectural problems".

Software providers can try to improve the quality of their product to reduce the need for patches, but there is no chance to eliminate the need for a patching mechanism. This is still not the main story to tell here. It is about a dangerous attitude of "we-can-fix-it-later" that is wide spread in software development that needs to be understood.

"We have to ship it now; we can provide a fix for it later!" Sound familiar? It is a valid and vital approach from business perspective. You cannot develop until you eliminate all bugs. You will simply go out of business if you do not follow a more pragmatic approach.

The real issue is – not everything can be fixed later. This is sometimes overlooked or ignored. Core architectural decisions like the programming language and model, interface technologies and protocols cannot be easily changed later. The basic architecture decisions will determine whether a system will perform and scale as expected, how it will harmonize with other systems or software components, how expensive it is to operate the software, and even whether it can be patched at all. In other words, the attitude "we can fix it later" has functional issues in mind. Non-functional requirements, like performance and scalability, are ignored.

These non-functional aspects of the software require careful consideration. They are usually harder to grasp and less tangible than functional aspects. From our experience we see that discussions around go-to-market or delivery of software products often focus on the functional aspects. Non-functional aspects are often not actively driven and understood as essential ingredients to make the software successful and sustainable. This behavior makes the non-functional aspects an endangered species. As non-functional aspects currently do not seem to be self-evident they need to be covered by a corresponding governance process. It should be obvious that the non-functional aspects become increasingly important with the growing inherent complexity of software systems.

Like the examples of the stock market or other patterns in the economy that lead to malfunction or even a breakdown, the system has to be controlled by corresponding governance activities. Software development is no exception and a too pragmatic approach to the patching issue is such a pattern.

2.4   The Evolving Role of Software Architects

> *"This time the rock has won, but the scars will remain forever."*
> *(sign at a view point of a Canyon in Canada)*

Many years ago, Gregory Naizirk, as the principal architect responsible for the architecture of an important product line, was asked by Kai Salvish, his CIO, on behalf of the top management their company to conduct an architecture assessment in another area.

"You can reach out to us many experts as you need. The executive board needs to know, whether the architecture guarantees a stable foundation for a sustainable software product. A first draft result is expected in 2 weeks." Kai said.

Two weeks sounded like a reasonable timeframe. And, hey, Gregory could involve all the experts he needed. "Fantastic!" Greg thought. "This is quite an unusual architecture task. It is exciting and thrilling, and it is certainly a good experience for my career."

Greg was very excited about this challenge, but he soon became aware of the reality of the task before him. He had to analyze the software architecture of a product he has never seen. The development team developed the product with technologies and tools he has never used.

"It is important that a reliable and neutral assessment is done." That was the reason for selecting him, Greg thought. He has reviewed architecture before. The tiny difference was

he knew the underlying business processes, which should have been covered by the software. He has never done an independent architecture review for an unknown product. "How do I judge the architecture?" came into his mind. Following that first question his thoughts were filled with successive questions – "What did top management understand by the term 'stable foundation'? What is their expectation? Stable for what purpose? And who should be involved? Certainly experts from the specific development area would be on top of the interview list. But will I get an unbiased result? How should I treat their input when this assessment thread may badly influence the results? The top management emphasized the objectiveness and neutrality of this exercise." Many, many more questions flooded Greg's mind.

At the end, he approached two other principal architects, hoping they have experience with both independent architecture assessment and top management expectations. He was wrong, totally wrong. He seems to be the first person in his company to start such an arduous journey. And it was not the last one. It was the launch of a new era of software architecture.

The world has changed. Software assessments that include its architecture have become quite common nowadays. And still, we notice that many software architects, even senior ones, have few experiences with such assessments. Plenty of pitfalls are along the assessment road. And if you have never seen or heard of these pitfalls before, you will certainly struggle or fall.

2.4.1   Role Enrichment #1: From Techie to Business Man

Each software developer and software architect is used to using a bunch of development tools, acting like a juggler with all these tools. The juggler is always excited to implement new technologies which improve development efficiency, that add value to the product or even give the product a dramatic new shape. This has always been part of every software architect's job. It was one of the technical tasks of a technical job. It is no longer sufficient to execute technical tasks proficiently. You also have to balance business needs with technical challenges. You are asked to understand the business. Strategic thinking has now become important. From the context information you are given you are supposed to derive the objective of your assessment. Like the example above, a few hints of the context were given by the top management: "A stable foundation", "sustainable product". Certainly the top management is going to decide on a strategic direction – a direction that could impact all software development participants. Some investments for new products or new development might be warranted. The question now becomes whether the software can still be used with a change in strategic direction. The business decision could be to further invest in the software for quite a new product, or quit and start again. Each of those alternatives has investment impacts and risks. Hence, it is not sufficient to check whether the architecture is okay. Advice is asked for by management on potential business options. Welcome to the business team!

2.4.2   Role Enrichment #2: Processes Are a New Area of Responsibility

Let's look a bit deeper in Gregory's first investigation of that kind.

This challenge was the first of its kind for Gregory. Yes, Gregory was quite experienced. But would his experience be sufficient? Greg decided to establish a small team of senior software architects who were neutral and independent as he was. He called it the core review team. Every day they met to lay all of their findings on the table and discuss how to evaluate options and how to proceed. Very early on, they reached a point, where they were faced with an unusual situation. The architecture of the software seemed suitable for what they understood it should do. Actually, it was very good considering the circumstances the development team had to live with. "Good foundation for a sustainable product" was the general consensus; however the management expectations worried Greg. Good architecture under the given circumstances: Is that the result that is asked by management? Eventually, he has to advise on how to proceed, and he thought the current architecture may not be good enough. They discussed this in the core team. They concluded that this was not the right question to be asking. Rather, they should ask themselves, whether the given architecture combined with the given development processes will result in reliable software. They had to question the processes, evaluate the past processes and how they influenced the software architecture. And, they should analyze how they will impact the future. They definitely had to start with the architecture relevant processes.

In the past we used to take the current development processes as a given. It was management's responsibility to adjust development processes when and where needed. We almost always reluctantly adopted process changes. It has worked, hasn't it? Why do we need to change what works? Frankly speaking, we didn't care too much about the processes: to work on software and its architecture was and is much more fun.

The new role of a software architect changes that we cannot take processes for granted any more. We have to review architecture from other areas and we have to put given software development processes on the test bench. It can be the processes, which improves or destroys architecture. It is important to understand that we have to take care of architecture relevant processes. Software development processes have become part of software architects' responsibility.

2.4.3   Role Enrichment #3: To Convince Management Is Key!

At all times software developers and architects have been asked by management to provide their viewpoint. Good managers always include expert views before deciding on future steps. This consulting role was important and will become even more important in future. The consulting service will grow to a more responsible service to convince, where advice is no longer enough. As the complexity of software architecture increases, management responsibility increases too. And with the rise of new management challenges, managers are getting more disconnected from software architecture knowledge. Good software architects are required to convince their managers by all means, if they see the potential irreversible damage of a decision.

Let's continue the insights of the architecture review in the case study above and see how management decisions can affect architecture.

It was one of Greg's daily core team meetings. During discussions of the principle architecture with experts, the core team identified and questioned the purpose of a couple of layers in the software.
"It is certainly a good idea to introduce an abstraction layer, if you want to achieve loose coupling. Did we need loose coupling here?" asked Greg and his core team: this seemed to be a very obvious question.
Following this line of questioning further, they learned more about the layers themselves. They understood how and why the layers were built – and how management decisions led to some peculiar architectural objects. Some of the software layers were important, to hide architectural decisions, and to build a robust shell around fragile pieces.
"The implementation of the architecture was finally successful, but we still recognize the scars from past decisions!" was Greg's final remark.

2.4.4   Role Enrichment #4: Don't Get Caught Up in Technology, Make Unbiased Judgments

One consequence of taking the business persons view is the requirement of judging objectively. How can a software architect assess an unknown architecture objectively? He has to rely on the evaluation of experts. All of them have their own vested interests, whether they are defending their architecture decisions, or their favorite path forward. Objective criteria for ones assessment are required, but often difficult to obtain.

Balancing business needs with technical issues becomes part of the duties for software architects too. That means that modern software architects accept management tools like risk evaluation. Drawing the picture from a business perspective is just one answer of staying unbiased in a world of conflicting objectives.

In this book we will discuss the necessary means to operate as a software architect effectively and to deliver reliable and measurable results.

2.5   Governance to the Extreme: Proper and Effective Measures

From the examples above we have learned that governance of software development is essential to limit risk. Even gaps in governance can lead to damage. All the patterns, which we see in the world of economics, are valid for software development as well. If we want to develop software products with prominent quality characteristics, we need to implement software development governance to achieve these properties. As indicated in the accounting scandal events, we can over correct. We can govern more than required. This is at the very least inefficient, can lead to low acceptance of the principle among involved parties, which is a prevalent mood against governance.

2.5.1   Govern What Is Essential

In many cases the introduction of governance is the result of a problem that should
be avoided in the first place. The start of governance is accompanied with the
optimism that accompanies the launch of something new. Loaded with this enthu-
siasm, architecture governance is seen as the answer to all issues related to risk.
Wherever risk is assumed, this risk is expected be covered by governance. We have
the governance pendulum swinging to the other extreme, and governance to the
extreme can be the beginning of the end of governance.

So, we recommend that all involved overcome this temptation to over govern.
Keep governance simple and govern what is essential. Limit your set of rules to
cope only with the highest risks. Don't allow too many rules, which will inevitably
not be completely followed – as we have seen in the examples in Sect. 2.2. Instead,
institute fewer rules and make governance of those rules effective. Let things go,
which are not in your focus. Carefully determine the scope of your governance!
When you define your governance scope, identify what is worthwhile to be
governed, selecting only those topics which cannot be achieved otherwise.

2.5.2   Keep It Simple but Adequate

Keep the scope and process simple. Determine which measures are needed to insure
your governance scope. Limit your efforts to essential activities. Architecture
governance is not universally accepted by everybody. If the introduction of architecture governance is too bold, to limiting, acceptance will be low. Low acceptance
results in resistance and architecture governance will be ignored eventually, if not
widely accepted. So, carefully select the methods you want to use in architecture
governance. If you notice that something cannot be grasped universally, make it
simpler.

2.5.3   Tackle the Risks

How do we find the right balance? We should start simple; we should avoid
strangling software development. Architecture governance is supposed to tackle
major risks. Proper guidelines are those which address these risks.

2.5.4   Do You Know Your Weakest Points?

We have learned that it is prudent to start architecture governance carefully. We
should resist the temptation to load up architecture governance with lots of
guidelines and measures. We should start simple. However, there is another temptation to resist, in other words there is a trap we ought to know and prevent. The
effectiveness of governance should be apparent to all! This means that we should

successfully be able to cope with the top risks which we identified and which are addressed by our architecture governance scope. In other words, we should not take on too many scope items, and what we take should be successfully completed.

Here we can also learn from the economy. Basel II failed at its weakest point. And the weakest point is a danger for architecture governance as well. When we review the architecture governance set-up, we should look for the weakest points. The weakest point could be a product component, where it is difficult to execute architecture governance. If we fail at this point, this has a major impact on the whole product. We must take care of this particular component. Another weak point could be identified within the governance process. Again, if we fail with a process step within governance, then the overall success of the product can be endangered. Before you improve the other parts of your governance approach, before you start to optimize anything, identify your weakest points and strengthen them. The risk assessment in Chap. 10 will give you some hints and guidance on how to identify your weak points from a risk perspective.

2.5.5 Plan Process Improvements

From the Greek insolvency risk we learned a few things. It is better start process improvement right from the beginning. Whatever governance approach you set-up, learn from the issues early on and iterate on your approach. In Europe we did this late. Many economists knew about the risks and weaknesses of the Euro trading zone. And though it was identified and seemingly accepted, once the risk of Greek insolvency became evident, Europe had to deal with two challenges at the same time. The Euro countries needed to identify the biggest gaps and fill them urgently. And they needed to help Greece with special measures and treatment.

There is another lesson we can learn as well. Don't allow violation or exceptions to rules from the beginning. If there is a need to get exceptions early on, your rules might be too strict. At this point it is better to reconsider your rules. If there are early request for deviations, this is an indicator that later someone will make the case for ignoring your rules all together. It is also better be strict as possible at the beginning to demonstrate the importance of the new governance.

In order to avoid these type of situations for newly launched architecture governance, plan "lessons learned" sessions from the beginning. Learn from gaps and potential risks and start improvements. These lessons can also identify opportunities to get rid of wasteful practices to streamline the process.

2.5.6 Correlation Between Efficiency and Effectiveness

There is a balance between efficiency and effectiveness of governance. You can be more efficient by omitting or simplifying activities and reducing governance measures. While you may save costs by these means, you may increase the risk of undetected damage. It is a decision about different cost types. You substitute immediate costs with risk costs, which mean costs from potential damage.

The governance perspective could be: *Don't reduce governance measures, accept the governance costs, as governance will prevent higher damages later.* You might think that increasing efficiency will eat up effectiveness, but you raise the risk of not achieving the quality properties you had defined in your architecture governance scope.

However, reducing or simplifying governance activities can also increase effectiveness. In the end, governance effectiveness is more than the number of activities defined in its process. Governance effectiveness includes how participants are willing and able to follow the process and to comply with the rules. The more complex architecture governance is, the lower acceptance you find among the participants. Low acceptance leads to a more formal compliance and less quality awareness, and higher the risk that you are not effective.

There is an additional correlation between efficiency and effectiveness. A change in efficiency can worsen or improve your effectiveness. It is the right balance we need to find and define.

2.5.7 Architecture Governance: Is There Still Room for Innovation?

And the final point is to highlight innovation. One of the early apprehensions is that architecture governance will kill innovation. And it does, if you do not implement it carefully. But if you balance architecture governance correctly, innovation can be kept alive and grow.

2.6 Summary

We have learned that governance and audits are never in place from the beginning. We encountered some patterns in the global economy and derive guidance from these patterns for software governance. We explain the related – but local – situation in software industry and its impact. We continue with illuminating the changed role of software engineers. A case study in corporate governance followed to let us understand the advantages of architectural governance. Some words of caution to avoid extremes completed the introductory picture of a changed world of software development.

References

1. Braudel, F. Sozialgeschichte des 15.-18. Jahrhunderts. Band III: Aufbruch zur Weltwirtschaft, Kindler Verlag, München 1986, ISBN 3-463-40027-8.
2. Home page of Bank for International Settlements. http://www.bis.org/publ/bcbs128a.pdf.
3. Home Page of CNet News. http://news.cnet.com/2100-1001-816880.html.
4. Home page of the Federal Reserve, press release from 30 Sep 2005. http://www.federalreserve.gov/boarddocs/press/bcreg/2005/20050930/default.htm.

Are You Connected: CIO, Architect, and Auditor?

What's in It for Me?

CIOs, architects and auditors have common interests in software sustainability audits. We will carve out these common interests, look at the different perspectives and define how to link these three roles together, making your tasks more effective.

CIO/CTO

If you want to know what can happen in your company, read and enjoy the story in Sect. 3.1. You can also jump to the end of Sect. 3.1 and briefly learn what you and the internal audit department have in common. Section 3.2 details corporate governance and its application in software producing companies. From Sect. 3.4 you better understand how you and internal audit functions can co-operate. Some final statements about the roles are described in Sect. 3.5.

Software Architect

The story in Sect. 3.1 could be déjà vu for you or a possible new experience waiting for you around the corner. Whatever your situation, the story explains some approaching tasks in software development. Read the story to be prepared. Section 3.2 gives some background about corporate governance and its relevance in the software industry. Section 3.4 can be read to understand where to find federates in auditing tasks. Some final statements about the roles are described in Sect. 3.5.

(continued)

R. Gutbrod and C. Wiele, *The Software Dilemma*, Management for Professionals, DOI 10.1007/978-3-642-27236-3_3, © Springer-Verlag Berlin Heidelberg 2012

> **Auditor**
>
> As independent internal auditor you keep a certain distance to development processes at your company. And though, there might be activities similar to your internal audit tasks. Start with the story in Sect. 3.1 to reveal the audit services in software development. Section 3.2 explains corporate governance background. Skip it or take it as recall. Section 3.3 indicates how your department and software development areas can co-operate. Some final statements about the roles are described in Sect. 3.5.

Software development and internal audit services are two absolutely different departments. Once in a while, if at all, an internal auditor visits the department of software development. But most time they spend on stuff like accounting, fraud or how the CIO runs IT. Software development and internal audit services are two different worlds – at least had been two different worlds in the past. Both areas are evolving. The software development complexity requires new methods to manage sustainable software. And also internal audit services are taking new orientations. Internal audit departments have discovered value adding services which they can provide software development departments. Unnoticed, the two areas have approached each others. If common interests are not immediately recognized, both of them can come into conflict with each other. Before we will explain the common interests and resolutions, we would like to take you one step further. What will happen, if both emerging tasks from software development and internal audits stay inwardly?

Let us start to explain the connective interests by telling a story about the opposite extreme: When the common interests collide.

3.1   When Common Interests Collide

This is a short story about an unresolved conflict of interests. The parties are:
- *Brian Steinherch, mediator in charge of resolving conflicts (the interested reader may learn more about this methodology in [1] or [2])*
- *Kai Salvish, CIO and initially an unnoticed partner in the conflict*
- *Gregory Naizirk, principal architect and main participant in the conflict*
- *Sam Tamies, auditor and main participant in the conflict*

Brian Steinherch arrived at the company. He parked his car in the parking garage for guests and went to the reception. "My name is Mr. Steinherch. I have an appointment with Mr. Kai Salvish at 9", Brian introduced himself.

Brian is a mediator. He had been called by the company's CIO, Kai Salvish, to facilitate the resolution of an ongoing conflict. He has used an initial phone call with Mr. Salvish to get a basic understanding of the conflict. The conflict concerns differing opinions about auditing roles for auditing tasks at the company. An auditor and an architect doing auditing tasks are involved in the conflict. The CIO might have some stake in resolving this role conflict, Brian thought. Brian still has a lot of open questions and is curious about the relevant facts and the persons involved in the conflict.

Brian usually prefers to do mediation sessions outside the company. This way the conflict parties get some distance from their work. That lets them be more relaxed and lessens the overall session tension. Most clients agree to his proposal. This time the CIO insisted on using company space. "It is the only chance to get all parties together", he argued. In the phone conversation Mr. Kai Salvish agreed on three conflict resolution sessions with one working day for each session. Today, the first meeting starts at 10, so Brian has some time to prepare the meeting room for the mediation session.

"Good morning Mr. Steinherch". The CIO appeared and welcomed Brian. "I hope you have had a good trip."

"Good morning, Mr. Salvish. Nice to meet you! It is fine weather today. The sun is already with us."

There was some more small talk till they arrived at the meeting room.

Brian looked at the room. "Very good, this room looks very good! Do you mind, if I take some time to get ready for the meeting?"

"Not at all! See you at 10."

Brian just finished his last preparation for the meeting, when the invitees arrived. "Good morning! My name is Gregory Naizirk. You must be Mr. Steinherch."

"Good morning. Yes, I am Mr. Steinherch. I am going to facilitate our meetings about 'company auditing'."

'Company auditing' was the title to take for the series of meetings, Brian and Mr. Salvish decided.

"Hello! I am Mr. Tamies, Sam Tamies. I am from the internal audit service team."

"Nice to meet you, Mr. Tamies", said Brian.

Kai Salvish, the CIO, joined the team. "Is everything okay?"

"Yes, everything is perfect. Thank you!" Brian nodded. "Please let's have a seat and get started."

After some further welcome exchanges, Brian introduced himself, the concept of mediation as a professional means to clarify and resolve conflicts, his mandate and the conflict as he understood it, and the history of contacts with the CIO.

"I had a short call with your CIO, Mr. Salvish." Brian started to unveil his knowledge about the situation. "I gained a brief understanding about the conflict. I understand that there are two different auditing tasks at your company, and this has caused some irritation around your audit roles. I also understand that software development is an important theme at your company. You develop a major part of the software in use at your company to cope with your core tasks. Frankly speaking, I am not an expert of software development and not an expert of auditing within a business. I would like to know more about each of your contributions and your view of this tense situation. I am sure all of you are certainly keen to share your stories with me. While I see each of your needs to tell me your views, I first would like to hear each view completely before moving on to the next persons view. This process helps me to listen carefully to each of you. Mr. Salvish, why don't you start to explain why you asked for this mediation and tell your view of the situation? I suggest continuing in a clockwise manner after you are finished."

"Yes, of course. Thank you Mr. Steinherch for you cordial introduction. I am the CIO of this company. As such, one of my tasks is to take care of the software we buy and the software we build in-house. In the past, I encountered several situations where I have needed a clearer picture about the status of our own software and their related risks. Let me give you an example. I made a decision to continue our in-house software development for a certain product instead of replacing it by available software in the market. Our in-house built software was tailor-made to our company's needs, the business liked the software a lot which was the major reason for our decision to continue in-house development. Later, however, it turned out that the foundation of our software was too old. The software could not be enhanced easily. We now bore the risk of not being competitive in our long term business plans because our software was difficult to enhance. It took us too long to add new *required business functions, and we had some security issues as well. Our CEO was not amused about this situation. I don't want to experience such a situation again. I want more transparency about our complete portfolio of the software we use. I want to know, where we are in covering the requirements of our business, the architecture robustness, what the risks for the company are, and be enabled to make informed decisions in the future."*

"Mr. Steinherch, I see that the unclear information you had in the past still makes you very angry." Brian interrupted.

"Yes, indeed. That was a very ugly situation. I need to get a clear picture of the software status in future." Mr. Salvish almost exploded.

"I understand that you did not feel comfortable at that time." Brian tried to summarize Mr. Salvish's perspective. "You are supposed to make informed decisions about software investments and you need transparency of your software architecture to make sustainable decisions."

"Yes, that is exactly what I mean. I can only make sustainable decisions, if I get clear information about the state of the software architecture." Mr. Salvish has become calm again. He felt that his point was well understood. "Anyway, after a series of those experiences I ordered a comprehensive assessment of our software. I asked Greg, I mean Mr. Naizirk, to conduct software audits of everything we have. Greg is my principal architect. I want to know the foundation stability of each software product, and all major risks I bear with the current software components."

"I understand. The software audits you requested are important for you to eventually be enabled to make informed decisions." Brian summarized again. He nodded his head and looked to the auditors, Mr. Naizirk and Mr. Tamies.

"Yes, that's the point. And here is where the conflict started as I see it. There are two things which bother me. While I need transparency about our soft-ware situation, I don't want any interruptions in the software departments. This is conflict number one. Gregory Naizirk is a brilliant principal architect. But these damn software audits brought too much disturbance into our software development. One department manager after another came to me with almost the same question, can't we assess the architecture without disrupting our development projects? Conflict number two is caused by our internal audit department. When Mr. Tamies heard about our software audits, he claimed to own these audits. Auditing is his business, he said. However, I never received information about our software risks from our internal audit department and I t need this kind of information."

"Please let me summarize to see if I have understood your issues correctly, Mr. Salvish." Brian thought that he understood the major points from the CIO. "You first are irritated because of reported concerns from the development teams. It is important to you and your development teams that they can work in peace in order to produce high quality products."

"Right" Mr. Salvish nodded.

"You are also annoyed by the intervention of the internal auditor. You definitely need clarity about the software situation in your company and you fear that the discussion concerning the auditing responsibility in your company could endanger this transparency." Brian looked at Mr. Tamies.

"Absolutely correct" Mr. Salvish agreed again.

"Fine", said Brian. "I think I have got a good insight of your view of the situation by now, Mr. Salvish. I noticed that Mr. Naizirk and Mr. Tamies have resisted sharing their views thus far. Thank you for your patience, Gentlemen. Let's move on to Mr. Naizirk.? Tell me Mr. Naizirk, what is your take on the situation?"

"Well, first of all I must confess that some of the things said so far is new to me." Mr. Naizirk started his thoughts. "I never heard that I should avoid bothering the development teams. Now I understand why I never got a response from Mr. Salvish when I wanted to escalate the development teams' lack of response to my auditing their area. But that makes me even angrier. It is a tough job to do an assessment. Not everybody is willing to unveil the facts. Especially if the teams fear that their development could be stopped.

The developed software is their baby. They do everything short of not telling the truth to keep the dangerous risks in their software a secret. I really need the CIO's support in these situations. He must decide what is more important to him. If transparency is as important as he claimed, then I expect full support to make the development teams co-operative."

"I see that you are very disappointed as you relate your last assessment to us." Brian started to capture the main thought.

"Yes, absolutely" Mr. Naizirk continued expressing his anger. *"It must be clear that looking into the existing software will make the colleagues nervous. The developers and their managers want to safeguard their jobs. The software audits break into the development process like a foreign object. If I am supposed to find the risks I need full support and co-operation from all concerned."*

"I understand." Brian repeated. *"Such a software audit is a very difficult task. You have to deal with emotional factors in the teams. You need your CIO's support to successfully deliver the required results."* And Brian looked at the CIO briefly.

"Yes, that is perfectly stated. The job is hard enough by itself and is doubly difficult with the emotional conflicts. A software audit is more than just judging the architecture. It is also about people. The minimum I need is the CIO's support. I need Mr. Salvish's support to get the co-operation from the involved teams. Furthermore, there was the confusion with the internal audit department. Sam Tamies is a good friend of mine. I asked him how he conducted internal audits. I told him that I have been asked to do similar tasks. I thought I can learn from him. Sam got really upset immediately and I am still not sure why. I thought I can learn from his methods. Although software audits and internal audits have similar processes, they are still different in some respects, aren't they? I don't know how a software audit could interfere with the services of internal audits, but somehow there must be a conflict because Sam got really upset."

"It is incredible that we start a new team for internal audits!" Sam could not hold back any longer, he had to intervene.

"Okay, okay." Brian interrupted the outburst. *"I understand that we need some discussion about the two types of audits. Mr. Tamies, I am sure you have some valuable insights into the situation and I will turn to you soon. I still would like to fully understand Mr. Naizirk's perception first. Would you mind waiting a few more minutes with your statements?"*

"Yes, sure" Mr. Tamies nodded.

"Thank you, Mr. Tamies", Brian gave Mr. Naizirk a signal to move on.

"As I said, Sam and I have been friends for some time. But when I told him about our software audit approach, he became really weird."

Brian tried to paraphrase what he understood. *"For you, Mr. Naizirk, the recently initiated software audit was a new task. You see these software audits as integral part of your architecture job. I understand that, beside the necessary support you need, that you even feel enriched by this new task. At the same time you noticed that there might be some overlaps with internal audits. Is that what you gathered from Mr. Tamies' reaction?"*

"Yes, absolutely" Mr. Naizirk confirmed. *"I just wanted to get some information from Sam. In fact, it seemed that we have some overlaps in our tasks."*

"You said it seemed that there are some overlaps, do you mean that you felt that Mr. Tamies recognized some clashes between your tasks?" Brian wanted some clarity in this topic.

"Yes. I felt that Sam was irritated by my new task. For some unknown reason it made him nervous."

"How did you feel, when you noticed that Mr. Tamies was irritated?"

"I was confused as well. I went back to Mr. Salvish. I asked him, whether I or colleagues from the internal audit department should do the audits. After I spoke with Sam, I thought that the approach of software audits was aligned with the internal audit department."

"I understand" Brian summed up. *"It was awkward for you to do a job that could have been assigned to your friend Sam Tamies, wasn't it?"*

"Yes. I felt terrible after the conversation with Sam."

"I see. First you were shocked about the intense reaction of your friend. Second, you felt bad and were uncomfortable about your task, but you want to do a good job. Last, you need clarification about the difference of your job and the one of your friend Sam Tamies. You see software audits as an important means to get insight of the software, and at the same time, you don't want conflicts with the internal audits of your friend."

"Yes, that's right." Mr. Naizirk felt for the first time that the discussion went in the right direction. His problem seemed to be recognized.

"Mr. Tamies," Brian moved on to the internal auditor. *"Thank you for your patience. It must have been hard for you to listen all the time, without voicing your view on the situation. How do you perceive the introduction of the new service of software audits?"*

"Thanks!" Mr. Tamies took a deep breath. *"I don't know how to start. I was really shocked, when I heard from Greg that our CIO started his own internal audits. In companies worldwide there is just one internal audit organization. The internal audit department makes sure the company does not get into trouble with fraudulent activities, compliance with regulations, and even how effective and efficient our processes run. And then this new audit task for Greg"*, Mr. Tamies took again a deep breath. He was deeply moved by the CIO's initiative.

"Mr. Tamies, I see that the introduction of software audits affected you directly. Is there anything else you would like to tell us on why you were so concerned about these software audits?" Brian granted Mr. Tamies a break.

"Look, auditing internal processes is a classic internal audit topic. That is our job. Of course, we are more focused on legal and compliance aspects. We currently don't have the required technology knowledge to assess our software in detail. But basically that is our job. With our internal audits we need to address major company risks. And there can only be one independent internal audit team in a company. I still can't believe that our CIO launched a new internal audit team. That is unbelievable!"

"I see that this really bothered you, Mr. Tamies. A unique and independent internal audit team is important for you to guarantee reliable audit results." Brian tried to understand Mr. Tamies' thoughts.

"Yes.", Mr. Tamies replied. *"Yes, we have to report our audit result. I don't know how we can report reliably, if there are other audit teams in this company."*

"Thank you, Mr. Tamies.", Brian was going to sum up the interests of all participants. *"Before we have a short break, I would like to summarize what I understood so far.*

Mr. Salvish as CIO is supposed to make decisions about software development. To this end, he needs reliable information about the software architectures of in-house built and bought software. For this reason he initiated software audits. Software audits for all existing software products shall provide him an overview of the overall architectural situation and enable him to make informed decisions. This is supposed to be a means of quality assurance. While having initiated software audits, it is important to Mr. Salvish that the development teams can continue to do their software development without a large distraction.

Mr. Naizirk is responsible for the new service of software audits. He is very interested in bringing transparency into the architectural situation. He is in charge of the new service of software audits. He sees a challenge in the fact that software audits not only deal with software, but also with people. He needs the co-operation of the development teams to fairly judge the status of the products. To this end, he also needs the CIO's support in critical situations. While Mr. Naizirk sees the value of software audits, he is irritated at the same time, because he felt an overlap with the internal audit services. Both, Mr. Naizirk and Mr. Tamies, need clarity about distinction of the two audit tasks: the new software audits and the internal audit services.

Mr. Tamies is worried as well about possible overlaps of both audit tasks. For him a unique internal audit team is essential to cope with external requirements for internal audits. The internal audit team must be an independent unit. The reports of the internal audit team are considered comprehensive. Missing facts, which are provided by other audit teams could question the reliability of the internal audit services."*

We could let the mediator, Brian Steinherch move on with his conflict resolution. He will identify more common and conflicting interests. Most certainly, he would end up with a result, which we intend to introduce here: The commonalities and differences of software sustainability audits and internal audit services; and proposals for collaborations between the two service teams.

There are two conflicts of interests touched in the story. One is a conflict between Greg, the principal architect, and Mr. Salvish, the CIO. Their conflict is about how to conduct an audit in software development. This has a conceptual component of software audits, for instance, how to define the right scope and early alignments with stakeholders. We will learn about that in the next chapters. And it certainly has a communication component, even if not mentioned in the dialogues yet. How communication matters is explained in Chap. 13. The second conflict that we will take care of in this chapter is the one of interests between software development and internal audits. We can take the mediator's summary to understand this conflict:

- The CIO needs transparency about software development. As such, he started software audits to get insights into the status of software development projects and the expected sustainability of the products.
- Auditing is the primary task of the internal audit department. According to Sarbanes-Oxley act (SOX) and international audit standards an internal audit team needs to be independent from operations. Hence, the recently defined software audits contradict both, the audit authority of the internal audit department, and the legally required independence.

3.2 Software Development: On the Radar Screen of Corporate Governance?

We have seen in Chap. 2 that a crisis is often followed by the call for increased governance. As a result of some financial incidents and crises in the past, rules and requirements for companies for effective governance have been established – the so called corporate governance. Let us look how this governance framework relates to our topic of software development.

The headline connects two things that might not be obviously connected: software development and corporate governance. "Ah, you are talking about audit capabilities we have to build into the software" is what might come to your mind when you see the terms software development and corporate governance in one sentence. Surely, when you develop software you have to ensure that the software itself allows the fulfillment of legal requirements, for instance, of audit ability. But this is not what is meant.

Your initial reaction could also have been different depending on your background. As a software architect you might have a clear idea what software development is about, but corporate governance? This is not an idea that you may have come in contact with yet. Are you an auditor? You probably know about corporate governance, but what about the specifics of software development? This most likely has not been your primary focus. As a CIO or CTO you hopefully have a rough idea of both. But how do they relate? It still might not be obvious to you.

There are different viewpoints on the same topic – this is an example of why we address this book to different target groups. Software architects, auditors, CIOs – all have to step outside their classical domains and get to know the other domains, respectively. At the very least it will make your life easier, so join us on this journey.

There is a deeper relation. Software development can have a severe impact on a company's operations and thus it is relevant for corporate governance. So we have to understand this relation.

3.2.1 Corporate Governance: A Closer Look

First of all we have to understand more about corporate governance. In very general terms, corporate governance covers processes, customs, policies, laws, and institutions affecting the way a company is directed, administered or controlled. Corporate governance is often discussed vividly in the context of financial accounting of publicly traded companies. This is basically a result of several accounting scandals having occurred in past years. Corporate governance is to some extent an approach to establish principles that make a "good" company for its stakeholders, the shareholders and employees.

While corporate governance is a broad area with many facets, we will focus only on certain aspects that are relevant in the specific context of software development. To be more precise, we focus on the consequences of corporate governance for companies whose core business is software development. It is also valid for companies where software development represents at least a significant part of the business, or who run strategic software development projects to support their core business.

3.2.1.1 Corporate Governance Principles

In many countries corporate governance is codified into law. We do not need to look into the individual laws of different countries, but rather focus on the core principles behind corporate governance. As a set of good corporate governance practices the Organization of Economic Cooperation and Development (OECD) has defined and published the *OECD Principles of Corporate Governance* [3]. These principles provide the basis for more specific national corporate governance guidelines in many countries. But for our discussion it is sufficient to look at these general principles.

Many principles relate to the way a company has to report and handle financial data and how to interact with stakeholders. Nevertheless, there is one more generic section relevant for us that is dedicated to the responsibilities of the board listed below:

OECD Principles of Corporate Governance [3]

[. . .]

VI. The Responsibilities of the Board

The corporate governance framework should ensure the strategic guidance of the company, the effective monitoring of management by the board, and the board's accountability to the company and the shareholders.

A. Board members should act on a fully informed basis, in good faith, with due diligence and care, and in the best interest of the company and the shareholders.

[. . .]

D. The board should fulfill certain key functions, including:

1. Reviewing and guiding corporate strategy, major plans of action, risk policy, annual budgets and business plans; setting performance objectives; monitoring implementation and corporate performance; and overseeing major capital expenditures, acquisitions and divestitures.

2. Monitoring the effectiveness of the company's governance practices and making changes as needed.

At first sight these principles seem to be quite abstract and there is nothing specific about software development mentioned. Nevertheless, these few sentences imply direct consequences for software developing companies.

3.2.2   Corporate Governance Meets Software Development

Let us understand in which way the above principles affect software developing companies. There are two central themes – the informational basis and governing the execution of the strategy.

- *Information basis*: There is an unmistakable requirement given in the above principles: "*Board members should act on a fully informed basis (. . .)*" [3]. As we have already seen software development has become a much more challenging task. We have to cope with increasing complexity and requirements to make new software fit into an existing landscape. This does not only imply the risk of failure, but it becomes increasingly difficult to judge the real status of a software project or product. Wrong assumptions about the status of a software development project or product – and thus an invalid basis of information – can have severe impact on the company. What makes a valid basis of information in the context of software development? The basis of information does not only refer to the financial data, but includes anything that is relevant for the company's welfare. The board requires information that relates the technical details of a software product to the potential business impact. To provide valid information in the sense of corporate governance, these technical details and the resulting complexity have to be translated into a business impact and risk that can be understood by top management and the board. Only insight into the (potential) impact will allow for educated decisions. This sets new expectations for people in software development – especially for architects as we will see further in our discussions. In addition to this translation process, a valid basis of information requires the ability of an independent assessment of the provided information. In other words the internal audit function needs to be extended accordingly. The requirements for such an audit function are described later in the context of software sustainability audits.

• *Governing execution of the strategy*: The second – related aspect – focuses more on the operational and direct governance aspects. The principles above require the board to review and guide the strategy and the corresponding execution. Moreover, the board is required to monitor the governance activities. The latter simply implies that there actually *is* governance available to ensure execution according to the strategy. In other words corporate governance implies effective governance of software development processes according to a defined strategy. It does not mean simply having any development process. As we will see later on, achieving effective software development processes – processes that ensure the development of sustainable software – is not an easy task. For that reason we introduce the concept of process validation audits in the context of software audits.

So, where are we? Corporate governance – originally driven from the financial point of view – has direct consequences for developing software. Still – to our experience – companies have not embraced this idea to the required extent today. There is much room for improvement to utilize internal audits in the context of software development which requires shaping the audit function accordingly. Furthermore, the translation of technical issues into business risks and impacts is not yet a natural skill expected from software architects.

3.3   From Corporate Governance to Effective Control

Now, here we are: First, there is the area of internal audit function headed by the Chief Audit Executive (CAE). This internal audit department takes an important role in corporate governance.

> "The key role of internal audit is to assist the board and/or its audit committee in discharging its governance responsibilities by delivering:
> • An objective evaluation of the existing risk and internal control framework.
> • Systematic analysis of business processes and associated controls.
>   (...)
> • Recommendations for more effective and efficient use of resources.
>   (...)"
> [4]

But internal audit departments intend to extend their service offering. They usually cover standard audit areas [5] like accounting, fraud, management, information technology, business processes. While software development becomes an essential part of several companies, the processes of software development have just started to be covered by internal audit services. And though, according to general principles of internal audits as described in [4] the company risks of software development need to be evaluated, too.

Furthermore, internal audit departments are supposed to give "recommendations for more effective and efficient use of resources" [4]. We see that this task is intended to being extended as well. Beside the evaluations and analysis, consulting services is likely to be offered by internal audit departments. Transparency to enable the board to "act on a fully informed basis" [3] should be enriched by consulting on how to manage the unveiled risks.

While both enhancements are in the spirit of corporate governance, internal audit departments are still limited to provide these service extensions. Resources are available for auditing standard audit areas. To offer audit services also for the area of software development, more resources are required.

In addition, the new auditors need capabilities in software development. Skills and experiences from software development are required. This is even more important as software development is not as standardized as other business processes. For accounting and even IT processes, questionnaires and check lists are available, e.g. IT Infrastructure Library (ITIL®) [6], Control Objectives for Information and Related Technology (CobiT) [7], which can be used in internal audits. Software development processes are only weakly covered by those standards.

On the other hand, internal audit organizations bring along valuable assets to audit software development and add consulting services. They have proven frameworks and tools, which can be utilized. The internal auditors have the right audit process skills. Moreover, they also have the abilities to present issues in terms of business impacts and business risks – a language needed to ensure that the board members can "act on a fully informed basis" [3].

The right ingredients are there in internal audit departments to grow from assisting in corporate governance to offering effective control in software development.

Secondly, there is the IT department or the department of software development, headed by CTO or CIO. A CIO is naturally interested in understanding the situation and the current risks of running software development projects. As head of these software development endeavors, CIOs need transparency to stop or change development projects, whenever needed.

Furthermore, the CTO and CIO is responsible or effectively involved in the two corporate governance principles as mentioned in Sect. 3.2 – providing adequate basis of information and governing the execution of the strategy with respect to software development. Software audits could be effective controls to retrieve the essential information to make informed decisions, or to provide the board the appropriate information to enable them to make informed decisions. Also, software audit activities help to monitor the status of strategy execution.

There are just a few facts, which hinder a CTO or CIO to establish software audits. First, in development teams audits are rather unknown. Quality assessments are tolerated as software quality can be improved early. However, the spirit to pro-actively validate software products and processes to achieve transparency of business risks and impacts are rather unpopular.

Second, knowledge about internal audit frameworks is missing in development areas. A quality management system typically offers a framework to check process compliance. But to validate software and related processes, a framework like internal audit functions is required.

Third, the translation of technical issues into business risks and impacts is not yet a natural skill expected from software architects.

On the other hand, the CTO or CIO has people with the right technical skill-set. Software architects can understand and validate used technologies and designed software architectures. They have a broad experience base with software development so they are able to assess efficiency and effectiveness of defined and executed development processes.

Thus, software development can grow to offering effective controls as part of corporate governance.

There is just one question to clarify. Who will be responsible for these new audit services? The approach is taken from internal audits. And the expertise can be found in the software development departments. It is an audit service, where two executives benefit: The Chief Audit Executive (CAE) and the CIO.

Both are interested in the operational risks which could endanger the business. The CIO is interested in these risks to manage his business to be successful. The CAE is interested in the same risks, to make everyone aware of potential risk and to mitigate these risks from corporate perspective. Both have different motivations to assess the risks, but both could lead to the same result, increase the company's prosperity and appropriately manage certain business threats.

Having understood the common goals, there is one restriction left that needs to be considered while answering the question of responsibility. "The internal audit function must be independent of the activities being audited and must also be independent from everyday internal processes" [4]. Software development expertise from the CTO area is needed, but software auditors from there will violate the requested independence rule of internal audit functions. A co-operative working model between these two areas can avoid this conflict and can utilize values and assets from both: development knowledge, audit experience and internal audit frameworks. A co-operative working model can delegate tasks to the CTO area and report results to both the CTO and the internal audit department.

The Software Sustainability Audit approach, which we introduce in this book, is actually a combination of the values of these two areas.

3.4   Roles in Your Company

Depending on the industry in which your company is involved, your relevant role may differ. If you major business is software development, you most certainly find yourself as CTO, Chief Technology Officer, of the company. If software development is a service you provide within your company, your restore yourself as CIO, Chief Information Officer. Below we will write about the CIO. Of course, CTOs of software companies are covered in these statements as well.

Similarly, the role of a software architect could be called differently in your company. You might find yourself as product manager or product owner with responsibilities which we identify with that of a software architect. Product managers and product owners, please find yourselves in the role of the described architect.

3.5 Summary

We have seen that the CIO, architects and auditors have common interests in software audits. The CIO needs software audits or software sustainability audits, as we will refer to them in this book, to get transparency about the software products and to make informed decisions, if software needs to be enhanced, rebuilt or acquired. On the contrary, the internal audit department has interest or even needs to offer their audit services for software related processes as well. Legally, the internal audit services need to stay independent from operations. A well-defined co-operation between software audits and internal audit services, can result in their overall efforts being even stronger.

References

1. Thomann, C., & Prior, C. (2007). Klärungshilfe 3, Das Praxisbuch, Rohwolt Taschenbuch Verlag, Reinbek bei Hamburg, ISBN 978-3-499-62214-4.
2. Bähner, C., Oboth, M., & Schmidt, J. (2008). Konfliktklärung in Teams & Gruppen, Junfermann Verlag Paderborn 2008, ISBN 978-3-87387-679-8.
3. Web site of OECD, Organisation for Economic Co-operation and Development. http://www.oecd.org/daf/corporateaffairs/principles/text.
4. KPMG. (2003). Internal audit's role in modern corporate governance. Thought leadership series, Hongkong 2003.
5. Kagermann, H., Kinney, W., Küting, K., & Weber, C.-P. (2008). Internal audit handbook, Management with SAP®-audit roadmap. Berlin/Heidelberg: Springer, ISBN 978-3-540-70886-5.
6. Home page of ITIL®. www.itil.org.
7. Home page of ISACA®, COBIT framework. http://www.isaca.org/Knowledge-Center/COBIT/Pages/Overview.aspx.

Building the Foundation

4

What's In It for Me?

Everyone in software development certainly has gained some experience with some form of architectural assessments. In this chapter, we lay the foundation for understanding the essential elements of successful architectural or Software Sustainability Audits. We describe typical pitfalls and must-have steps in your software audits.

CIO/CTO

If you already have had experience – whether positive or negative – with software assessments, you can jump directly to Sect. 4.2 and skip 4.1, which tells a motivating tale, about how missing methods can become problematic. Section 4.2 compares formal and less formal approaches of architecture reviews. Section 4.3 gives an overview of essential methods for any successful software audit. You may skip Sect. 4.4, which enriches Sect. 4.3 with additional hints. However, don't miss 4.5, where you'll see how Software Sustainability Audits are related to other methodologies like CobIT or ITIL. Section 4.6 summarizes the meaning of the Software Sustainability Audit concept.

Software Architect

The example in 4.1 provides and initial description of the value of an audit framework. Section 4.2 lists several formal and less formal approaches. 4.3 describes a toolbox that is helpful whenever you need to start a Software Sustainability Audit or some similar activity. Section 4.4 enriches 4.3 with valuable hints. You may skip 5.5 and complete the foundation with summaries in 4.6 and 4.7.

(continued)

R. Gutbrod and C. Wiele, *The Software Dilemma*, Management for Professionals,
DOI 10.1007/978-3-642-27236-3_4, © Springer-Verlag Berlin Heidelberg 2012

Auditor

The example in 4.1 and 4.2 describes a scenario that can be avoided if you use a proper internal audit framework. 4.3 will remind you of the aspects of your internal audits, and gives you some insights to the specific nature of architecture reviews. You may skip the hints in 4.4 and move on with Sect. 4.5, which defines how Software Sustainability Audits enrich other methodologies like CobIT and ITIL. In, 4.6 we summarize the basic meaning of architectural audits.

4.1   The Usual Suspects: Lessons Learned from Reviews

We don't want to rush into the theoretical aspects of Software Sustainability Audits, listing essential methods that we advise, without first providing some insight into why these methods are important or could be important for you. Before we provide a useful toolbox for any kind of software audit, it makes sense to discuss a fictional example about an architecture assessment, to help illustrate some potential challenges that could occur, which are inspired by actual experience.

This example shall impart a sense of what can go wrong in architectural review projects. Furthermore, we explain why this example review encountered some difficulties and how you can avoid similar tribulations. This example starts at the beginning, and provides some background for the architecture review. We will run through major steps of an architecture review. And we finish with an outlook of a potential aftermath of this architecture review.

This example features Gregory Naizirk, a principal software architect. Gregory has been asked by his CIO, Kai Salvish, to conduct an architecture review.

4.1.1   Have You Selected the Right Experts?

Greg plans a kick-off meeting for an architecture review. He is just a click away and the meeting request has been sent. He has carefully selected all the key experts needed for this review. His CIO, Kai Salvish, emphasized in the last preparation call that being neutral is extremely important.

"Yes, I am neutral", thought Greg. He is sure about it. But is he also perceived as neutral? He understands that perception is reality. So, he checked the list of participants again. Is anybody missing? Which questions need to be answered? Who are the right people to get proper and reliable information? Greg looked at the questions he has already gathered. Yes, he thought, he has selected the right people. But another aspect is important as well. Has he omitted anyone who would object that they have not been included? He checked his list of matter experts again. Yes, the list seems to be complete. He has even invited more experts than he expected to be needed, just to be balanced, he thought. He wanted to avoid any conflicts of interest. At the end of the review, the results must be reliable. Also, at the end of the review, Greg must prove his neutrality to his CIO Kai.

After having checked several times, Greg feels comfortable with his invitation list. And . . .

"here we go". He pressed the enter button. In an instant the colleagues will have received

the invitations. The architecture review can begin, and he will soon get feedback about his selection of experts ...

For several reasons, it is important to include the right experts. Of course, correctness and fairness stipulates a fair balance of participants. Every opinion should be heard and respected. Furthermore, at the end you want to have complete coverage of the subject. No significant snippet of information and examination should be missed. So, there are actually two key aspects to consider, and two traps to avoid.

First, identify the people you need to get answers to your questions. To meet this objective, start by compiling a comprehensive set of questions. Consider the root cause of some significant issues or concerns. Is there a history of the area you are reviewing? What is the reason, that you were asked to conduct an architecture review? You might look into the course of events that have led to the current state of that which you are investigating. Were there some specific decisions or actions that contributed to your suspected the root cause? You might get a different view of the real cause. After having identified a root question or main theme of your review, consider further related questions. Consider stakeholders of the theme. Stakeholders can be helpful to identify both questions you need to be answered, and specific experts that should be invited.

Secondly, consider any infighting. Are there different strategic directions which are unclear or unsolved? Are there silos, covering similar topics? Whenever you might get different answers from different departments or teams, it's better to include more experts, in order to form a more complete picture, especially when conflicting viewpoints may be presented. Redundancies are allowed: an extra interview can pay off.

4.1.2   Can You Explain Your Mandate?

Soon after Greg sent the invitation to the kick-off meeting, he was almost overrun with questions and requests. Adam, a software architect of the affected software, came into Greg's office. "I received an invitation for an architecture review. We have already looked at the architecture. What is the reason to do a review again? Is there anything different that will be done? Why are you in charge of such an architecture review? And – what is the scope of this review anyway? I saw that a lot of people invited to the kick-off meeting. Product managers are even on the list. This is certainly not an architecture review. What kind of political game is this?"

Greg sensed Adam's aggressive posture. Adam is a key player; he definitely needs him in the review project. But Greg is in hurry to get to a meeting he cannot miss, but he also feels that he needs to calm Adam down before he leaves his office.

"Adam, I understand that you are quite surprised by my e-mail.", Greg started.

"Yes, I am very much surprised about what's going on here. What is the damned reason ...?" Adam gasped for breath. Adam was very agitated.

It was difficult for Greg to maintain his composure, to avoid an emotional reaction. He felt uncomfortable, very uncomfortable. Something seems to have happened in the past. Greg has not yet checked the complete context of his mission.

When Adam panted for air, Greg took the opportunity to interrupt him very calmly. "Adam, I understand that you feel very uncomfortable. You have received just a short explanation with my invitation. You definitely want more clarity about the reason and the context of the review. It is essential that you can explain it to your team as well. I understand that. And I will be more than happy to provide you with all these details. It is also important to me to explain the rationale to you. And I would like to answer all your questions. That is the reason, why I have invited you to the kick-off meeting at short notice. And you are one of the most important participants there. Can I count on you in the kick-off meeting? There will be other colleagues, who certainly have similar questions and would like to know the answers of questions you ask. Could you allow me to answer all these questions in the kick-off meeting?" Greg noticed Adam's soft nod of apparent agreement. "Thank you for your understanding, Adam. See you in the kick-off meeting, then."

Preparation is important. Once you have sent an announcement mail of the intended review, you'd better already be prepared for the review to begin. A common attitude is to invite to a kick-off meeting, where you want to explain everything, and you think you have time till then to get prepared. That can turn out to be difficult. Once colleagues are aware of an imminent review, they will come to you with all kinds of questions. And you definitely should be sure about your mission. What has happened in the past that is relevant to understand? What is the rationale for an architecture review? You will be well advised to collect these basic background facts before you officially start the review. Thus, the review starts before the kick-off meeting. It is already underway at the time, when you send the invitation. The most frequently asked question is "why". It's crucial to be able to explain the nature of the initiative and its objectives. Don't hesitate to start gathering information from your sponsor in the early stages. Ask for the context, the history, the reason for the review. Don't settle for answers like "it is confidential", or "it is irrelevant". It is relevant to be able to explain the mission. Reviews are typically met with skepticism. You need to explain "why" and "why now".

4.1.3 Are You Aligned with Your Stakeholders?

The conversation with Adam taught Greg one important thing. He is not yet aligned with his stakeholders. Yes, he understood the tasks he would undertake. And he understood that neutrality, objectivity is very important. But he still wonders, why? What is special with this architecture review? Greg needs to know the history. What has happened that led up to this point? Even more important to know, what is the scope of the review? What is in, what is out of scope? It is a complex area, where your investigations can go in many directions. Jim, the senior manager responsible for the area under review, certainly is a key stakeholder with respect to this review. Are his interests the same as those from the sponsor, the CIO? Jim will have two roles at the end of the review. His area is going to be reviewed. And he will eventually judge Greg's objectivity in carrying out his tasks. Greg recognized that it was important to check with Jim.
Next, Greg sought a meeting with Jim. "Hi Jim! How are you doing? Thank you for taking your time to go through the background of the scheduled review. I would like to understand, what you see as in the scope of the review, and what is considered to be out of scope."
After a short talk Greg understood Jim's position. The software product subject to review comprises several components. There is one main component, which serves as foundation of the product. There is also a collaborative application standing aside this foundation. The collaboration part, even though important for customers, is considered out of scope.

Jim also added some constraints. Finally, Greg summarized his understanding of the discussion.

Greg had some doubts about the scope and the given constraints. Why should he exclude something that is required by customers? He got back to Kai, his CIO. He presented the scope as aligned with Jim. Kai agreed on the proposal. He explained that it is most important to verify, whether the foundation is stable and flexible enough to be used for the next generation of applications.

"Ah, good information", thought Greg. That more clearly defines the objective of the review.

And Kai appreciated Greg's approach. "It is good that Jim is already involved", he said. "Jim will be heavily involved in any follow up actions that may be necessary depending on the results of the review".

For every project it is a good idea to align the scope with the stakeholders; this is also the case for architecture reviews. It is helpful to avoid misunderstandings, which could result in conflict-prone situations later. It also improves the comprehension of the objective and the scope. It can also prevent people affected by the audit from engaging in political maneuvers. By being well prepared with aligned scopes, you can show proficiency in all related discussions. You may encounter situations where the experts involved are skeptical, and by aligning the key objectives and scope with stakeholders in advance, you are in a better position to build a convincing argument.

Stakeholders typically have different roles, and thus they may have different interests, and different views on the architecture review and its expected results. Lay all these interests out on the table. Make them transparent and lead the stakeholders toward a joint objective. In all further discussions, this will serve you well whenever you can refer to a mutual agreement with a stakeholder.

Additionally, gaining alignment early in the process ultimately empowers you. With their joint agreement the stakeholders pass on their power to you, power that you may wield effectively to resolve difficult situations.

4.1.4 Stick to Your Topic: Just Look at the Architecture!

Greg was in the middle of the kick-off meeting. The team members were introduced, the architecture review briefly explained. There was a short discussion about the objective, where Greg had to convince the team about the significance of this review. It was advantageous that he was able to refer to the objective, which had been previously aligned. Some of the participants of the meeting stated some minor complaints about the scope of the review. Again, he explained the objective, and how the scope and scope limitations indeed support the objective. Greg knew that successful communication often means repeated communication. Perception is reality. What is not heard has not been effectively communicated. The project structure presentation went quite smoothly. Thus, all these standard items had been presented and discussed.

Greg moved on to the review plan. "In a first session, I would like to learn the underlying business. Who can present the basic business requirements, explain the business processes, which are covered by the software or should be addressed in further releases?"

Greg elaborated a bit more about his expectations of that business session, which now triggered a lively discussion.

One of the participants chimed in, "I thought this is about architecture", "Why do you need the business requirements and the business goals? Please focus on the given objective – the stability of the architecture".

The conversation continued in this direction, and Greg could sense it was escalating. However, Greg was able to gain control of the proceedings.

"Look" Greg said. "At first glance your architecture might not reveal any flaws. If we better understand the business processes, however, we also understand non-functional requirements like performance, flexibility, and so forth. We even might be able to make some reasonable assumptions about future requirements, when we compare your business process with others from our experience. Looking at the business helps us to understand whether the architecture is capable to support the business process. The architecture might be stable with respect to current business requirements. However, future requirements could pose problems for this stability."

"That was close", Greg thought. At the end his argument "stable architectures need to support business requirements and foresee future business requirements" was convincing.

It is a frequent misunderstanding, when architecture is defined or should be inspected. What makes a particular architecture good or bad? There are certainly architecture patterns, which disclose some weaknesses. When is architecture stable? A stable architecture supports business and assumes future use cases. Just one additional requirement, one unexpected use case can de-stabilize your architecture. And there are other influencing factors. How solid are all assumptions? How effective were the processes around and beyond architecture? Insights into processes allow you further insights into architecture. The architecture embeds scars of processes and decisions!

4.1.5 Are You Supported by Management?

As Greg moved forward in his project to examine architecture, a mail from Jim arrived. "I think it is fine, now. I need my experts for other tasks. Could you please finish your review?"

Greg was puzzled. He has just started. Of course, he needs the experts for his investigations. And there is still a lot of time till the agreed deadline for the final report. And there is a lot to do. Greg got back to Jim. "I understand that these experts are crucial for your next development projects. While I respect your position, I still need to include them into my review work. I understood that at the moment the review had highest priority, because it will lay the foundation for our future. Certainly I may be mistaken. Please let us get back to the CIO to jointly define the proper priorities."

No further objection occurred after this mail exchange.

In the course of architecture reviews, or even in other endeavors, whenever you are likely to find major deficiencies and imperatives to improve things, you may experience various forms resistance, intimidation, or other types of disturbances. And by the way, your architecture assessment is also a disturbance for others. Instead of continuing smoothly with software development, they are interrupted by your architecture assessment. But nonetheless, you are charged with executing on your objectives You are expected to deliver reliable and useful results. And, if there is anything essential to improve, that has to be reported. But for many other items with medium risk or impact, it is a matter of balancing the business risks, which you might identify, with the potential costs involved in addressing the concerns.

Whatever situation you are in, it is important to understand your sponsor's expectations for the amount of effort to expend in executing the review. And it is important to have full support from management. In the course of the review, you may encounter critical situations, where you need to go back to your sponsor. Therefore, it's important to ensure upfront who are the managers for your review initiative, and to clarify escalation paths.

4.1.6 Look Outside the Box, But Stay Focused!

It is often discussed, how business needs and architecture should be balanced. And this is just an example for a family of discussions. Architect, auditor, reviewer, are you still focused? Are you yet working within the given scope? It is a slippery slope.

Whenever you review architecture or audit anything else, you should work with an attitude of openness. You are expected to collect observations, even if they are beyond the concrete scope. Prioritization comes later. First collect what you find, and often you need facts "outside the box" in order to judge elements" inside the box". You need other views to come to a valid conclusion.

While thinking outside the box, there is certain risk that you lose focus. You may end up with discarding the predefined scope. Even more, a change of focus can be desired by review participant, since distracting from the given scope can help them to keep secrets concealed. Whatever the reason is that causes you lose your focus, there is one additional effect: Results that are clearly out of scope, are perceived as unprofessional, while reviewers are perceived as subjective or biased. Objectivity is a precious value. It is hard to gain and easy to lose. Ultimately, perception is reality. Hence, whenever you look beyond the defined scope, ensure that objectivity is still granted.

4.1.7 And He Turns and Was Forgotten ...

Greg carefully proceeded with the review, interviewing all the right people who had involvement with, or responsibility for, the software product under review. He performed diligent analysis and assessment of all relevant concerns, and compiled the necessary information into his report. Carefully he went through all his findings, and he double-checked all his recommendations. He felt sure he could prove all the facts he listed in his final report. There were 10 major action items he defined and recommended. He assigned each action item to responsible persons. In follow up discussions, all owners of action items agreed to both the facts and the recommendations. Greg received appreciations from all parties including Jim and Kai for his tremendous work. "Real work from a leader", the CIO said. The architecture review was finished.

Half a year later, Greg crossed paths with some people working on the software product he reviewed. Some new people are working on this topic now, and Management changed as well. Greg became curious: What has happened with his review results? Was his document properly handed over to the new responsible persons? Have the decided action items in fact been considered? Greg spoke to an architect of this area, and he was quite relieved to hear that his document was used in the next development planning phase. Kai, his CIO, has already checked its implementation status.

Architecture review, like any other review or audit, does not stop at the delivery of the architecture review report. When you turn, you are forgotten. If there is no control for implementation of the recommendations, implementation just will not happen. Many things can go wrong. There can be changes of responsibilities, and a proper handover may not take place. New priorities can be set, with lost action items as result. If no one is charged with periodically checking the status of the action items, there is a risk that they will not be addressed, for various reasons. A mere "hello, what has happened with . . ." is a very good first step to make sure important recommendations get successfully implemented. Appealing to people's conscience can actually drive implementation.

4.1.8 And the CIO Had the Final Say

"Just another urgent and important task on my plate", Kai thought. As CIO he has a complex job; He has to manage many projects running in parallel featuring and several interdependencies. He has to evolve this product, make it ready for the next IT generation including cloud enablement, collaboration and so forth. "Is the basic architecture ready to take this product to the next level?" He is glad that Greg took on this task of an architecture review. He had a brief discussion with Greg about it. It was the first review of this kind, and Kai didn't have enough time to brief Greg on all important aspects of the product before he began his review. . . "Greg will hopefully get back to me, if he identifies any open questions" Kai thought.
Kai also appreciated the alignment of Greg with Jim, the development lead for this product. Jim was able to elaborate a bit more on the goals and the substantial elements in a follow up discussion. It was good to see both Greg and Jim on the same page. He wasn't sure how this architecture review would be perceived by Jim, but the results were impressive. It was clear that this was not a mere criticism of the architecture that was reviewed; Greg provided much more than a simple list of weaknesses from architecture point of view. Firstly, all the observations could be clearly understood, as proof points were provided for all of them. Moreover, the business impacts were made clearly transparent. Kai recognized the value of the prioritization of the relevant action items that was provided. "Good sense for business", he thought. It would reduce the preparation time needed to convince his colleagues from top management of the necessity of the proposed investments. Furthermore, it gave clear guidance to Jim, what steps to take in development. "It's now my turn", Kai thought, "to guarantee the implementation of the recommended activities." With this in mind, Kai sent a short mail to his COO, Greg's report attached, to ensure the required next steps.

4.2 The Basics: Never Start a Voyage Without a Plan

The examples in the last sections illustrate essential success factors in architecture reviews. Some potential snafus were included as well. Certainly the examples above are just fictional examples, to give you an idea of the sorts of things that can go wrong. Additionally, some ideas how to handle (or prepare for) a situation have been included.

Have you ever prepared yourself for a long voyage? Let's say you want to travel to some interesting places for 4–6 weeks. Have you ever gotten the travel bug and spend several weeks in America, Asia, Africa, Australia, or Europe? Perhaps as a student, or right out of the university, you took the opportunity to travel extensively for weeks or even months at a time?

Phileas Fogg travelled around the world in 80 days in the novel of the same title by Jules Verne. Even though he normally lived his life with mathematical precision, he made a bet about a worldwide journey, and left London the next day. Now, did he start his journey with a plan? He obviously did not have enough time for planning. But, if you follow Mr. Fogg on his travels, you always sense that he has a plan. He always knew what to do, where to go. Take a balloon or a train? Which shipping routes would be the most direct ones for him to utilize? Mr. Fogg always knew. And even more, he was always prepared for all circumstances. There was no disruption, for which Mr. Fogg is ill-prepared; he was always ready to switch to a back-up plan at a moment's notice. Jules Verne did not disclose in his book, how well prepared was Phileas Fogg when he started his voyage. We can only assume that he would not have survived without a plan.

And that brings us back again to the complex world of software development. Let's dive in the matter of architecture reviews again. When you start a review, whether it takes a week or 80 days, you never know, what awaits around the corner. One thing is key: you'd better be prepared. And we will help you to be prepared for all kind of architecture reviews.

4.2.1 Different Flavors of Architecture Reviews

How can you get prepared for the journey of a software audit? One helpful resource is a checklist. This can take the form of a list of key activities; this will help prevent pitfalls.

Before we present such a checklist, we need to say some words about how to use it. If you are an architect, what kind of architecture review are you supposed to perform? If you are a CIO, what kind of architecture review work do you expect from your architect? If you are an auditor, what does an architecture review means for your audit plan? There is not just one type of architecture review. In fact, there are many flavors.

We have seen architecture reviews which were executed once, as they were requested for a very specific reason. This type of architecture review is reflected in the previous example, where Greg was asked to verify whether a stable foundation is in place to support future releases. These types of architecture reviews can initiate some decisions or action items, which need to be tracked. Or they can simply provide an overview of the software architecture without any further action required.

We have also been involved with architecture deep dives for the sole purpose of judging the architecture quality of a single product, in order to estimate risks for further developments. No further context was provided. "Just go, look, and tell me what you find . . .!"

Finally, we have gained experience with architectural audits. Such architectural audits comprised deep dives and reviews, and the subjects were carefully selected. The overall aim of these software audits was to identify risks in software development, and to define means for mitigation. Such architectural audits closely resemble other forms of internal audits. In the cases of reviews and deep dives the reviewer defined their own methodology, and selected their own methods individually and from case to case; on the other hand, all architectural audits were well defined and conformed to a specific framework. Such a framework can describe in advance, how an architectural audit will be conducted. Furthermore, it can prove the objectivity of the auditors, by referencing results to the original software audit plan.

There are many other forms of architecture reviews. Many different methodologies are valid. They all have advantages and disadvantages. They are like architecture and design patterns; design patterns are not valid per se. With each design patterns there are pros and cons. The context provides information about valid or improper usage.

4.2.2   Some Definitions

In the rest of the book, we refer to *architecture reviews*, *architecture assessments*, *architectural audits* or *architecture deep dives*, whenever we refer to a one-time assessment without having a common framework in place. In other words, a one-time architectural due diligence with limited subsequent activities. The effort is finished and completed with the report on the results.

On the contrary, we refer to a *software audit* when a framework for such an assessment task is given. With this definition, there are recurrent audits based on this commonly used software audit framework. Software audits are planned in advance; further ad hoc audits can be added and complete the software audit plan.

Moreover, we will introduce a specific framework for software audits in Chap. 6. We call our suggested approach *Software Sustainability Audit*. This approach shall help to build qualities for sustainability into your software and software delivery.

4.3   The Architecture Review Toolbox

We can compare architecture review styles and the methods utilized with agile development methodologies and their methods. Consider Scrum, a methodology many development teams employ nowadays. Just 10 years ago, trendy development teams tried to use XP, extreme programming. Both are agile development methodologies, and there are many more of them. Both address agility factors; in other words, they take care of the uncertainty of requirements that can occur during the software development lifecycle. They take a unique shape out of a toolbox of agile development methods. They both feature paired programming, an iterative approach, prototyping, daily status meetings, team spirit as a key value, putting the customer and customer value in focus, etc.

All of these agile methodologies have advantages and disadvantages – as with any method. They can be used independently or may be utilized in conjunction with other agile techniques. About 10 years ago, it was common to find two conflicting approaches being debated. One approach was to use a fixed set of tools out of the toolbox of agile methods, like XP. Another approach was to define up-front the valid set of methods to be used for each individual development project. While the former approach guarantees stability of the methodology, which can even be improved over time, the latter approach allows a better fit to specific environment. It is more flexible to adapt to the given conditions.

Now we can argue about the one or the other approach in regards to software development methodologies. If we consider the principles involved – a highly structured approach irrespective of the specific project, versus a more flexible methodology tailored to the specific situation -, we could easily extend these same concepts to the realm of architecture reviews. Within the context of architecture reviews, both approaches are needed. For certain requirements, we need a fixed framework to be evolved and improved over a relatively long period of time. We also need a pragmatic approach, flexible to adjust to given requirements, while providing guidance and support along the way.

A toolbox of architecture review methods is needed, which provides an invaluable starting point. What are important elements for architecture reviews of any flavor? If you have this list of methods, you can prepare yourself based on the situation you face. Later in the book we will define a bundle of those methods and call it *software audit*. A software audit is more formal – like XP and Scrum – with all their respective advantages and disadvantages. Then, it is up to you to decide on what better fits to your situation, what better suits your requirements. Do you need a stable but fixed framework for architecture reviews? Or, do you like the freedom to select appropriate methods? The toolbox will help you in all cases. It can be even used as check list for your individual preparation.

At this juncture, it makes sense to define a list of methods you most certainly will need. We can separate these methods into three groups. First, there are the organizational methods. They detail the specific actions to take in architecture reviews; most of them are relevant in the planning phase. Secondly, there are substantial methods. They will provide guidance on the content while performing certain activities. Finally, there are communication methods providing advice about appropriate communication styles. Communication matters in all parts of an architecture review. Reviews frequently suffer from negative perceptions as in, "there must be something wrong, if a review is performed", in other words, emotions accompany the review in all phases. Due to the importance of appropriate communication, we cover this part in more detail in a separate chapter "Communication Matters".

4.3.1   Set Objective

Whichever way you start an architecture assessment, your first thoughts should be with the objective of your task. Why is this assessment requested or needed? What is the rationale of this assessment? Equally important is the answer to the question "what will be the possible consequences?" What will happen with the results? Will there be any impact?

Goal: The goal of setting a clear and transparent objective is to explain to all participants and stakeholders the rationale of the assessment project.

Advantages: A clear objective compels motivation in all people involved. It helps to convince the participants to support the effort. Experts, who need to be included, will be much more open in all discussions and analysis work, when they understand reasons and potential impact. Any reluctance to reveal true facts will be reduced. They will be even more motivated, if they see advantages for themselves, e.g. if they can expect improvements in their environment. A comprehensive objective minimizes hindering emotions from the beginning, and makes the assessment an accepted endeavor.

Limitations: In rare cases, it may not be possible or feasible to provide a transparent objective. For instance, when providing a clear and valid objective would reveal strictly confidential information. Another possibility might be the effort to elicit the true reason for an assessment request, or the pure effort to properly describe it. This could be the situation, if availability of the requestor is limited.

Best Practices: The draft objective should be defined when reaching out to the stakeholders. Work on a refinement with the stakeholders. The objective should be final when the architecture assessment is announced.

4.3.2   Define Scope

Defining the scope may look like a no-brainer. But an architecture assessment can be very broad and deep. There is always the risk of getting bogged down in details. Set clear boundaries to limit your effort. Define the scope of the investigation. What is in scope of your examination, and what is out? Are there reasons for taking items out of scope? If so, explain them.

Goal: Defining the scope helps the auditors to stay on track during the architecture assessment, and to deliver as expected by stakeholders.

Advantage: It ensures that the relevant parts and views have been taken into account at the end. It clarifies stakeholders' expectations and supports delivering according to those expectations. The ability to reference to the scope at all times shows the proficiency of the assessment work. Moreover, it proves objectivity of the auditors.

Limitations: It is common that important detections happen during architecture reviews, which should be followed up. If the scope has been defined too narrowly, then many discoveries might lead you beyond the borders of your scope. If the scope is too wide, you might struggle to present results in time.

Best Practices: The scope should be defined before you reach out to experts. The scope depends on the given objective. A draft scope should be available for stakeholder alignment.

4.3.3   Identify Stakeholders

Most of the time you think you know your stakeholders. The review requestors and your manager are natural candidates. And that is it – or so you might think. There are many cases where other stakeholders exist, but they are not obvious. Anyone who has interest in your results and should receive your final report should be considered a stakeholder. A stakeholder recognized late can force you into some extra work or even invalidate some of your results. This is due to the fact that an additional stakeholder can have an impact to both the set objective and on the defined scope.

Goal: Identify all relevant stakeholders to ensure that all important interests of the architecture assessment are covered.

Advantages: A complete set of stakeholders helps ensure that the objective and scope are valid throughout the architecture assessment. It prevents any disturbance based on outside interests. Moreover, contrary positions can be identified and handled early.

Limitations: Sometimes stakeholders are first identified during your investigations. If you identify somebody late, give alignment top priority.

Best Practices: Stakeholders shall be identified before you start the architecture assessment.

4.3.4   Align with Stakeholders

Align the objective (as you have understood it) and the scope of your architecture review with all identified stakeholders. You are well-advised to start alignments with prepared objectives and scope proposals. On one hand, your proposals should be clear enough to streamline the discussion with the stakeholders. The best possible outcome is certainly for the stakeholders to simply agree with and approve your proposals. On the other hand, be open and consider the stakeholders' input.

Goal: Alignment with stakeholders tightens the objective and scope.

Advantage: Aligned objective and scope are prerequisites for any smooth running architecture assessment. In all situations you can refer to this stable foundation. Furthermore, alignment sets up a good relationship between the auditors and the stakeholders. This will be effective in critical situations.

Limitations: There can be opposing views on objective and scope, which can be difficult to align. If no agreement is possible, the sponsor's decision has to be accepted.

Best Practices: It is important that the alignment has happened, before you start to announce architecture assessments.

4.3.5   Prepare the Right Questions

During an architecture assessment, you typically conduct several interviews, and your brain gets fully laden with all the answers. Numerous branches of discussions have occurred. Have you considered all relevant and important aspects? Good preparation includes the formulation of the right questions. The right questions are ones which nicely cover the complete scope. You can go even further and figure out which specific prepared questions should be asked to the particular people you plan to interview.

Goal: The goal of preparing the right questions is to define a set of leading queries, which cover the architecture assessment scope as completely as possible.

Advantage: Preparation of questions guides you through a jungle of open discussions, while ensuring comprehensive coverage of the given scope. It strengthens your position, so that you have a good chance of being on the right track during all discussions. It also aids as checklist at the end of each session, so that you can determine whether you in fact have asked all important questions. Altogether, it helps you to relax during the interviews, knowing you are well prepared.

Limitations: If questions are too detailed, and the list of them is lengthy, then their advantage might turn into a disadvantage. You run the risk that you will stick more to your questions instead of focusing on the answers given in the discussions. You may lose an open attitude, which would limit the potential discoveries.

Best Practices: A set of guiding questions should be prepared before you conduct an interview. However, the set of questions can be revised throughout the process of architecture assessment. Information provided and experience gathered in the interview process (and in other research) can be leveraged to improve your list of questions. Just ensure that the full coverage of the scope is still respected.

4.3.6   Select Experts to Discuss All Topics

As with the comprehensive set of questions, it's a good idea to select all experts you need for your architecture assessment before you start. Take your defined scope and consider relevant roles. Sometimes those roles may not be obvious, however. You typically need developers and software architects. But what about business experts to help understand the business processes to be covered by the architecture? Are there any project or people managers, who may bring some insights into difficult subjects and scope?

Goal: Select all experts which are needed to analyze the complete scope.

Advantage: Having the right experts defined before you start your endeavor allows you to set the consistent order of interviews. You might need answers from one expert before you contact another one. An initial list of experts allows you to set up an efficient plan. In addition, it allows you to ensure the completeness of your assessment. Finally, it lets you estimate your effort and plan possible milestones for delivering your results.

Limitations: Sometimes the appropriate experts are not known in the initial phase. Depending on the importance of these experts, you can identify them on your way, or add a pre-analysis phase. Also, the right experts could be available outside your company. Depending on the scenario, it might be valuable to contact customers or partners outside your company, especially if it becomes clear that their input is essential.

Best Practices: The list of experts should be defined before you start your assessment. Some new experts might be found along the way of your investigations, however; they might be needed for further clarifications. Generally, it's OK to involve new experts during the course of the assessment, but be careful not to extend too much, or you run the risk of getting lost in an ever-expanding project.

4.3.7 Identify Experts to Balance Views

Coping with all topics is one facet of selecting required experts. Are you sure that those experts are not biased? Are there other opinions which might contradict your findings? Try to balance views by adding more experts to your list whenever you identify teams or individuals with different perspectives, different experiences, or different goals.

Goal: Add other experts to your invitation list to ensure balanced viewpoints.

Advantage: Attempting to combine different views often leads to entirely new insights and new facts. More importantly, a consideration of balanced viewpoints is required in order to construct results that are sustainable, results that can be proven independently from the any one individual you have interviewed.

Limitations: It is quite difficult to detect opposing views from the beginning. In some cases, you may sense some snide remarks about others during interviews. Use these comments as opportunities to detect further interviewees who could potentially provide additional useful information.

Best Practices: Ensure a balance of viewpoints as soon as possible in the process. Involving of experts with different views late in the course of the assessment may run up against conclusions that have already been formed, which may make it difficult to come to a fair and valid assessment.

4.3.8 Get Empowered

Difficult and demanding situations happen. Your scope might be questioned. "Stick to the architecture. Your questions are not relevant", is a frequent refrain you will hear, which is often an attempt to block further investigations. The validity of your approach could be impeached, or your authority may be questioned. For whatever reason you may find yourself in such an objectionable situation, your empowerment must be made clear. This could take the form of some sign of your authority – which could be a mere e-mail from the right manager or executive. Having well-defined escalation path is important; make sure you clarify your empowerment with your sponsor before you start.

Goal: Clarify your empowerment and your means to be prepared for escalations.

Advantage: Discussions can lose momentum or focus, if individuals perceive a lack of empowerment. You can avoid such obstacles with clearly defined empowerment. Appropriate empowerment can be like a trump card, you can play it if and when you really need to.

Limitations: Actually using the escalation path should only be done in exceptional cases. Frequent usage of this path will not only delay the process, it will lead to questions about your aptitude.

Best Practices: Use the alignment with the stakeholders to clarify the proper treatment of escalations upfront.

4.3.9 Analyze the Context of the Architecture

Have you ever rented an apartment or even bought a house? While looking for potential places to live, the center of your search includes questions like "how many rooms?", "how large?", "is there a garden?" and so forth. These are types of architectural questions, within the context of buildings. In your search, you certainly asked other questions as well. "Where are the nearby schools, and what is their quality of education?" "Which shopping malls are nearby?" "How old is this house?" "Why is this house on the market?" Usually, nobody argues, why these questions are relevant. The context of your house is important. Period!

It's a similar case with software architecture. If you want to understand the architecture, try to understand its context. Most of the context, where the architecture is embedded, is defined along the path from strategy to code. Start with the company strategy to understand how the architecture should conform. Continue to look at business objectives on different levels, like business objectives from the company, from the department, or even the development project, depending on the situation. A business case for a development project should provide important information. Continue your research by looking at the development goals. Why is something going to be developed? What is the main reason for starting this development? Finally the requirements define anchor points for the architecture.

This path, from strategy to business objectives/goals and to requirements, is a golden line of context for architecture. Interviews with involved parties may unveil other constraints which need to be considered. Whatever context information you excavate from the soil of business directions, the architecture should at least match and should reasonably reflect the context.

Goal: Identify the relevant context of the architecture and include this context in your analysis.

Advantage: You only determine whether architecture is sound if you understand its influencing factors. Serious flaws are often embedded in the context.

Limitations: Concentrating on the context too much can distract from the architecture itself. Carefully balance architecture analysis and the assessment of the context.

Best Practices: While preparing your questions, consider the context. Context should be well represented in your list of key questions.

4.3.10 Stay Focused

A healthy curiosity can serve you well when assessing architecture. You look into different aspects of the architecture, following different paths in the course of your investigation. While this is good and normal, you run the risk of spending time and energy analyzing aspects which are far beyond the originally defined scope. Don't allow diversion. While looking left and right, stay focused at all times.

Goal: Proceed with a flexible and open approach, but stay focused on the aspects which are most in line with the given scope.

Advantage: Focusing on the scope prevents deviations. Deviations may delay your assessment. Also, deviations can be a tactic participants use to hide information about issues. Another reason to remain focused on the scope is objectivity. If you predominantly leave the scope, your objectivity is endangered.

Limitations: Being focused must be balanced with openness; otherwise you can miss important points, if you concentrate too much on a narrow scope.

Best Practices: Defining a proper set of questions can guide you to the right degree of focus.

4.3.11 Think Outside the Box

"Think outside the box" is good advice, when you design new architecture. While this is valid for creation, it is also valid for assessments of architecture. Of course, the review scope is still important. However, it's OK to sometimes reach beyond your scope to include an item that should not be ignored. Keep an open atmosphere, and be always prepared for information beyond your radar screen.

Goal: Do not unnecessarily limit your exploration, while remaining focused on your scope.

Advantage: You can collect more information with an outside-the-box approach. Indeed, the most important fact can actually lie outside the defined scope.

Limitations: While gathering facts beyond the scope might be fruitful, it can be risky at the same time. If you are not sufficiently mindful of the given focus, you can get lost in details which take you far beyond your scope.

Best Practices: Fostering an open and relaxed atmosphere opens the door to looking outside the box. When auditees are invited to talk about burning issues rather than answering given question, they might reveal facts that are worthwhile to consider.

4.3.12 Communicate with Empathy

When the subject of the audit is already well-known to you, and you have heard rumors about it, you easily become biased. Even worse, there is a risk that your concerns may become apparent to the people who work in the audited area, and it could taint their own views. Negative attitudes are disservices; they confine the space of results. They even may lead you to wrong conclusions.

Approach the people with empathy. They certainly have had good reasons for their decisions and actions, and they did their best. Try to understand the colleagues in the audited area. Indeed, try to understand their motivation first.

Goal: When talking with people, try to understand their interests and needs, and appreciate their work.

Advantage: When you face people with empathy, they are more open to your questions and will answer your questions frankly. When you appreciate the individuals' work, you create a positive atmosphere, where everybody feels comfortable. This prepares fertile ground for your root cause analysis.

Also, don't underestimate the chance that you will cross paths with the people in the audited area in the future. Operating with empathy and appreciation for other's work fosters good will that may be helpful in future situations that you cannot foresee.

Limitations: If serious issues are already recognized, or if they are even the reasons for the software audit, you may feel distracted by these bad circumstances. Avoid being swayed by negative energy. Think positive right from the beginning.

Best Practices: People should feel from the beginning that they are taken seriously. It's difficult to establish an atmosphere of empathy and appreciation if you have an unfriendly start to the proceedings. Also, it's important to be authentic in order to establish a good working relationship and modus operandi.

4.3.13 Describe the Business Impact

All findings need to be fully explained. Also, you must explain, what you conclude from those findings. Additionally, you must explain why the findings are important. Ensure the importance is described in terms of what this means for the business owners. Why is the finding important to the manager, who is supposed to follow some actions? Why is the finding important to the company? The potential business impact answers these questions in most cases.

Goal: Describe the business impact, or potential business impact of your finding, to explain the importance from the business owner's view.

Advantage: When you annotate observations with potential business impacts, you automatically take a neutral view of the situation. You show that this is not just your favorite topic, but you explain the significance for the company.

Findings which have business impact descriptions attached are easy to understand and easy to accept.

Limitations: Together with the potential business impact, a risk description is
helpful and recommended. When the risk probability is too low, potential
damages are often hard to accept, even though risk exposure could be calami-
tous. In those cases, the potential impact and further consequences need to be
described even more clearly.

Best Practices: Typically business impacts are described together with the
associated risks or as part of a risk. It should be clarified, whether the responsible
manager has alternative options to mitigate the risk in order to avoid the
mentioned business impact.

4.3.14 Define Clear Actions

Managers don't like to hear about issues without proposals to improve the situation.
Reporting sole issues is like complaining. You lay out problems, because you like to
detect and talk about problems. A better approach is to ensure that your service attitude
is perceived. Advise the business owners by providing clear recommendations on how
the situation can be improved. Instead of being puzzled, managers rely on your report.

Goal: Add clear actions to your observations, which helps responsible business
owner to resolve issues and improve the situation.

Advantage: Defining clear actions puts you in the driver seat for a moment. It is
your chance to improve a situation. Additionally, you are perceived as professional auditor with service orientation. Your constructive attitude is perceived
and appreciated. Furthermore, business owners, who usually deal with many
issues a day, are enabled to react quickly.

Limitations: Actions need to be defined clearly and precisely to be understood and
to be followed. Unclear or imprecise mitigation steps will be either ignored, or
your recommendations will not be properly executed, which can actually worsen
the situation.

Though clear actions are advised, manager's authority still needs to be accepted.
Recommendations may have two parts, one with soft advice providing different
options to execute, and one with a recommended alternative, which gives clear
guidance. This approach leaves business owners the freedom to define other
actions, if they want to. Additionally, it provides clear guidance when they are
willing to follow your proposal.

Best Practices: The rationale behind recommendations should be provided, directly
or indirectly. You should articulate why the guidance will lead to the intended
correction. Such a rationale can be detailed simply by describing the observation.
When the rationale cannot be derived from the finding, an illustration may be
useful.

4.3.15 Demonstrate Sustainability

"You turn and your software audit was forgotten." This should not happen!
A successful audit is not completed with the delivery of the audit report. The

audit report just marks the end of the first phase of your audit. Real success is achieved if you can demonstrate *sustainability*. In other words, show that your results will not be forgotten after the delivery. Plan and communicate that the agreed actions are going to be explicitly pursued and monitored. This may result in your being actively consulted during the implementation of those actions. Furthermore, there could be a further audit to verify how the actions have been executed, and how the situation has changed – and hopefully improved.

Goal: Plan and communicate further activities after the delivery of the audit report to ensure that the audit results are implemented effectively.

Advantage: When communicating audit actions beyond the delivery of the results, you increase the probability that audit results will be taken seriously and executed effectively. In addition, you show your professional attitude and your interest in resolution of the issues.

Limitations: Such sustainability of audit results can hardly be achieved on a project basis. If you are asked to do a software audit as a one-time approach, it could be difficult to gain this success factor. Basically, there are two options. When software audits are embedded in a permanent organization, you easily can offer services and activities after the software audit occurred. When such an organizational foundation is missing, you still can look for an overall owner of the audit report. A neutral instance or person, who has a stake or interest in the resolution, could take over the results and guarantee sustainable steps.

Best Practices: It is recommended to think about this sustainability factor at the beginning. Before you actually start the software audit, the steps after this endeavor should be clear. In the initial opening or briefing meeting of you software audit, you should explain what happens next. "We will now start an architecture analysis – and we also explain what comes next."

4.4   Every Journey Begins with the First Step: Including Yours!

In the previous section we prepared a checklist of recommended activities. We learned *what* to do. This toolbox of software audits will now be extended by hints *how* to perform the proposed activities. We still offer tools from a software audit toolbox. We leave it to the interested reader to adapt these measures to their own needs. We still provide flexibility while adopting the methods before we make them more precise and strict and suggest a concrete approach for software sustainability audits. For the moment, we will dwell on this more open toolbox and enrich it with some further hints and food for thought.

4.4.1 Objective and Scope

We already introduced the idea that software audits should comprise both process assessments and product due diligence. However, we can emphasize one or the other part. Both can be the driver for initiating a software audit. Hence, the first thought should be on these two parts. Objective and scope shall clarify the focus of the software audit. Do you intend to inspect an important development process and do so by verifying this process with a few product samples? Or were concerns about a product the cause of the software audit and a few specific processes should be considered, because they are essential for the product in question?

Whatever your primary focus is, specify both the processes that are in scope, and the product parts that are in scope.

Keeping your focus can be difficult. It typically turns out to be a challenge when the number of crucial observations tends to explode, threatening to lead you in different directions. Thus, a scope reduction or a prioritization of scope items could prevent the software audit from becoming too big. Look at the high-level architecture of the product. Are there naturally separated components? Do these components differ according to importance? Select the crucial components and declare them as in scope. Explicitly classify the other components as out of scope.

It can be helpful to plan your software audit with a preliminary scope and iterate on your scope by using this audit plan. Such established work plans can contain elements that are worthwhile to be further developed in the scope. The draft work plan can contain essential questions to be asked which narrow the objective or scope. Also participating teams could be derived from a first audit plan, and this information is helpful to specify the scope as well.

Most software audits are not unique. They are not unique in execution methods, and they are not unique from a planning perspective either. Why don't you prepare a template, or for specific types of software audits a set of few templates, which specify the scope? There are key questions, which are always the usual suspects. There are key architecture characteristics, which you will assess every time. A template for scope definition defined once will accelerate future software audits, and improves their quality. You seldom will miss important pieces in your scope if you use pre-defined content.

4.4.2 Stakeholders

When you prepare your list of stakeholders, you usually have two questions. Who are my stakeholders? And after you have identified your candidates, you will ask: Is this list of stakeholders complete?

There are two groups of stakeholders. The ones who are included in your software audit from the beginning. These are the ones that you in invite, or they come from teams where you invite people. This first type of stakeholders can be described as those from whom you need information. These stakeholders are naturally identified – they are people who have responsibility for processes or product components within your scope.

The other group of stakeholders is defined by referencing action items from the audits. In most cases these two aforementioned groups of stakeholders are congruent. However in many cases there will be additional stakeholders. There will be different managers or business owners who will be charged with taking action based on some of your audit results. It can be helpful to try to look ahead and anticipate this. Also, consider customers and partners outside the company. Additionally, imagine possible observations and to whom you would need to address corresponding recommendations.

Is the scope set? Or, do you need stakeholders to not only align, but also to specify the audit scope or even the audit objective? You certainly remember one or the other scenario, when you wanted to align something. We have included two alignment scenarios for illustration purposes.

4.4.2.1 Alignment Example 1: The Individual Approach

Greg approached his two stakeholders Adam and Britta individually. He wanted to define a software audit scope which would be accepted by both. He first met Adam, who made it very clear that component A is the foundation of the product. Whether the product was robust or not depended to a large extent on component A. Greg should focus on this central component A. "The remainder was irrelevant", thought Adam.

Afterwards, Greg talked to Britta. He explained the scope as discussed with Adam. The scope was about the robustness of component A. The other components on top were apparently out of scope. Britta exploded. "What nonsense!" The component A existed for years now. All the recent quality issues came from the applications on top of A. Britta assumed that the new applications just used the foundation component A incorrectly. "Set component A out of scope and concentrate on the new applications", was Britta's advice. Greg now turned to Adam again and explained the outcome of his alignment with Britta. Adam was very irritated and angry. "Why have you altered the scope? I thought we had a clear decision about the scope already?"

4.4.2.2 Alignment Example 2: The Team Approach

Greg was upset about the outcome of his first attempt at alignment. Next time, Greg tried another approach. He invited both Christa and Dan to jointly discuss the software audit scope. After a short introduction, Christa started to give direction. "I think, there is low risk with the architecture as it is. We should focus on how it was defined, how requirements have been collected and considered in architecture."

Dan interrupted immediately. "Rubbish! The requirement processes were executed as defined. Why do you always distract from your architecture?"

Christa went red. "I already told you. I don't like your hostility."

And Dan jumped in again ...

Well, we certainly described two extremes. Certainly, animosity is not encountered in all software audits. However, they show the essence of what you should consider when defining or aligning the scope with your stakeholders.

Both alignment methods have advantages. The first example helps you to get independent view from each stakeholder. Method two could have accomplished to understand different views.

So, why don't we combine the two methods? Start with the individual approach to get a list of independent proposals. Just ensure that this is a collection step and not a decision. Expectation management about the result is essential. Continue with a team session. Collect approvals or reasons for objections. If conflicts were revealed in the team session, be prepared for strong facilitation.

4.4.2.3 The Consulting Approach

Software audits do not always reveal conflicts as indicated in the examples above. Software audits are not necessarily based on evidence of a bad or perilous situation. Software audits can be used as real pro-active measures. Your stakeholders will cooperate and tell you where the highest probabilities of weak points exist. They will be interested in your results, as your observations are valuable to help improve their business.

4.4.3   The Right Questions

Normally, the right questions to ask are obvious. If your scope is defined, you easily will find the main questions to ask. However, there is one potential pitfall we should mention here: State open, not closed questions! Ask "Who?", "What?", "Why?", "Where?", and so forth. Avoid questions like "Is the architecture scalable?" A yes/no answer will not really add value.

This is a no-brainer, you certainly think – And you are right. However, in reality we tend to ask yes/no questions. Even if we do not ask them in interviews, there is another potential pitfall: It is simply easier to use closed questions when you prepare a list of questions that should cover the main audit scope. One closed question represents several open questions you need to ask. For example, a question on your list like "is your architecture scalable?" might be asked in the form "How scalable is your architecture?" in an interview. Other examples are questions like, "How have you designed your architecture to make it scalable?", or "What are the requirements towards scalability, which you need to cope with your architecture?". There are many more relevant questions. While you might represent a question in closed form on a prepared list of questions as a short form, the risk we see is actual usage. Once you have written a closed question, it's likely you will use it in the interview as well. It is a challenge to change the phrasing during an interview, since your brain has already stored a different version.

You find good questions if you refer to the following types of artifacts, which are typically valuable for audits:

- *Documents*: Which document provides insights, can confirm a fact, describes something in detail?
- *Processes*: Which process is in place to validate the architecture? To define the requirements?
- *Stakeholders*: Who was responsible, decided, proposed the architecture, and collected requirements?
- *Business Goals*: Which goals, objectives, strategy were driving the architecture?

4.4.4   Experts Needed

As with stakeholders, the primary questions are similar in regards to experts. How can you find and engage the required experts? How can you complete your initial list of experts?

The set of relevant processes answers the question about determining who the appropriate experts are that should be involved. All major roles that contribute to the relevant processes should be considered. So, start by determining the processes that drove the product development and architecture definition. Then select the important roles in these processes. Finally, identify representatives who were in these roles. These steps will yield a solid list of experts to start.

What has to be considered when completing the expert list? Ask who could have a different opinion or perspective (and the difference is important). Identify who might add something to the information already provided. Again, an answer to those questions can be derived by the relevant processes. While you can use the process definition to get the initial list of experts, we recommend looking at the executed processes this time. How are the developed processes used and executed in the real world? Which changes and deviations from the normal processes are known? The answers to these questions can lead you to additional experts who can help balance the view.

4.4.5 Empowerment

Some software audits run smoothly, while others face myriad challenges. It is not uncommon to encounter situations where people involved with the audit question the auditor's authority. There are various reasons that this occurs, from attempting to avoid the added workload imposed by the audit, or simply as a means of channeling some negative emotions.

The easiest way to demonstrate authority is to show it from the beginning. Don't let any question about your authority linger and clarify who the sponsor is of your software audits.

The first official letter or mail that will be circulated is your signifier of authority: the announcement mail. In the email that announces the software audit, the objective and scope should be clearly stated. Your empowerment begins with the statement of your sponsor. You can either mention the sponsor of your software audit. Better though, if your sponsor sends the announcement mail himself. If your sponsor is indeed interested in the software audit, he will be more than willing to send the announcement letter – provided that you have prepared the announcement content.

The announcement mail is the indicator of your empowerment.

4.4.6 Focus

The first time you perform a software audit, it can run much longer than planned. There is so much to understand and learn. There are often so many surprises, which are worth tracking. There are typically a huge number of indicators of potential issues that seem important enough to warrant further investigation. You need more time, but often time is limited. There are deadlines for which results have to be presented. An answer to this dilemma is the focus. Stay focused all the time.

The natural question that arises is: How can someone stay focused despite encountering evidence almost demanding to be followed-up? One solution can be provided in the execution of the software audit, one during the planning.

In the execution, the audit objective and the audit scope are naturally provide aid for staying focused. Imagine a fruit-bearing tree that becomes too big to sufficiently absorb water. The fruit is very small at harvest time. An experienced gardener cuts the branches of the tree yearly, to limit the extent of the tree's growth. The fruit becomes bigger and sweeter. Within the context of audit, you should behave like the gardener. Prune branches of investigation regularly. Derive priorities from the audit objective and scope, and cut off any direction you start to take where the priority is lower than other issues apparent in other evidence.

You may have a feeling when you are planning a software audit that it's likely to become too big, or the stated time frame is insufficient, or that quality would likely suffer with the stated deadlines. At this point you can divide the software audit in two or three pieces; you can run two or three software audits instead of one to cover the given audit objective and scope.

There is another option to limit scope during planning, an option based on risk analysis, which can be considered as well. You might consider planning recurrent software audits instead of running several one-time software audits. In other words, plan recurrent software audits, which address the same audit objective, but the scope differs every time. Every time you start a new audit, you analyze the risks and take those scope items with the highest current risks. You will never get complete coverage of the objective, but you will have samples which are representative of the objective. A risk based selection of samples provides you enough certainty that you have fairly considered the business risks. And responding to the business risks is the main driver for doing software audits after all, isn't it?

4.4.7   Reporting

When you report your results, the sequence of views makes your set of findings convincing. This sequence starts with an observation. A clear observation description explains what you have noticed. Most of the time these are many tiny observations, and therefore consolidation is necessary. This can present the first snafu: consolidation of many smaller findings into a main finding can result in generalization or abstraction of what you have indeed. Your conclusions can become part of the observation. Make sure you avoid putting any conclusions in the beginning. Even after consolidation, facts need to remain facts.

Once you provide facts, including your observations, it is fair to continue with your conclusion. What does this observation mean for the company's success? The observation should be judged and the business impact evaluated. Based on the evidence, what events could occur if steps are not taken to address the issue? What is the potential financial damage? What is the risk that this damage occurs? The potential financial impact together with the probability of such an event occurring describes the clear impact of your observation. In this manner, a technical finding is translated into business viewpoint. And the business view is the relevant information to understand the importance of the finding.

The third step is your recommendation. Define clear actions. Help management to act appropriately. How can the risk, which you described before, be mitigated? It is important for your success to separate these three parts carefully from each other. Facts should be stated as facts, and conclusions should be written in business language – we often refer to it as C-language, meaning appropriate for CEOs, COOs, CFOs, CIOs, CTOs, and the like. It should define potential business impacts and risks, include recommendations with your individual view, and it should express your experience with the particular matter.

4.4.8   Follow-Up

Sustainability is easy; you just have to do it. At the same time, it is difficult – because you have to do it. Convenience is the most important enemy of sustainability. You conduct a software audit. You write your report. A deep breath, – and the job is done. Is the job done? Almost!

You should plan an additional software audit with the same scope. Look at the findings and check how the responsible manager dealt with your observation. The follow-up audit objective purely defines the improvement of the situation in question. "We will check the how the prescribed measures have been implemented" is the basic scope of the follow-up audit.

4.5   Give It a Frame: Architecture Governance

There are many other measures and activities which are similar to software audits. Moreover, there are relations between those activities and software audits. Sometimes you find activities running in parallel to software audits, like architecture reviews, ISO audits, or internal audit. Sometimes software audits are framed by governance. Software audit can be seen as one means of applying governance. While there is certainly a long list of candidates, which would be worthwhile to explain, we will present some of them to clarify the role of software audits and put it in relation to other known activities.

4.5.1   Architecture Reviews and Software Audits

Architecture reviews are common instruments in software development. In contrast, a comprehensive framework like software audits is rather unusual, most of the time even unknown to the development community. When we notice such a difference in usage, then what is the difference in their characteristics?

Architecture reviews are often naturally embedded in the software development lifecycle. A senior developer, a software architect or a development manager wants to ensure a robust architecture. He verifies the proposed architecture of new development programs before he approves the start of the software implementation. It is a check performed at a particular milestone, where an architect or manager takes ownership of the corrective measures as required. It is part of the quality management aspects of software development. The lead of architecture reviews is also involved in the development and has responsibility for the architecture. Architecture review is an activity which is integrated into software development itself. The responsibilities of architecture definition and architecture review are not precisely separated.

Software audits, as we introduce in this book, are services provided from outside the development team. Architects external from the development organization assess the architecture. Based on this particular relationship, these outside architects have a neutral and different view of the architecture. They are independent from the development unit. They recognize defects, which may have been overlooked by people involved in the development. It is like the attempt to proofread a manuscript. The author of the manuscript can read it a dozen times and will not be able to find a misspelling. Someone else reviewing it can find those mistakes in an instant. These outside architects, or software auditors, typically find it difficult to drive the necessary improvements. Special handling is needed to steer the corrective measurements.

Another difference is apparent when we look at the nature of the approach. Architecture reviews typically are one time reviews. An architecture review completes the architecture definition process. In the SCRUM methodology, it is often planned to take place in one of the first sprints. The scope of an architecture review is quite narrow; it focuses on the quality assurance of the next software version.

Software audit, however, defines a framework of recurrent audit work. The audit objective and scope changes with each software audit. With software audit, the scope is normally sufficiently broad to ensure sustainability of the software application for several future releases.

4.5.2   Embedded in Architecture Governance

While software audits as framework for architecture assessments are rather unknown, architecture governance, in contrast, is being introduced increasingly more often in software development these days. Architecture governance is set up to ensure certain capabilities, properties and quality criteria of software components and software products. Typically, those requirements for software architectures are described in form of development guidelines or architecture guidelines. The requirements are also known as architecture qualities. Architecture governance is a methodology that combines several activities, starting from defining and aligning these qualities and guidelines, assuring adherence to those, and dealing with exceptions.

Software audits can be perfectly embedded into those architecture governance approaches. Software audits can be used as selective controls for ensuring that important characteristics are built into software. For instance, if certain integration requirements, like REST enablement, are claimed for all products, software audits can check on a case by case basis how these claimed features are implemented. Software audits can notify when guidelines are not considered, resulting in a negative impact on required product quality. They can also report if guidelines are not effective or not efficient, needing improvement. Thus, software audits can be chosen as an effective control embedded in architecture governance.

4.5.3 Software Audits and Other (Internal) Audits

A company has (or should have) some form of internal audits in place which verify compliance with external regulations. Many companies are voluntarily compliant with ISO standards. Therefore, ISO audits are performed to check compliance with these ISO standards. Thus, the question may arise "what is different with software audits? Why do we need an additional type of audit?"

First of all, it is interesting to clarify the roles of the different audit types. To be precise, internal audit services (according to the institute of internal audits, IIA) and ISO audits (according to ISO 900x) can be in conflict with one another, but there is a clear demarcation line between the two of them. ISO audits are part of an established quality management system. It is not necessarily separated from the operational teams, in most cases they belong to a central team which also defines processes of the quality management program. The purpose of such audits is to ensure the compliance of the defined quality management program.

Internal audits (as defined by IIA) need to be done by an independent unit, reporting to, and acting on behalf of, the CEO and the audit committee of the Board of Directors. Internal auditing is part of the corporate governance and corporate monitoring functions. "It helps an organization accomplish its objectives by bringing a systematic, disciplined approach to evaluate and improve the effectiveness of risk management, control and governance process." – from IIA Standards for the Professional Practice of Internal Auditing, Glossary. The main aspects of internal auditing are reliability of financial reporting, effectiveness and efficiency of operations, and compliance with applicable laws and regulations (COSO 1992).

Software audits could be considered as residing somewhere between the two auditing types explained before. Software auditing is established as part of architecture governance, an essential instrument for the quality management function in software development. Its objective goes beyond compliance, effectiveness, and efficiency. Software auditing extends those audit objectives toward a twofold validation: A validation of the software product, and a validation of the software development processes and guidelines. Software audits validate, whether processes and guidelines lead to high-quality software products with required properties.

They recommend changes to improve quality of all developed products. And software audits validate the products themselves. They assess development architectures and software products and identify causes for observed defects.

4.5.4   Why Not COBIT, ITIL, TOGAF or the Like?

If you are a CIO, you know the CobIT [1], ITIL [2] or TOGAF framework [3]. You certainly ask, why not utilize existing standards, or collection of standards, for this software audit purpose, as is? Why do we propose another framework with software audits? Software audits will definitely not replace the known frameworks. They are intended to enhance those frameworks with software relevant pieces, but there are massive differences. Processes in IT are generally established and standardized. CobIT [1] and ITIL [2] describe these standardizations, and provide compiled checklists for compliance.

Similarly, TOGAF focuses on the IT architecture "to optimize across the enterprise the often fragmented legacy of processes (both manual and automated) into an integrated environment that is responsive to change and supportive of the delivery of the business strategy" [3].

Software development is still in the early stages of achieving standardization. We have seen several attempts to standardize software development at least to some degree. With SCRUM methodology there is a new wave trying to standardize software development processes, which is itself a very promising approach. However, there is still a long way to go to define such standards. Still many degrees of freedom are visible in software development. Our software audit approach is a first step in the direction of providing a framework for auditing software development.

Moreover, software development often misses some kind of predictability or ability to plan. Seldom are there precise requirements given, leading to predictable software development activities. There are always surprises. When you start to develop your software product, things become clearer, which trigger further questions about the requirements. In other words, requirements are a moving target during software development. Our software audit concept considers this particular effect and though offers a framework for a stable audit framework.

4.6   In a Nutshell: What Are Software Audits?

Software audit is your health check for software products you are going to develop, you are in the process of developing, or you have already developed. At each step of the software development lifecycle you can assess the architecture and other factors influencing the architecture. We might think of it like a health check, where a blood test is performed to examine various indicators of wellness, such as liver function, cholesterol, etc. Similarly, you can define the scope of a software audit: To validate stability with respect to requirements, scalability of the solution, and so on. If your blood test shows a deviation of your thyroid indicator, you can request other blood tests for additional indicators to figure out what exactly is wrong in your body. Similarly, you can continue with additional audits, if your findings reveal some architecture anomalies.

While the health check reports information which bears risk for your health and your life, software audits respond to observations that carry certain risks for your product's success.

Software audits range from being a formal process to a validation of results following a pure compliance check. The formal framework is helpful to efficiently and effectively perform your software due diligence. It guides you through all obstacles which could block you from getting the right and necessary insights.

At the same time software audits allow a measure of flexibility, to not only to formally assess the architecture, but also do it substantially.

4.7   Summary

In this chapter we set the foundation for all types of architecture reviews and software audits. A fictitious example was provided to help illustrate the potential pitfalls. Then, we discussed how you can use different approaches to software audits. A key aspect is toolbox of essential methods, which we enriched with further suggestions. At the end we discussed how Software Sustainability Audits relate to known methodologies like CobIT and ITL.

References

1. Home page of ISACA®, COBIT framework. http://www.isaca.org/Knowledge-Center/COBIT/Pages/Overview.aspx
2. Home page of ITIL®. www.itil.org
3. Home page of Open Group organization, publication of TOGAF. http://pubs.opengroup.org/architecture/togaf9-doc/arch/index.html

Orienteering Race: Position, Direction, Go!

What's In It for Me?

You want to establish governance for your software development. This requires understanding and setting the context – where are you today, where do you want to go, what are appropriate measures? Find your road to success.

CIO/CTO

This is one of the central chapters for you if you want to take further steps towards governance of software development. We discuss overall success factors –defining your own path meeting the individual situation and requirements of your company and making up your mind on governance needs and direction. Sections 5.1, 5.2 and 5.3 helps orient you. Where are you coming from? What is the context in which governance is required? What are my strategy, information needs, and company culture? What kind of product issues do I have, and how are they covered by governance today? Sections 5.4 and 5.5 help you find your main route to governance. Section 5.6 sheds some light on practical aspects of your governance activities.

Software Architect

As software architect you might be involved in the setup or operation of governing software development processes or products. Although you are not responsible for the governance activities this chapter helps you ask the right questions and challenging the approach taken by your management. Read this chapter from your own and from a management perspective. Do you get to different answers? What route would you take? Try to discuss the governance direction with the responsible managers in your company.

(continued)

R. Gutbrod and C. Wiele, *The Software Dilemma*, Management for Professionals, DOI 10.1007/978-3-642-27236-3_5, © Springer-Verlag Berlin Heidelberg 2012

Auditor

Auditing itself is a central governance activity requiring a clear context. As an auditor you are familiar with different governance approaches. You may have helped setting up an audit structure in a company. Nevertheless, you might not be familiar with the specifics of software development. So you can learn the important aspects here. This chapter helps you asking the right questions. Read this chapter and match it with the situation of your company. Does a clear direction exist for governing software development processes and products?

5.1   The Journey Continues: The Road Ahead

In the previous chapter we introduced different means of assessing the state of a software product. We explained necessary prerequisites and tasks to make such a review successful even without a formal audit or governance framework. Typically a concrete incident is the trigger for such an analysis and assessment. A product might have architectural flaws and does not provide the required performance and scalability. Or the software missed meeting customer expectations otherwise. We have experienced over and over again that it is a challenge for architects to provide architecture-related assessments on an ad-hoc basis. Architects need guidance for making such a review or audit successful. To this end we provide a tool set for an architecture assessment.

But we experienced an additional pattern. The implementation of a successful review or audit lets the appetite for more grow. Executives and managers realize the value of the insight gained and the transparency created. The idea is born to institutionalize that kind of audit. Management wants a regular assessment of software products and related processes. But this imposes the next challenge. It is a great achievement to provide valuable results once, such as the best architect has been assigned to this task. But it requires much more for providing such a service with high quality and value on a regular basis.

The standardization of software audits requires a framework to ensure high quality. The direction of governance has to be aligned with the company's strategy and information needs. The approach and measures have to fit to the company culture. A variety of different aspects have to be considered. What we envision is a professional governance approach based on software audits. This leads to a shift in focus from an individual assessment towards the optimization of software development processes and products. The goal is to support the organization in providing sustainable software products.

We invite you to join us on that journey. As a first step you have to define a governance environment fitting to your company's needs. This chapter is intended to help you in this task. The journey continues with the introduction of Software Sustainability Audits in the next chapter. Software Sustainability Audits build a standard means and framework for software audits. They comprise the concepts of software development process audits as well as software product audits. Each type is introduced in depth in dedicated chapters. We complement the governance framework and approach through discussing dedicated aspects like risk management, communication, or the concept of Control Self-Assessment in subsequent chapters.

5.2   Make Up Your Mind!

Your have taken the first steps on your journey to software auditing. But now you reached a crossroad. Before you keep running, have a rest and look at the map. Make up your mind. Where are you coming from? Where do you want to go? What is the best route to take? We give hints in this chapter to make your journey more successful. Although we cannot promise that you will reach your goals one thing is for sure. Not making up your mind will yield ineffective governance. This does not automatically imply failure of your software development; however, you will have less assurance about the quality and sustainability of your software products. In this case your governance and audit effort might become simply waste.

Honestly, defining what you want to achieve by governance sometimes is a painful exercise. It is easily understood that there is at least some need for governance. The corresponding activities like audits have to fit to a larger idea. Also some high level goals might be easily defined. But making it concrete and getting it running requires many more thoughts. You need to be very clear about what you want. This impacts how you have to set things up. Otherwise you will not get the intended results. Even worse you will not receive the required acceptance and support of your organization. With audits you look at things in detail, ask nasty questions, and bring up painful issues. This may not be in favor of affected people causes resistance. Still, auditors can be well perceived and accepted (and thus be much more effective) if they can explain their task. We will see below what it takes.

Defining your goals and direction is the best exercise as preparation for Software Sustainability Audits. If you want to improve development processes you have to understand the intention behind the process or sub-process. You have to assess whether the goals – for instance ensuring certain product qualities – are actually achieved by the process. If you are not clear about your own goals and corresponding measures it is hard questioning others'.

5.3   Where Are You Today: The Context for Governance

What was the last software development project you have been involved in that failed? Do you know why it failed? Failure – by the way – is not meant to be a complete disaster. It is more intended to express that it was less successful than expected or possible. Are there issues recurrently showing up across development projects? What have you done so far to prevent such issues? Are you on track with your development strategy?

Questions like this immediately pop up when you assess your current situation. For any journey you have to know where you start, where you want to go, and which path you will follow. Consequently, the initial step is an honest assessment where you are. This exercise is not meant to lead to any kind of bashing or blaming. Always think about the future. What can you do better, regardless of your role? Analyze whether you are optimally equipped by asking yourself questions like:

CIO/CTO
- Do you get the information about software development projects or products that you need to make decisions? If not, what is missing?
- Is the information you receive on a product state reliable? Why do you think so?

All
- What issues did you face in the past despite your governance activities?
- What do you know about the effectiveness of your governance process?
- How do you assure software products are developed according to the strategy and corresponding rules?
- What is your company culture? What is the attitude of your development teams towards governance?
- Are developers used to strong rules, or are they reluctant to follow standards?

The better you analyze your current situation the better you will be able to define your needs for setting up or improving the governance frame for software audits. As you see from the sample questions above there are five main areas you need to consider:

- *Strategy*: Strategy is the central driver for governance and affects the software development process either directly or indirectly. For software companies the strategy directly relates to the software products. The strategy defines the target markets and the kind of software to be developed. The strategy has a direct impact on the architecture and requires corresponding governance. A strategic aspect having such an impact is the decision to build standard software. This requires different architectural considerations than implementing individual software solutions. For other companies, (internal) software development might be more or less important for the overall company strategy. There are industries like banking where software development is essential to support the core processes. Other companies might cover their main software related requirements through standard software packages. Internal software development is limited to fill some functional gaps in this case.

- *Information Needs*: As we have learned, corporate governance requires the board of a company to base decisions on a solid and valid basis of information. But also managers, product owners, architects, or the CTO require corresponding information – especially product related ones – to make decisions. Another requirement from corporate governance is monitoring the effectiveness of governance-related measures. Roughly speaking the strategy should be reflected in the development projects and processes which are complemented by corresponding governance activities. The board requires transparency about the state of the strategic objectives, and the related governance. If the basis of information about this is not sufficient you will not be able to take corrective measures. You need to assess how you currently assure a solid basis of information. Analyze your sources of information and their reliability.

- *Company Culture*: There are different cultures and corresponding organizational structures. Some companies are driven top down and very hierarchical. Others have an open atmosphere with a more bottom up approach for solving business problems. Employees might be used to strong governance; others see this as an impediment to their freedom. The company culture determines what kind of governance approach is most appropriate. In hierarchical organizations it is sufficient to define central rules that are followed by the employees. In a more open culture you need the buy-in from the people to be effective. If they are not convinced of the governance measures they will be reluctant to follow.
- *Product State*: The current state of your products is one of the main triggers for thinking about improving governance. If the products are successful in the market, your customers are satisfied and there are no major issues with supporting them. There is no reason for you to think of improving your governance. On the other hand, if you are constantly facing product issues you start thinking about your processes at some point in time. Product issues are varied. Customers might not buy and implement the software as it simply does not meet the functional expectations. It could be cumbersome to use. The support load could be very high as the product has many bugs or there is lack of an efficient and effective infrastructure to analyze problems. Maybe integrating the software into an existing landscape is too expensive, or it is very costly to operate the product. All these issues have some root cause which you might not know yet. But based on the list of issues you can decide which you want to address with an improved governance process.
- *Governance Process*: Look at what you have today. It probably depends on the size of your company. Small start-ups hardly have any kind of (formal) governance. The quality of products in such companies often depends on individuals driving the product and development process in a specific direction. In larger organizations you typically have at least some kind of governance. This can be development guidelines, formal processes, or standard review procedures. Further measures like a formal governance organization for software development or teams performing in depth product audits are rather rarely found.

The analysis will take some time. Don't rush; governance is not a fast business. It takes diligent consideration. Better preparation yields better results.

5.4   Where Do You Want to Go?: Goals for Governance

Now that you know where you are consider where you are heading to. (Okay, if you have a subsidiary in the Caribbean or the South Seas, the decision is pretty easy. No question, the governance process needs to be improved there with highest priority). With the inventory of gaps and issues you start making a plan what to address. In this step it is important to focus on *what* you want to achieve, not *how*.

- *Ability to Analyze Product Issues*: This is the most concrete and tangible scheme: You know the issue but don't know the root cause of it. Even if you currently have no concrete issue, be prepared for such an analysis. Such an analysis can be driven – not exclusively – in two directions. On one hand you want to resolve the concrete issue with a product. On the other you want to understand what lead to the issue in order to avoid similar problems in future. The term "product issue" needs to be understood in a broader sense here. It does not cover only bugs or other obvious deficiencies. It also covers any non-compliance with the strategic direction, or with other internal standards.
- *Understanding How Things Work*: This is a more abstract scheme. In this case understand how your development processes actually work. Assess the effectiveness of corresponding governance activities. Trigger could be some indications that something does not work as expected. But the issue might not be obvious. This is a building block for a broader approach focusing on optimizing your processes and procedures.
- *Safeguard Development Projects*: Maybe you have a strategic development project where failure is not an option. You are not sure how to safeguard the project but you are looking for additional means of assuring its success.
- *Assuring Legal Compliance*: Another scheme is the requirement to comply with some legal regulations. There are some regulations that have a direct impact on the development process. For instance if you want to sell and deliver your software to foreign countries your product is subject to export control regulations. One area is encryption. You need to control the usage and assure transparency of cryptographic components in your product. Another area affected by legal regulations is the use of open source components. The use of open source is very popular nowadays; but there are many open source licenses that basically do not allow the use of corresponding components in commercial (software) products.

Surely, the different goals have some commonality. At the end it is about building better, more sustainable products and being in synch with your strategic goals. It is rather a matter of your current main pain points making you think about improvements.

5.5 Different Routes to Your Destination: Governance Styles

Now that you know *what* you want to achieve you have to decide on *how* to achieve it. Let us briefly look at the options. Most of the remainder of the book will focus on the details.

- *Traditional Governance Approach*: This approach covers the well-known measures of governance. In software development process measures are process descriptions, rules, development guidelines, reviews, and code scans. When embracing these kinds of measures you have to be clear about their effectiveness in the respective context. As this is such an important aspect we will look in depth into this in Chap.12.

- *Product and Development Process Audits*: Audits are nothing new. Nevertheless, audits have not been used for an in-depth analysis of software products. The way we embrace the audit concept for assessing the effectiveness of development processes is rarely seen. A major part of the remainder of the book will focus on this specific audit approach – the Software Sustainability Audits.
- *Control Self-Assessment*: In addition to the product and process audits we introduce the concept of Control Self-Assessment (CSA) which is a concept known from the audit space. We have adapted the concept as a more effective alternative to classical reviews in the software development process. This concept is also covered by the dedicated Chap. 12.

We provide a set of methods and their advantages and drawbacks. At the end it is your choice. You have to decide what is best suited for your company and working environment. Try out different approaches to make your own experience. It is most convincing for people affected by governance and audits if you can explain your choice of methods. We assume that your goals and objectives for governing software development processes and products are quite stable. But the approach and concrete methods can change over time. Be open to adapt your approach if it has proven ineffective here or there.

5.5.1 Partner or Police

When analyzing your current situation we touched the point of company culture. The governance approach and style has to fit to this culture to be most effective. Although we focus on this in more depth in Chap. 13 about communication we briefly want to mention it here. The first approach – and probably the more traditional one – is what we call policing. You set up rules and check whether people and teams follow these rules. When you check compliance with the rules it is less important why the rules exist. But honestly, this is not a very successful approach in software development. Most people in software development have a good educational background and are smart enough to think about what they are doing. Governance has to be able to explain why certain rules exist and why development has to comply with them. Otherwise it is very hard to get buy-in from development teams and to enforce compliance.

An alternative to policing is the partner approach. Here the focus is on the common company goals and objectives. Both, development teams and governance teams have a common interest in the success of the company. Thus governance rather supports development teams in achieving their goals. For instance, instead of purely checking compliance with some rules, governance consults development teams on how to achieve compliance. This requires convincing arguments as to why respective rules are important and expertise in the governance teams to provide corresponding consulting services.

5.5.2   Governance by Example: Utilize Your Experience!

Governance activities are often considered having a negative touch, especially in software development where you deal with smart and creative people. Sometimes they consider governance as limiting their creative latitude. It is surely not always the case, and people also see the benefits of governance. Nevertheless, governance exists to direct software development in certain direction. It is the opposite of creativity.

Software development creates or shapes products. You have – hopefully – a positive and tangible result at the end. Governance is different. Governance activities – and especially audits – constantly expose you to things that do not work well – ineffective process, projects that fail, etc. Things working well do not need much attention (except when you try to figure out why they are working well). People working in governance can be impacted by the negative aspects of that job. Constant discussion with development teams about the sense or non-sense of governance activities can lead to attrition. Decreasing motivation in the governance team can be the consequence.

Governance is important and increasing in importance. Sustainable software cannot be reliably developed without governance. And approaches like Software Sustainability Audits require skills, expertise, and motivation. To attract and retain people with the required expertise you have to make up your mind also about the negative aspects of governance. The solution cannot be cutting back on any governance activity. You rather have to compensate for the negative facets.

Over time software auditors will gain a lot of insight about what work and what does not work. This is extremely valuable expertise you can utilize for improving products or processes. Auditors might participate in software development projects or related projects to provide their experience and expertise. Whether they act more as consultants or participate as normal members in a project is less important. In addition to utilizing their expertise this can be a compensation for the drawbacks of governance and auditing – a positive experience.

5.6   The Right Equipment: Tips for Your Journey

Now that we have investigated the territory of governance we want to give you some final hints for a successful journey. The single most influencing factor for the success of your governance activity is the quality of your work. Without quality you hardly get the acceptance required to cause a positive impact on your company. Quality has many facets so we selected a few to briefly consider here. For software audits we advise following a holistic approach. Clarify your mission, select the right combination of skills in your team, and consider the way you communicate and interact with other people and teams.

5.6.1 The Holistic Approach

When assessing individual products or development processes there is a single most important aspect to be considered. It is expressed by the questions "Why does this product or process exist?" or "Why is it built the way it is?" Without understanding the reasons behind these questions you will not be successful. In the context of governance success is the ability to drive positive improvements. It sounds simple, but experience shows – at least in software development – that many people do not really think about motivation and reasons. A process is established to achieve an objective in a controlled and repeatable manner. But how can you assess the process effectiveness if you do not understand what the intention behind the process? How can you assess the architecture of a software product if you do not understand its purpose?

Software architecture can only be understood in its context. With a software product you serve a certain market or customer expecting specific functionality. In addition the software has to fulfill non-functional requirements like scalability, performance, security, etc. These non-functional aspects mainly determined the required architecture. Try to assess the architecture with regard to its validity and sustainability without understanding the objectives for the overall product. You might discover that a product is basically built from spaghetti code or that there is no meaningful component structure allowing for reusing components. But whether this is an issue in the context of the assumed usage of the product cannot be determined.

The holistic approach extends and embraces the previous aspect of understanding the "why". The governance approach should take into account all relevant aspects, not only selected ones. For instance, if you audit your development processes do not only focus on compliance, i.e. whether development teams comply with the rules. Also question and challenge the process definition itself. Is the process suited to achieve the defined business objectives? In other words, if you follow the current process does it assure achieving the business objectives? Take an end-to-end approach from understanding the "why" to the final product.

The holistic approach is a key characteristic of the software sustainable audits introduced in the next chapter. The approach essentially acknowledges that business objectives, development processes, and software products are intrinsically tied together. This is discussed in depth in the subsequent chapters.

5.6.2 Define Your Mission

In Sect. 5.4 we recommended making up your mind about the goals you want to achieve with a governance approach. Make your goals transparent and write them down. This allows you assessing selected measures with regard to their effectiveness. Be clear about what you want to achieve and make this transparent. Governance can sometimes be a tough journey. You might discover things some people rather would like to remain undiscovered. You face nasty discussions about the sense of what you are doing. In these situations it is vital to have a guide that provides orientation, and helps staying on track. A mission statement supports this. Still you have to ensure that the employed methods are in synch with your mission.

> **Example.**
> *The governance and audit services provide a continuous, systematic, and holistic feedback mechanism to establish high-performance standard development processes and to deliver best-in class products serving our customers and supporting the company's strategic product goals.*
>
> *With our delivered services we add value by providing a clear and transparent assessment of current process maturity and product state, effectiveness and efficiency, associated risks, and by proposing management-oriented recommendations enabling informed decisions about corrective measures.*

5.6.3 Valuable Expertise: Skills for Your Team

Software development is a rather complex topic. There are a lot of influencing factors determining the success of products and the environment of today's business software has to fit into is highly complex in itself. Consequently, auditing software development processes and products requires many different skills and a lot of expertise. The diversity of required skills and expertise is enormous. It is almost impossible that a single person covers all these skills. So, when setting up an audit or governance team, it is not only important to have individuals with strong expertise. It is equally important to ensure a broad coverage and diversity across the team. Let us look at the areas required to cover with the corresponding skills and expertise.

- *Development and Technology Expertise*: By far the most relevant expertise is the one about software development in general. To perform effective development process and software product audits it is indispensable to have a solid understanding of how software development works, how developers act and think, and what the influencing factors for products are. Technical skills needed to understand the technological aspects of software are software technologies like operating and database systems, programming languages, software platforms like the different user interface technologies, or communication protocols. Without strong technical expertise it will be not only hard to effectively assess processes and products. It is also hard to get the required acceptance within the development teams as auditors. Sometimes it can be very beneficial if you are able to employ some hands-on as part of an audit to independently assess certain aspects of the development environment or the capabilities of software platforms.
- *Architecture Expertise*: Secondly, you need engineering and architecture skills and expertise. This covers all the aspects of architecting and designing software products according to defined requirements. This covers all the facets like technology platform selection, componentization of the software and reuse of

components, achieving non-functional requirements, and documenting and communicating architectural ideas.

- *Product Management Expertise*: Under product management expertise we subsume any customer and market aspect related to the software development process. Customers can be internal (like other departments) or external ones. Product management includes topics such as gathering customer requirements, prioritizing these requirements, creating business cases, and rolling-out software products to customers.
- *Field Expertise*: Field expertise covers sales and consulting expertise. Understanding how software products are sold and positioned can help identifying disconnects between expectations set by sales and the actual delivered products. Consultants work with the software at the customer side and know typical issues related to the products from an operational point of view. That kind of background can be very helpful in assessing the match of a product to typical customer expectations.

It might not be possible to cover all skills. But often audit teams have a certain dynamic of auditors coming and going. Developers, architects, or else work as auditors for some time and go back to software development afterwards. This gives room to try out different combinations of skills to find the one best suited for your environment.

5.6.4   One Voice, Coaching, and Communication

Imagine you are audited or reviewed twice by the same central governance team, but each time by different people. What kind of impression would you have if they follow different approaches for the assessment and the communication of results? One team might have a more formal style, the other a rather open one. Maybe the templates are different for presenting the scope, measures, and results. In the best case you would see some missing alignment within the team and a non-professional behavior. In the worst case you could conclude – or at least suspect – that the assessment is not objective, that the results highly depend on the people implementing the audit or review. You do not trust the results. And this is extremely hard to correct. Governance in software development is much easier if people trust in the independence and assume an objective assessment.

All your effort and competency can be undermined by the wrong appearance of your governance team. You can prevent this if you focus on a *one voice* approach. This requires additional effort but will pay-off through professional results and increased acceptance of the governance entity.

Whatever your governance approach is, there is a single person or a small group of people defining and shaping it. Whether a partnering or policing approach is embraced or what other important things are defined in a small circle. Ensuring that all team members act accordingly is the idea behind *one voice*. There are different measures and facets we would like to discuss here to give more insight about possible and effective approaches.

- *Coaching of Team Members*: Most emphasis should be put on the acting people in your team. On the one hand side they have the relevant expertise; on the other hand you have to ensure that they present the governance topic in a unified manner. A very effective way of alignment is a coaching approach. Schedule a weekly coaching session with individuals or audit teams to discuss relevant issues. These are questions that are open or unclear, or questions about how to formulate and communicate findings. The coaching is performed by the owner of the governance topic or someone close to the owner who has a clear understanding of the intended direction.
- *Process Description and Checklists*: Similar to your goals and objectives you need a clear description of your governance process. It should contain all important roles, process steps, and responsibilities. Especially when you employ an audit concept you need a formal framework. This framework has to be covered by the process description in detail. Although you need a comprehensive description a lengthy text document is not very practical for day-to-day business. To this end we recommend complementing the text document with a checklist. This checklist should cover the important process steps for your team members. You can link the checklist to the relevant passages of the text document and thus have a very efficient and effective control for your process. We will provide an example when discussing the audit framework in Chap. 7.
- *Communication Within the Governance Team*: With the coaching approach we introduced a very effective means of ensuring one voice. But there might be new topics you want to introduce for which the operational oriented coaching is not the appropriate choice. An educational style might be better suited (workshops, classroom training, etc.) in this case. We experienced that a single event is not sufficient to establish new topics. It takes several iterations of re-communicating new topics to the team. Keep this in mind to avoid disappointments. Whatever it might be that is important to you, communicate it again and again to your team. People are often overloaded with information and it is hard to determine for them what is of utmost importance. Information only communicated once can easily get lost. Iterating on specific aspects will help your team to get a better sense of what is important.
- *Communication to the Outside*: We have a dedicated chapter about communication but would like to put some emphasis on this topic here. Communication with people outside the governance team is essential to get the buy in from affected people. You need to explain the reason behind the governance activities and the findings and issues identified during audits. This communication needs to be consistent across team members and aligned with the overall strategy. On the one hand side you have to focus on facts rather than on opinions. On the other hand you have to communicate with empathy to take the situation of the affected colleagues into account. The people developing software and people running governance are required to bring the software products and so the company forward. Thus transparency on the steps you are taking is important. If you communicate consistently, ensure transparency on the governance process, treat

affected colleagues fairly, and are open towards feedback you will be most successful.

5.7 Summary

With the first successful software audits executives and managers experience the added value. This brings up the idea to establish this kind of audit as a standard and institutionalized service. This requires a governance frame aligned with the company's strategy and culture. We discussed different aspects of the governance framework as basis for software audits and gave hints on taking the first steps. Assessing where you are and where you want to go is an essential initial step in setting up governance. Furthermore we looked at different purposes of governance and introduced different possible styles. In the following chapters we will further detail the discussion and take a closer look at requirements towards an audit framework. Subsequently we introduce the Software Sustainability Audits as a standardized concept for auditing software development processes and products.

The Software Sustainability Audit

What's In It for Me?

In this chapter we introduce the new concepts of Software Sustainability Audits. This is a new and dedicated class of audits. These audits focus on the sustainability aspects of software products and their development processes. The concept follows one core question: *Where do we have to improve to make our software more sustainable?* Sustainability is understood in a broad sense, not limited to carbon emission. The concept comprises any limited resource like IT personnel, support resources, or IT budgets. The standardized concept comprises a holistic approach with unified assessment criteria, an audit framework, and a blend of process and product audits. The details will be discussed in subsequent chapters.

CIO/CTO

Understanding the basic idea is essential from an executive perspective. You have to set the appropriate boundary conditions for this audit approach. Read Sects. 6.1 and 6.2 for the core concept. Section 6.2.1 onwards discusses the details and can be skipped. Section 6.3 outlines the need and requirements for an audit framework. In Sect. 6.4 we discuss the relation of the software development process and corresponding products. This might be helpful for you to further deepen your general understanding.

Software Architect

Auditing is probably a new territory for you. It is essential to fully understand the concept behind Software Sustainability Audits. You already have a good understanding of software and how it is developed. Assessing software products and development processes from the outside is something entirely different. Read this chapter carefully. Section 6.2 discusses common criteria

(continued)

R. Gutbrod and C. Wiele, *The Software Dilemma*, Management for Professionals,
DOI 10.1007/978-3-642-27236-3_6, © Springer-Verlag Berlin Heidelberg 2012

needed to apply a holistic approach to an assessment. This could help you in assessing software even if you are not following a strict audit approach. Section 6.4 will help you sharper your understanding of how the development process and the resulting products depend on each other.

Auditor
As an auditor you are familiar with the core concepts of auditing and the need for a corresponding framework. This chapter details the specifics of software development auditing (the content of the audits). The audit objectives introduced in Sect. 6.2 are especially important. They build the backbone of this audit approach. Compare the audit approaches you are familiar with as you carefully read the chapter.

6.1   Taking the Final Step: Introducing a New Class of Audits

Our journey through the world of software audits and reviews started in Chap. 4. This introduction was based on our experience of how things typically evolve. Once in a while architects are confronted with the request to provide a technical assessment of a software product. In this situation, an architect needs guidance on how to proceed. We introduced a tool set for making such software reviews successful. Our discussion continued in the previous chapter. We looked at the boundary conditions for successful software governance.

Now we take the last step. We introduce a standardized class of software audits following a holistic approach. These new audits focus on all aspects influencing the sustainability of software products. The approach covers the specifics of software development. As we will see in Chap. 7 software development processes have a different character than other IT-related processes. This is why we need Software Sustainability Audits.

Sustainability in our understanding is not limited to carbon emission but has a broader meaning. Sustainability comprises all the aspects influencing the cost of development, support, and operation in the lifetime of the software. There is one core idea behind Software Sustainability Audits. This idea is providing transparency on the state of development processes and software products. Main focus – as the name indicates – is the sustainability of the resulting software. A central aspect of this broad understanding is the adequacy of products for their defined target market. Meeting customer and user expectations is a prerequisite for sustainable software.

What does the holistic approach mean? It means that all stages of the software development process are taken into account. The assessment covers the business objectives, the development process, and the final product. The audits are based on unified assessment criteria. A standardized audit framework ensures the required quality of the audits. And finally the concept comprises a blend of process and product audits as manifestation of the holistic approach. The concept of process validation audits is of particular importance. These validation audits assess development processes with regard to their effectiveness. This is by no means always ensured in software development as we will see in Chap. 8.

This chapter covers the holistic approach and the unified assessment criteria. The audit framework is covered in Chap. 7. We discuss process and product audits in detail in Chaps. 8 and 9.

6.2   From One End to the Other: Take the Holistic Approach

The holistic approach is the heart of the Software Sustainability. We briefly introduced the holistic view in Chap. 5. There we recommended the holistic approach in a broader context of the governance framework. We now continue the discussion by formalizing this holistic view. This will make it more tangible in the context of auditing. To this end we need a process model generic enough to cover all software development processes.

This process model is outlined in Fig. 6.1. The model is built by four core constituents:

- The business objectives,
- The plans and process designs to achieve these objectives,
- The execution of plans and processes, and
- The results or final software products.

We will now explain how these constituents are inter-dependent in specific ways. At the center of all activity are the business objectives. The term business objective might sound quite abstract but it comprises the reasoning for anything that is done in software development. Business objectives cover the "why" and the "what" of anything you want to achieve with your products and development processes. This can be a certain level of security, addressing a dedicated market segment, or a specific performance goal.

Achieving the objectives will enable success of software products. We talk about *enabling* success as the success depends on more than the product itself and its qualities. The go-to-market strategy, sales, roll-out activities, etc. are equally important. But we solely focus on the development aspects here. Objectives can be related to all products developed by the company. For example, all products have to be secure. Objectives can also be specific to a single product. For example, a product has to fulfill the specific security requirements for the banking sector; another product might require a highly competitive user interface to match user expectations.

Product-related standards can also be established at the business objectives level. If performance is essential for the product success you can establish a standard. This standard could define that any end-user interaction with the system shall not exceed a certain response time. Standards can be considered as *derived objectives*. A high-level objective could require meeting the performance expectations of

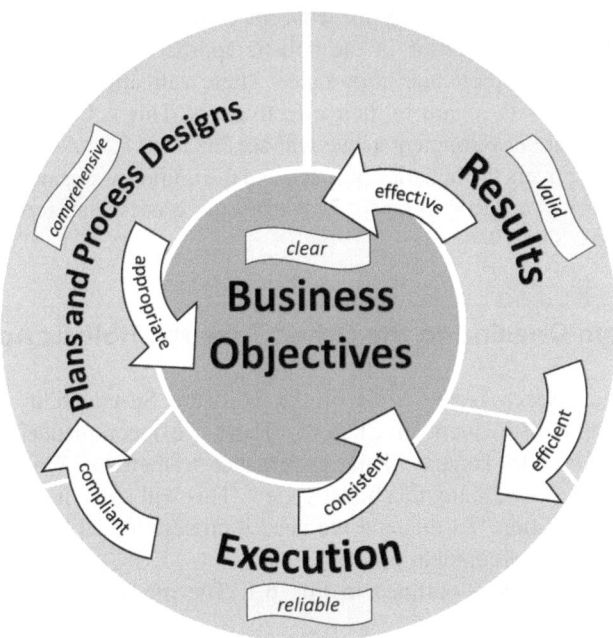

Fig. 6.1 Process model and audit objectives for software sustainability audits

customers and users. The concretization of this objective would be the requirements of the standard.

If we want to achieve a specific objective we need a plan or a process. A process has a generic character and applies to all software development projects. Take the example of secure programming. This process comprises secure programming guidelines and other rules. Furthermore, so called controls (we come to this in Chaps. 8 and 11) are required. The controls should assure that the objectives are actually achieved, or deviations are detected. Think of code scans for security vulnerabilities, code reviews, or security training.

Plans are more specific to individual software projects. Think of classical project plans or product roadmaps. But the term plan also comprises more specific documents. The architecture document used to implement a software product can be understood as a plan in this context. We have introduced both terms – plans and processes – to cover process and product audits with a single model.

The plans or processes do not need to be formally documented. Especially in smaller companies, one often finds a rather pragmatic approach here. There is a kind of common sense of what should be done. Nevertheless, it is important to ensure that the processes and plans are aligned with the given business objectives. What you have defined or what is common sense needs to be suited to achieve the corresponding objectives. Again take the example of a secure programming guideline. The guideline is only suited if it is up-to-date and covers all relevant aspects.

What will happen otherwise? Even if people exactly follow the guidelines you will not achieve secure products.

Now we have our plans and processes. What's next? Next we run our software development projects. This is the execution part. The software gets implemented. Hopefully this is done according to our plans or processes, i.e. compliant. Unfortunately, development projects not only have to achieve a single objective, there are many competing objectives. On the one hand, this requires prioritization of the objectives. Is it more important to deliver a certain feature or to provide better performance of the products? Development projects constantly have to make decisions in the magic triangle of time, resources, and quality. This comprises features and non-functional requirements. Decisions have to be taken in accordance with the defined priorities of the objectives. The holistic approach requires assessing both. Does a prioritization of objectives exist, and do project teams make decisions accordingly?

Last but not least, at the end of the development process we will have a completed product. There is a single most important question to ask. Have we accomplished our product-related objectives? Here the holistic view is vital. Imagine the product does not fulfill the objectives (or at least some). The product could have derailed at different stages. The objectives were not defined well or concrete enough. Maybe the prioritization was missing. The plans or processes were not appropriate to accomplish the objectives. And finally, the project team did not follow the process. Or they did not make decisions in accordance with the priority of the objectives. We have to take all these aspects into account when assessing software products.

But what if the product meets the objectives? Can you assume everything to be fine? The astonishing answer is "no". Surely, for the product at hand it is all right. But it does not necessarily mean that your plans and process are valid and okay. Maybe the project team has recognized that the processes are flawed, and following them would not lead to success. They ignored the process and simply did what was right to do. You are lucky with such a team. But what will happen to the next project? They might follow the process as designed and will miss the objectives. So, even you have no current product issue, it can make sense to review your processes. Maybe a process is not required at all and it could be removed without negative impact. In this way you can optimize your organization.

So far we have explained the basic concept and interdependencies of the software development process and the holistic approach. We will now turn to a more formal discussion. We introduce audit objectives as unified assessment criteria. Understanding the ideas behind the unified assessment criteria is vital for successful Software Sustainability Audits.

6.2.1   Unified Criteria: The Audit Objectives

In this section we introduce a set of common assessment criteria for Software Sustainability Audits. These criteria are called audit objectives. We have to be careful not to confuse the different types of objectives. In the previous section we introduced the business objectives. The business objectives define what we want to achieve with our software development. Audit objectives on the other hand define what we want to assess with an audit. Defining a set of common audit objectives is the basis for making a consistent assessment across different audit implementations.

Look again at our process model Fig. 6.1. We introduced the four constituents: business objectives, development plans and process designs, process execution, and results. In addition we defined nine different audit objectives in Fig. 6.1. These audit objectives cover the complete process – more specifically the software development process. Please keep in mind when we talk about processes this refers to software development processes. These are not the business processes covered by the software.

We have defined four audit objectives that focus on the individual constituents. The remaining five establish the relationships between the constituents. Looking at Fig. 6.1 you might have found there is a missing direct connection between the results and the plans and process designs. This was intentionally left out as there is no such direct connection. The results are only indirectly connected through the underlying business objectives.

We now will discuss all the different audit objectives, starting with the audit objective related to the center of gravity – the business objectives.

6.2.1.1 What's the Purpose?: Assessing Business Objectives

Sam, our auditor, is requested to conduct an end-to-end audit on a software development project. In the course of the audit he analyses the relevant documents. To clarify some aspects of the business objectives defined for the software project, Sam schedules an interview with the product manager Sonja Payonne.

Sam:"Sonja, as part of my preparation I have looked at the objectives you have defined for your development project. I was a little puzzled with one of your objectives. Can you please explain what is meant by the objective to create a 'world-shattering space age application'? I haven't found much of an explanation for this."

Sonja:"Well, what's so hard to understand about this? Our company is not known for really sexy applications. And we will change this with our new release. We have to keep pace with our competition."

Sam."But how do you assess whether you have achieved this objective?"

Sonja:"Oh, this is simple. We implement the new release using the Thunderbolt technology."

Sam:"This is all? That stack is used by the competition as well."

Sonja:"Yes, but not by us so far."

Sam:"Okay, let's turn to your other objectives. In addition you set two objectives. On the one hand, you want to clean up your portfolio by harmonizing the existing technologies used. Then you state you want to seamlessly integrate your product with two other products. This sounds quite challenging. What is the priority of these three objectives?"

Sonja:"All are equally important. If we miss any we will fail in the market."

Sam:"With the support of the existing products, do you have the required resources to really achieve all objectives?"

Sonja:"Again, we cannot miss any."

This little example leads us to our first audit objective – *clear business objectives*. Audit objectives describe the expectations we have with regard to relevant artifacts. A "world-shattering space age application" is probably something everyone would like to achieve when developing a software product. Unfortunately, as long as you do not explain what makes an application "world-shattering", this objective does not help in your developing such a product.

- What are the required functional and non-functional objectives?
- What kind of user interaction do you expect?
- How can I assess that the objective has actually been achieved?

One thing that we have at our disposal is the expectations we have towards individual business objectives. Another essential aspect is the prioritization of these business objectives. Any software development project has to balance time, features, and resources. What will happen without prioritization? Development projects will make random decisions in case the scope has to be reduced. This could be required to keep the delivery date.

The example above focused on the business objectives defined for an individual product. The same expectations pertain to the business objectives of a development process. We have to be clear about what we want to achieve with a process. Otherwise it is not possible to design an effective and efficient process accordingly.

The following table contains a summary of the expectations towards clear business objectives. An audit focusing on this audit objective would assess the business objectives with regard to the given criteria.

Audit Objective: Clear Business Objectives

Business objectives are any explicit or implicit expectation associated with the result of the process. This could be the compliance with external or internal regulations, or a product with certain qualities.

The business objectives have to be defined in a clear and transparent way comprising several aspects. The first is that the set of objectives has to be complete. No objective must be hidden or implicit. If people have implicit assumptions about certain objectives the development team cannot act accordingly. For instance the product requires a specific scalability to serve a defined market segment but this is not made transparent.

Furthermore, objectives have to be well documented and communicated. It also has to be clear how the achievement of an objective is assessed. Still, it might not always be possible to define them according to the SMART criteria (specific, measurable, attainable, realistic, and timely). Uncertainty in the assessment of objectives will lead to discussions and missing guidance for the development teams.

Development projects face multiple, competing objectives which have to be accomplished. To enable reliable decisions, a prioritization of the objectives is required. Otherwise random decisions might occur. In this case the easiest and not the most important objective will win.

The audit objective of clear business objectives is the most important one for Software Sustainability Audits. Our experience shows that products without clear objectives face a high risk of failure. They lack a clear landmark. Similarly, development processes without clear objectives and purpose are ineffective and inefficient.

6.2.1.2 Paving the Path: Assessing Plans and Process Designs

In our company we faced some severe impacts from security vulnerabilities in some of our software products. As a result, our auditor Sam is asked to conduct an audit. The focus is on the processes that should assure the delivery of secure software.
As part of the audit execution he has scheduled an interview with Homer Certos, the owner of the secure development process.
Sam:"Homer, from my analysis I understood your objective. It is to ensure secure software products to the extent possible with state-of-the-art technology."
Homer:"That's correct. We invest a lot into security related education of our developers. We also use guidelines, code reviews and the like."
Sam:"Well, I read the guideline for secure software development. It covers only the two main development languages we currently use in our development. But it lacks any description about some others."
Homer:"Yes, that's true. We currently decided to focus on the two main ones."
Sam:"The other thing that I noticed is that you solely rely on code reviews. As your objective is to ensure security to the state-of-the-art wouldn't it be more appropriate to introduce code scanning as a better means?"
Homer:"Maybe yes, but we currently do not have the resources to master such a project."

The little example above gives a first glimpse of what has to be assessed when auditing the design of processes or development plans. The first step is making up your mind what to achieve by defining the business objectives. The second step is deciding on the appropriate way to achieve the objectives. Processes require a corresponding design. The design covers the process steps, required guidelines, and procedures. But the design also covers controls assuring the achievement of the business objectives. Auditing a software product, we have to look at development plans, schedules, test procedures, etc. They are established to achieve the corresponding product-related objectives.

These plans and process designs have to fulfill two main criteria. First, they have to be comprehensive – covering all important aspects. Secondly, they have to be appropriate. By following the plans and process designs there will be assurance that he defined objectives will be achieved.

Audit Objective: Comprehensive Development Plans, Process and Control Designs

Let us distinguish the difference between process and product related designs and documents.

In the case of processes, a comprehensive design is required comprising an understandable and complete documentation. This includes all relevant roles, the process steps and their respective sequence, as well as all required deliverables. The complete context also has to be defined. This comprises any required input from other processes or groups, the expected output to other processes or groups, and any important boundary conditions.

The process design also needs to cover corresponding internal controls that assure that the corresponding business objectives are achieved. Controls in the context of software development are the description of the process flow itself, as well as things like quality gates, mandatory code scans, or reviews.

The reason for having processes is to achieve a dedicated objective in a reliable manner. If the design is not comprehensive, it cannot be effectively executed, and the outcome might not meet expectations.

In addition to the process and control design, other documents are required as input for a process. These documents typically depend on a specific product. This comprises project plans, but also things like product backlogs, architecture concepts, and design documents. Most of these documents are the outcome of corresponding development related processes like requirements engineering. But when looking at the comprehensiveness of the documents, the focus is the content and not the process of creating the documents. When we require the product backlog as input for a development process we are looking only on the content of the backlog, not how it came into being. Take this as an example that documents can take on different roles in an audit depending on the scope and objective of the audit. Sometimes a document is considered as the result of a process, in a different context the same document can act as the input for further processes. In both cases the role of the document must be differentiated and is assessed based on different criteria.

The development-related documents required as input for a process need to fulfill similar criteria as the process description. Documents have to be complete and consumable. Process documents usually change infrequently. Development documents are much more volatile and have to be up-to-date.

Audit Objective: Appropriate Development Plans, Process and Control Designs

When assessing the comprehensiveness we only focused on the formal aspects of process designs and documents. When looking at the appropriateness we assess the processes and documents in the context of the corresponding business objectives. In other words we consider the purpose of the processes and documents.

A process design with corresponding controls is appropriate if it assures achieving the business objective at hand. If you follow the process as it is designed you will – at least with high probability – achieve the intended objectives. For instance, your objective is to develop secure software products. But the development process does not ensure that developers are equipped with the required skills. In this case the process is not appropriate – or at least suffers from certain deficiencies. But the example of security also reveals the limitations. There is no process guaranteeing absolute secure software– at least not at reasonable cost. Security vulnerabilities cannot always be prevented. Thus assessing the appropriateness is restricted to current best practices, existing technology and knowledge. The assessment also has to set the costs of the process in relation to the possible impact when failing to achieve the business objective.

Similarly we have to assess relevant development documents. Again take the security example. We might need to assess the architecture of a software product. If the architecture is not appropriate to ensure a secure product, the subsequent implementation will not lead to a secure product. For instance, if the architecture design does not foresee encrypted communication channels, the development teams will not implement them.

Overall, the audit objective of appropriate plans and process designs is probably the second most important one. The main risk of not having appropriate plans and process designs is a process running with the perception of being appropriate. You comply with all the steps and requirements of the process, and then late in the process, you realize you have not arrived at the intended objective.

6.2.1.3 What Are You Doing?: Assessing the Execution

In our process model a software product is built based on the execution of plans and processes. We introduce three audit objectives for assessing different aspects of the execution part. The first two and most important of the three are *reliable* and *consistent* execution. The third objective of *compliant* execution is very popular but less important in the context of software sustainability audits. We will come back to this in Chap. 8 about process audits.

Audit Objective: Reliable Execution

The first objective focused on execution is the one of reliability. This audit objective comprises general aspects required to execute a development process. These aspects are independent from the process design, or the business objectives at hand.

People require certain skills and expertise to develop software. If these required skills are not available, it is obvious that the development process cannot be effectively executed. This aspect covers any different aspects like programming languages, technologies, but also project management skills, and others.

Secondly, reliable execution covers organizational aspects. Roles and responsibilities need to be clearly defined, assigned, and communicated. Required management decisions have to be made in a timely manner, well communicated, and executed. If the development team is spread across different locations, efficient and effective communication has to be established. This is required to ensure information is exchanged and decisions are aligned. The organizational aspects are mainly independent from a specific product, or process at hand.

And last, a reliable execution requires a working infrastructure. Developers need computers to implement the code. The code needs to be managed by a corresponding infrastructure. Related documents like specifications and designs need to be managed, as well as required communication enabled.

Audit Objective: Consistent Execution

The second audit objective with respect to execution is the one of consistency with given business objectives. During the execution of a process or project decisions must be made. With regard to software development these decisions might be related to the scope of a product, the delivery date, or the prioritization of features to be implemented. But it could also affect the resource allocation, or the technology selection for a specific product. All these decisions have to be made consistent with the affected business objectives and their prioritized correctly. If this is not the case the project is at risk in meeting its objectives. For example, let us look at a software product that is intended to be sold globally. During the implementation phase a user interface technology is selected that does not allow for bi-directional language support. This decision is inconsistent with the globalization requirement. Alternately, the programming language might be chosen with regard to the existing skills in the team, but not with regard to the requirements of the product objectives.

Audit Objective: Compliant Execution

The objective of compliant execution relates the execution of a process or project to the corresponding process design or development plans. A process or plan is set up to be followed. If this is not the case the risk of failure is increased.

Here a word of caution is advisable. As explained in Chap. 8 compliance audits are of limited use in software development. It has to be guaranteed that the process design or plan is appropriate to achieve the corresponding business objectives. Otherwise compliance with the defined rules will give a misleading sense of security, and the risk of failure is not transparent.

6.2.1.4 Where Have We Gone?: Assessing the Result

Finally, we need to look at the results of a process or development project. We started off with our goals and business objectives. We went through the development process. And now the main question is: Have we achieved our goals and objectives? This question is covered by the audit objective of *effective achievement of objectives*. Furthermore, we introduce the audit objectives of *validity* and *efficiency*. They are typically less important than the *effectiveness* in the context of software sustainability audits.

Audit Objective: *Effective* Achievement of Objectives

The foremost reason to run a development process or project is to achieve certain business objectives. You want to have a product with certain qualities, whether it is the final product or any intermediate step required on the way to a final product. Assessing the effective achievement relates the actual product or step to the corresponding objectives at hand.

The assessment – especially if it involves a software product – is everything but easy and straight forward. It often requires deep insight and experience, a good understanding of the underlying technology, as well as thorough analysis of the business objectives. Take for example the objective to guarantee a certain through-put of a business application. You can run internal tests and review the specification and design. But the final judgment might only be possible if the application is deployed into the customer environment, operational with live customer data.

Audit Objective: *Valid* Results

The validity of process results comprises all aspects that ensure the consistency of the result in itself. These are aspects especially independent of the business objectives. For instance, if the process result is a guideline, this guideline has to be free of contradictions.

Audit Objective: *Efficient Achievement of Results*

The last audit objective is the one of efficiency. This objective relates the result to the effort required to achieve it. Efficiency is no end in itself; it always has to be assessed in the context of the specific process or product. You try to relate the actual effort to a – probably theoretical – minimal effort to achieve the same result.

6.3   The Road to Success: Audit Framework and Roadmap

Software Sustainability Audits require a solid framework ensuring a high level of quality. We will go into the details of the framework in Chap. 7. But as an initial step we have to make up our minds about the purpose of an audit framework. What is it exactly that we expect from an audit framework? There is nothing more worthless than a formal framework without purpose.

The purpose of the audit framework is supporting the achievement of the goals and objectives set for in the audit function. So, before thinking about the frame-work, we have to be clear about what we want to achieve with our audits. After that we can discuss the appropriate setup.

Auditing is a tool within the governance framework of an organization. Thus there is a primary goal and – depending on the philosophy followed – a secondary one:

- *Transparency on the State of Affairs*: Whether a software product or a related development process – the primary goal of the audit function is to create transparency. Providing facts to management enables informed decisions and corrective measures if required. Audits provide the highest value if they cover the most important topics. As an example, the selection of a topic could be based on risk exposure.
- *Support Improvements*: Depending on the philosophy of the audit team the audit goal can be extended. Besides creating transparency, supporting the resolution of issues could be a goal. This could be achieved by meaningful recommendations. Auditors are not responsible for resolving the identified issues. But they often

have a lot of relevant and valuable expertise and experience. They are able to act as consultants supporting the responsible managers on improving the situation.

Achieving these objectives requires assurance of certain aspects by the audit function. The most impact can be achieved if findings are accepted and resolved by the responsible managers. The audit framework can be used to support these audit objectives by assuring:

- *An Independent and Fair Assessment*: The results generated by an audit have to be based on an independent and unbiased assessment of the topic at hand. The auditors must not have any other interest than a fact-based assessment. Auditees have to be treated fairly. If this is not the case, you cannot be assured results would be accepted by auditees.
- *Transparency on Scope and Approach*: Support of the above objective with full transparency on the scope and the approach of the audit has to be assured.
- *Reliability and Traceability of Results*: Only if the results are based on facts and the audit team is able to prove this basis, will the audit results be accepted as valid. This also requires that each audit finding is supported by sufficient evidence.

Fulfilling the requirements of an audit framework requires discussion of the following aspects. Except for the assessment criteria we will discuss these aspects in Chap. 7, which is dedicated to the audit framework:

- *The Organizational Setup*: The organizational set up determines the ability to independently assess a software product or corresponding development process.
- *The Assessment Criteria*: Assuring an independent, fair, and transparent assessment requires unified and consistent assessment criteria across different audit teams. We embed these criteria into the audit objectives. These have already been introduced in the previous section and will not be re-discussed in the next chapter.
- *The Set of Audit Activities for the Assessment*: Audit results have to be based on facts. These facts are gained by implementing certain audit activities like interviews, document analysis etc. We will look at the different activities required in the context of software development.
- *The Audit Roadmap*: All activities have to be embedded into a general audit process – the audit roadmap. The process ensures reliability and traceability of the results, as well as transparency. This includes important steps like audit planning, the execution of audit activities, and the correct and traceable identification of audit findings.
- *Further Aspects*: Additional aspects like documenting audits and checklists must be taken into account in our audit approach.

6.4 Two Sides of a Coin: Process and Product Audits

A long time ago, when Gregory just became a principle architect, he was asked to assess a given product architecture. It was a product that was new to Greg. He first met some colleagues who could explain the business. He needed to understand what the product was supposed to do. Comprehending the business processes covered by this application was important to him. So he discussed the business function with some experts. Then he looked at the prototype. The experts enthusiastically showed him the user interface prototype. Greg wondered as he looked at the UI. "What users are supposed to use this front-end?" he asked one expert. It was an accounting application. He asked what is the expected business expert using the application. "Accountants" was the answer. "What technical background do they have?" Greg continued. With each question, he was trying to understand more details of the targeted users. An expected user profile and the knowledge of the user base seemed important to him. "Actually, they are business guys. Don't expect them to know too much about any software details" was the reply from another expert. "And what are these technical database names?" Greg had become curious about some fields on the screen. "How can the users understand what they represent?" He couldn't see how the users' business profile and these technical terms in the application would match. "That's all right" was the answer. "These database terms are very well-known by the users." "If I am frank with you, this is very strange. I thought the users don't have any technical background." Greg was confused by the answer. "Don't worry, Greg" was again the appeasing answer. "We just met a customer. The users there were very aware of these technical terms. He could use the prototype without any problem. The usability should be okay."

Greg still did not believe the story. Something must have gone wrong. Yes, he knew that he had only scraped the surface of business operations and left the architecture aside. However, he couldn't ignore it. He proposed a follow-up meeting with a business consultant to clarify the situation. "That's fine with us" said the experts. "Jack is a business consultant for this application. He certainly will confirm our business user base and requirements."

So, Greg setup another meeting to include both Jack and the product experts. Greg started the meeting. He explained what he understood from the business requirements. He referred to the technical database terms he found at the front-end user interface and his expectations. "Wouldn't the application be easier to use if the technical fields would be replaced by some business information? I am not the business expert, and I do not know the exact terms, but I would find it easier with the following information on the screen." Greg started sketching his ideas. The business consultant was excited by Greg's proposal. "Yes, that is exactly what the users tell me all the time. They want to get rid of technical terms." The experts – obviously irritated by the turn of events– interrupted. "We don't understand. Whenever we have joint sessions with users they don't have any issues with these types of fields." The business consultant explained this paradox. "From the beginning, the users were adamant in their complaints, that they do not understand those fields. Over the years they got used to them, but still would prefer something more adapted to their business language."

What went wrong? Based on the knowledge of the experts the application was all right. Yet, at first sight a strange user interface behavior was recognized. But the experts verified the front-end prototypes with users. The users could easily use the prototypes. So, everything was okay, wasn't it? Apparently not! That was the outcome of the deeper investigation. So what was the issue here? Which mistake was made? How could such a situation be prevented in future?

There must be more than just the architecture itself when you validate a product. "Architecture is good, but only when it meets business requirements." This frequently used statement was true in the story above. At first glance, the architecture was assumed to be valid for the business requirements, but on closer inspection, the business requirements did not meet the user's expectations.

6.4.1   Digging Deep: Root Cause Analysis

6.4.1.1 It Might Be the Product: Product Deep Dives

The story shows a common pattern of a hidden root cause. This can be treated by different means. The most common guidance is to dig deeper. "Ask why five times" is a famous rule. That is basically what Gregory did above. He dived deeper and deeper. If the business consultant would have confirmed the experts' statements, Greg could have contacted the users. He also could have challenged the experts with the "why-rule". He could have asked why the users understood the technical terms. And he could have continued with his deep dive.

This is one option to identify the root cause. Dig deep into the product architecture. Look at the product from different angles. Challenge every single item where you are not convinced that the root cause is identified.

6.4.1.2 It Might Be the Process: Process Assessment

There is another alternative route to identify root causes. Sometimes the direct path of assessment is not as valuable to learning the root cause. Alternatively, take an indirect way. Don't ask questions about the product, instead, ask how the creation of the product was accomplished. Figure out how the results were achieved.

In the example above, Gregory could have figured out how the processes were designed and executed to involve the end users. He could have challenged the design and execution of the requirement management process. He could have looked at the usability tests. Instead of validating the specific product Greg could have audited relevant processes for developing the final product.

6.4.2   Going Together: Unified in Software Sustainability Audits

The two approaches of root cause analysis show how software products and the corresponding processes are intrinsically tied to each other. Both approaches may be required depending on the actual situation. Software Sustainability Audits comprise both aspects – products and processes by respective audit types. Ignoring one side of the coin would leave you partly blind.

6.4.2.1 Process Audits

Process audits are intent on assessing the processes relevant for sustainable products. The sustainability is defined by the core architecture of a software product. In process audits we start understanding the business objective of the process. Then, we look how the process is defined. We take two or three products as samples to concretely check the process execution. Valid processes ensure that the final product and its architecture meet the defined business objectives. This is why assessing the results is a vital part of process audits during Software Sustainability Audits.

Process audits focus on the processes, not on the products or the product architecture. Whatever we find out here has potential impact on all developed products. This broad impact of development processes is reflected in the concept of process validation audits. These special audits are a core element of Software Sustainability Audits.

Process audits – as sample products are always included – still could reveal issues and findings in the sample products. These findings can be independent from the audited process. For instance, the process definition itself might be fine, but the particular execution in the project does not follow the defined route. This possibly has a negative impact on the sustainability of the product architecture. This is the touch point between process and product audits.

6.4.2.2 Product Audits

Product audits put the product and its architecture in the center of interest and investigation. The audit focuses on the stability and sustainability of the product architecture. When assessing a particular product and its architecture, some relevant processes can be added to the audit scope. Focus is the execution of these processes during the development of the audited product. An important process included into a product audit is the requirement management process. The central question to ask is: "How were the business requirements identified?" Depending on the product other processes might be considered. Take the example of a product storing credit card information. In this case the security process should be included into the scope.

Summarized, process audits take products as samples to validate the efficiency and effectiveness of processes. Product audits, however, have the products and their architectures as center of gravity. Most relevant processes of the particular products will be considered with focus on implementation of these processes within the product development.

6.4.3   The Trigger for Audits: Planned and Ad-Hoc Audits

Gregory, the principal architect, and Kai, his CIO, discussed their first experiences with Software Sustainability Audits. "It takes quite a lot of effort to complete a Software Sustainability Audit" Greg started. "Yes, we need to plan the effort for Software Sustainability Audits more carefully this year" Kai stated. They both looked at potential candidates. Soon, they had a perfect plan of candidates for Software Sustainability Audits to be conducted within the current year. "Let's finalize this as our plan for the year" Kai decided.

Shortly after Greg and Kai decided on the Software Sustainability Audit plan, a business owner contacted Kai. "I have experienced a lot of trouble with application X. Unfortunately, this application is absolutely crucial for the business. I have heard that you do some Software Sustainability Audits. Could you do me a favor? Could you please audit the architecture of this application?" Kai agreed.

Kai went back to Greg. "Greg, we need to do an urgent Software Sustainability Audit for product X. The architecture seems to be unstable and causes some trouble for the business owner" Kai explained. "Ok" Greg responded. "But we already have our plan and have assigned all of our resources for Software Sustainability Audits, didn't we? We did the planning with respect to our learning from last year. All products with high risk should be addressed, shouldn't they? How does this new audit fit into our plan?"

We need two audit types with respect to planning. There should be a plan of Software Sustainability Audits based on the company's risks. In addition, we need some slots to cope with additional Software Sustainability Audits for ad-hoc requests. Often, urgent requests pop up. Unforeseen issues or unidentified risks are reported. We need capacity to cover those requests. It is a good idea to balance both planned and ad-hoc Software Sustainability Audits at the same time. Not allowing ad-hoc Software Sustainability Audits is not a good idea. Screwing up the plan of scheduled audits is not a good idea either.

6.4.3.1 Planned Audits

Planned Software Sustainability Audits should address standard risks. The goal is the mitigation of development risks. We described above that Software Sustainability Audits cover the product and process dimension. We look at the processes which have high impact on architecture and sustainability. And we consider products which are essential for the company. We plan Software Sustainability Audits with focus on both, processes and product architecture. We collect risk information to identify high risk exposures of process and product combinations. We aggregate the risks with the view on processes. And we consolidate the risks for each identified product. For those process and product combinations with the highest risk we plan Software Sustainability Audits. So, planned Software Sustainability Audits address the forecast on the risks.

6.4.3.2 Ad-Hoc Audits

On the contrary, ad-hoc audits take care of risks which are identified spontaneously. You cannot foresee all future risks. However, when planning your Software Sustainability Audits there will be unknown gaps. A new high risk or a major issue needs to be tackled. Imagine that you plan the development of a software product. Imagine further that during your software development a business owner identifies that a very important feature is missing. Without this feature the product cannot be used. Will you continue developing according to your initial plan? Certainly not! You will identify efforts that can be skipped and use the freed resources for developing the important feature.

Similarly, urgent risks need to be addressed by ad-hoc audits. High risks can be identified by everybody. Hence, we recommend allowing everybody to submit a request for an ad-hoc audit. Risk assessments of those requests help integrating the most crucial ad-hoc audits into your Software Sustainability Audit plan.

6.5   Summary

We introduced a new and dedicated class of audits focusing on the sustainability aspects of software products and development processes. The standardized concept of Software Sustainability Audits comprises a holistic approach with unified assessment criteria, an audit framework, and a blend of process and product audits. We discussed the core idea and concepts and learned about the common audit objectives. The need for an audit framework was explained as well as the relationship of software development processes and the resulting products. The latter is important to understand why product and process audits are two sides of a single coin.

While this chapter focuses on the core idea of Software Sustainability Audits, the detailed discussion of process and product audits will be presented in the following chapters.

Put a Frame Around Your Work

What's In It for Me?

In this chapter we discuss the need and the details of an audit framework. The audit framework builds the core audit process and sets the required boundary conditions. The selection and discussion of the topics is based on the author's experience in the context of Software Sustainability Audits.

CIO/CTO

From an executive perspective it is important to understand why a solid audit framework is needed and what organizational aspects are relevant for efficient and effective audit work. It is sufficient to concentrate on Sects. 7.1 and 7.2. The remainder discusses the audit framework in details focusing on important operational aspects.

Software Architect

Audit and architecture work are typically quite different things. It is not expected that you have experience in this areas. Nevertheless, if you want to step into auditing of software development processes or products, you have to get a solid understanding of the audit framework. This chapter is mainly written for your support in getting the required understanding without having to consult additional literature. Reading this chapter for the first time we recommend going through it rather quickly to get a feeling about the topic of auditing in general. If you want to setup a corresponding audit team you can take a more detailed look later on. You can also use this chapter for reference later on. Even if you are not following a formal audit approach for an architecture assessment you can take ideas from the audit framework and adapt them to your individual needs. Especially Sects. 7.4.1.1 and 7.4.3.4

(continued)

R. Gutbrod and C. Wiele, *The Software Dilemma*, Management for Professionals, DOI 10.1007/978-3-642-27236-3_7, © Springer-Verlag Berlin Heidelberg 2012

about scoping and Sects. 7.4.4.1 and 7.4.4.4 about findings and reporting have a general validity and should be considered even in less formal cases like classical reviews.

Auditor
As auditor you should be familiar with the basic ideas of an audit framework. So, for the main part you can skim the chapter or pick individual parts to compare it to your experience or setup. For the specifics of auditing software development processes and products we recommend reading Sect. 7.3 for the audit activities and Sect. 7.4.4.1 for scoping.

7.1   Why an Audit Framework?

In the past, our model company had no audit group focusing on software development processes and software product audits. Nevertheless, some central activities existed to assess the architecture of the products developed by the company. One day, our principal architect Greg was asked to participate in a technical review of one of the products. This review was a follow-up to a previous review that had been conducted some time ago on the same product. New to this review process Greg tries to figure out how to proceed. He meets with Peter, the owner of the review process.
Greg: "Peter, I am trying to understand the review process and our authority during the review."
Peter: "Okay, what do you want to know?"
Greg: "Where can I find the documentation of the process to familiarize myself with it?"
Peter: "We have not documented the review process. Usually we ask the area that we review to prepare an architecture document. When the document is available we invite the participants to a 2 hour review session. Anything else?"
Greg: "Well, I know the product under review to some extent and I expect to find some issues. If we identify anything severe, are we authorized to stop the development project?"
Peter: "Hmm, good question. Don't know if this has been defined."
Greg: "And what about the action items from the last review. Where can I find the documentation of what was found last time? What was the agreement concerning the actions with the product team?"
Peter: "I don't have anything. Ask Carl, he ran the review the last time."
Greg walks over to Carl's office to ask for the documents.
Greg: "Carl, I am looking for the documents and meeting minutes of the last review. Can you help me?"
Carl: "Well, I think we created something. Let me check. I will send it to you."
A little later, Greg receives a slide deck with few slides about the last review. Unfortunately, no action items have been agreed upon, and no details about the review have been documented. Only a very high level declaration of intent has been documented covering potential improvements of the product.
Greg starts the review with very limited information about the past review and not much to base the new review on. During the review process Greg and his colleague notice that what was actually developed has very little to do with the high level goals set for the development

project. They schedule a meeting with Eric Ligumaag, the responsible manager for the product.
Greg: "Eric, we have reviewed the product and your current development plans. We are trying to understand how your plans fit to the overall goals you have set for the product."
Eric: "Oh, this is not your job. Only assess the architecture and technical aspects of the product. The rest should not be considered by you."
Greg: "But we doubt that with your current plans you will achieve your goals."
Eric: "This is a pure architecture review. You are not authorized to look at anything else."
After some more discussion the review is stopped without any concrete finding and tangible results.

This little story gives some hints why governance – be it a formal audit or some other kind of review – requires a clearly defined framework. If there is no clearly defined framework, the process might be inefficient, ineffective, and much more drastic – the results might be questioned. The framework has to ensure that the authority of the governance or audit team is clear, that the process is transparent, and that all findings are traceable. If you step into the shoes of the audited or reviewed area, how would you feel? It makes an unprofessional impression if the process is not supported by a solid framework and the corresponding authority. You could easily doubt that the review or audit is conducted in an open, fair, and independent manner. You might even be reluctant to trust the correctness of identified issues and thus won't accept any corresponding action item. This is basically the worst case that can happen to an audit or review function. Losing the trust of stakeholders – and the audited areas are important stakeholders – is the end of any audit function.

In the following sections we give an overview of the most important aspects of an audit framework. Even if you do not intend to implement a formal audit team and process you should look at what could be important in other – less formal – approaches. This chapter is not intended as a full description of an audit framework. Other comprehensive books exist on this topic. We focus on a general overview, and the aspects specific to auditing software development processes and projects.

7.2   Being Independent: Organizational Aspects

All of us are aware, by way of public discussions, that opposing groups have conflicting interests. Unions want to achieve higher wages for the employees, but employers are reluctant to pay more. Environmental activist are at odds with non-environmental lobby groups wanting to influence politicians to change legislation. Typically both sides will support their arguments by research studies – astonishingly exactly reflecting their respective position. Do we believe in the independence of these research studies? Well, most probably not.

Software development processes and products are also subject to different interests. The managers, the CIOs, the product owners, architects, developers – all have different interests. The sales people are pushing for a fast release to customers, while the development team wants more time to implement more features or to improve quality. A CIO might want to harmonize the use of technologies, while developers want to always use the newest technology to keep current with new trends. A responsible manager wants to make his product shine bright, while a colleague after another's job tries to unveil some issues.

In all these situations imagine an audit report that is suspicious of being created in one of the opponent's interest. Such a document would be useless. And the audit function flawed. Besides the requirement to base audit assessments on facts, the potential impact of the audit function depends on the trust people put into the generated results. Independence of the audit function is a central pillar of this trust. Although we only briefly touch this topic it is of utmost importance.

There are two different aspects of independence that need to be taken into account and assured by the audit framework and the organizational set up:

- *Independent Selection*: The first step in auditing is the selection of audit topics – software products and related processes – to be assessed. The selection needs to be independent, unbiased, and based on transparent criteria. If a manager is able to influence the selection in his interest – for instance dropping a specific software product from the list of audits – the independence is impaired.
- *Independent Implementation*: The auditors implementing an audit have to assess the state of affairs in an independent and unbiased manner. This requires that they not function as any kind of stakeholder for the audited topic. Sometimes it is required to involve experts for dedicated topics – for example an architect providing a specific expertise – as auditor in an audit. This expert must not be involved in any way in the audited product or be the owner of the audited process. The organizational boundary conditions also have to ensure that the content of an audit report, i.e. the identified issues, will not bear any positive or negative consequence for the auditor – be it financial, career-wise or others.

Full organizational independence is not always possible to establish. There are a limited number of board members required to cover a large set of topics. The ability for a complete independent audit organization might also be limited by legislation. There are also counter arguments for a complete organizational independence:

- *The Required Network*: As described in this book, auditing software development processes and products is a complex and challenging issue. The ability to assess this purely from the outside is limited. The better you know the internal processes and habits, the better you can perform an assessment as auditor. Being an insider to the organization increases the ability to sense issues better than as an external auditor. In a large organization a well-connected network helps to sense important topics, issues, or trends.
- *Attracting Talents*: Auditing software products and processes requires deep technical expertise and experience. While it might be attractive for experienced architects focusing on something like audits for some time, most of them will not see this type of work as a long term goal for their career. They will at some time prefer to return to software development creating new products. While working as an auditor they will need to stay current with new trends and technologies. A complete and independent audit organization is not attractive for these experts. But an audit team without this kind of expert is useless. The team will

not be able to reveal the relevant issues for a product or process, and will not gain the required acceptance by the development organization.

There is no silver bullet in the organizational set up. To some extent it is always a compromise. There is no optimum organizational set up. Still, the independent assessment by no means must be compromised. To ensure the independence, additional controls can be implemented to ensure the correct balance. Here are two options:

- *An Audit Committee*: The role of an audit committee is to control the audit function. This is a typical function ensuring a transparent and independent selection process of audit topics. The audit committee also monitors the independent implementation of audits.
- *Auditing the Audit Team*: Another control could be to audit the audit team itself. This audit could be implemented by another internal audit team or an external audit team. Such an audit would focus on the selection process of audit topics, and the independent assessment during audits. Basis for such an audit are commonly accepted audit standards.

7.3 Getting Information: The Right Activities

In the previous chapter we introduced the audit objectives as the basis for standardized Software Sustainability Audits. In the next step we identify measures and approaches appropriate to gather evidence about the state of software products and processes. These measures are called fieldwork activities. The most important activities are interviews and document analysis. But there are also other useful activities providing valuable insight. The following table contains the activities relevant in the context of Software Sustainability Audits. The table activities are listed with a short description.

The fieldwork activities for a specific audit are selected during the preparation phase. The selection is based on the audit objectives that define the scope of the audit (Table 7.1).

We stated before that the intention of this chapter is not providing a comprehensive introduction to auditing with all its facets. There are different auditing standards provided by audit organizations like Institute of Internal Auditors (IIA) and Information Systems Audit and Control Association (ISACA) covering also the different audit activity types. For further information we refer to corresponding literature.

7.4 The Audit Roadmap

The audit objectives and activities build the foundation for assessing software development processes and products. In the next step we have to embed both into a formal process. You can use the audit objectives and activities within a classical review, but only a formal audit process ensures the transparency and independence

Table 7.1 Fieldwork activities for software sustainability audits

Fieldwork activity type	Description
Interviews	Conducting interviews is one of the classical audit procedures. Interviews are the most flexible activity. Interviews can always be conducted even if no other activity is applied. While it is easy to meet with a person to talk about a topic, making an effective audit interview requires some effort
	A very powerful approach is the semi-structured method. Auditors prepare a set of core questions for which they are seeking answers. These core questions build the foundation and structure of the interview. But the questions are not simply asked in questionnaire form. Instead the auditors ask open questions leaving enough room for additional topics or issues brought up by the interviewee. In contrast to closed questions – which can be answered with yes or no – open questions require a full answer. For example, a closed question would be: "Do you handle non-functional requirements during the development process?" In contrast the open approach would be: "Please explain how you handle non-functional requirements during the development process"
	The typical time required for an interview is 60 min. If more time is required we recommend scheduling a follow-up interview. This leaves room for the auditors to rethink open topics they want to cover during the follow-up. The preparation and post-processing of an interview requires effort. It is recommended to limit the number of interviews per audit to 10–12. Meeting the audit objectives requires a careful selection of interview partners. The selected people and their assigned roles have to fit the audit scope
Document analysis	Document analysis is the second most common activity in Software Sustainability Audits. From a process perspective, relevant documents are process descriptions, guidelines, or any kind of policy. For software products relevant documents are the product strategy, requirements specifications, or architecture and design documents. Further documents could be organizational charts that provide insight about responsibilities. Auditors analyze the documents with regard to the audit objectives of *comprehensiveness* and *appropriateness*. In case of documents describing the business objectives (like product strategy documents) the *clarity* of the objectives is in focus
	Document analysis provides the basis for understanding the process or product at hand. In the course of the audit the content of the document is assessed against reality. This allows identifying inconsistencies or deficiencies
	Documents can be comprised of physical documents (printed material), but also web pages and electronic media should be reviewed. During the audit, it would be good to understand document change management, since it is important to assess the most current version of a document. Auditors should seek confirmation about reviewing the correct version. Ensuring the traceability of audit findings requires storing all relevant and analyzed documents in a central audit store. Each document is numbered with a unique identifier/index
External confirmations	External confirmation takes responses from outside the company into account. This could be feedback from customers, partners, service providers, or external auditors. This type of confirmation provides an external assessment of a certain development process, state of affairs, or software product. There are different confirmation types like customer satisfaction

(continued)

Table 7.1 (continued)

Fieldwork activity type	Description
	surveys, feedback about the implementation of customer requirements, an external audit report, or an external security assessment by a specialized security company. The external confirmation can be received in written form or by interviews
	The external confirmation requires a careful selection of the information source to ensure the reliability of the information
Sampling	In many cases it is not possible to take all artifacts of specific type into account. Typically a software product has to fulfill a high number of customer requirements. It is not feasible to assess the implementation of all requirements during an audit. This requires selecting a sample set of requirements. For this sample, the development process from gathering, to requirements engineering, to the actual implemented code is assessed during the audit. Other examples could be the handling of customer support requests or deviations to defined guidelines and standards. These examples are used to assess a process – like the requirements management above. But sampling can also be applied to assess a product in certain cases. A software product exposes many external interfaces. A sample of these interfaces could be analyzed to assess compliance with given guidelines and standards
Statistical analysis	In some specific cases a statistical analysis can be used in Software Sustainability Audits. Relevant data in this context could be the number of customers for a specific product, the number of customer support requests, number of escalations, lines of code, revenue planned and generated by a product, and others
Walk-through	A structured walk through refers to the assessment of a process or a product from the users perspective. A product manager could walk an auditor through a mock-up created for a new product. In this case the auditor could assess how certain customer requirements are reflected in the development plan. A process could be the focus of a walk through. For instance a developer could walk an auditor through relevant development tools when the auditor tries assessing the tool environment for efficient software development
Code analysis	Code analysis is an activity very specific to the software development process. The auditor can manually analyze the code, or the code could be automatically analyzed through a code scan. Code analysis is performed to check for compliance with certain programming rules and guidelines, to ensure compliance with open source licenses, or to detect security vulnerabilities. While these activities can be part of the standard development and quality assurance cycle, they can also be used to gather audit evidence

making the results reliable and traceable. The core constituent of the audit process is called the audit roadmap. The audit roadmap comprises five phases: planning, preparation, execution, reporting, and follow-up. We will briefly discuss these phases with the focus on important aspects for Software Sustainability Audits. For a more general and detailed discussion of the audit roadmap we refer to the *Internal Audit Handbook* [1].

7.4.1 Making Up Your Mind: The Planning Phase

The first phase – audit planning – differs from the other phases. While the remaining four phases are specific to an individual audit, the planning phase concerns all audits conducted by the audit team. The main goal of the phase is the selection of audits to be implemented in a specific period (for instance the next year). The challenge is selecting the audits providing the highest value for the company. This is not an easy task. The selection process has to be transparent and requires accepted selection criteria to ensure that audits are not selected based on individual preferences – for instance, of the auditors. A question often heard from an audited organization is "Why us?" A good and convincing answer helps in getting the support and buy-in from the auditees. Auditees should not be under the impression that an audit is conducted based on personal interests and preferences. Otherwise they could refuse to accept the results. They could claim there was a bias of the auditors impeding the independence of the assessment. There are different approaches to ensure an independent and objective selection process. Here are some examples:

- *Concrete Information Needs*: The board, the CIO, or other top management might have a concrete or documented need of specific information to make strategic decisions. This audit could be the need to understand the state of a specific product.
- *A Concrete Incident*: A specific incident in the past can be the trigger for an audit. As examples, customer escalations, security incidents, or failed projects fall into this category.
- *A Risk-Based Planning Approach*: The risk-based selection of audits can be a very valuable approach. Audits are selected according to the risk exposed by the audited topics. This is such an important topic that we have reserved a dedicated chapter (Chap. 10).
- *A Random Selection*: If there are no other criteria available, or different possible audit topics don't expose a major risk, a random selection could be applied. For example drawing lots would be a possible solution.
- *Equal Distribution*: Another approach could be equally distributing the audit topics. An option would be selecting a product to be audited from every development area of the company.
- *Base Lining*: You could run an audit on every development process to get a baseline of where you are. This could be an option if you start with a new audit function – for instance establishing Software Sustainability Audits.

The typical audit planning process is based on a combination of the above examples. Your process description for the audit process should contain the selected planning approach. The selection criteria for each individual planning round have to be clear and transparent.

7.4.1.1 Scoping

As the first step in the planning and selection process you have to make up your mind regarding possible audit topics. The scope of a Software Sustainability Audit is defined by three core dimensions – the audited process, the software product, and the audit objective. Although not directly part of the scope, the point in time of the audit can play a significant role in some cases. So we will take this aspect into account here.

We already discussed the audit objectives in depth in Chap. 6 and will not repeat them here. We rather focus on the remaining two dimensions and consider the aspect of time. The goal of the planning process is to get a list of processes and products you want to audit. This list also contains the corresponding audit objectives and the expected time of the audit.

Scoping of an audit is typically performed in three phases. In the first phase you create an inventory of existing and audit-relevant development processes and products. The second phase is the annual planning where a high level scope is defined as outlined above. The final scope is defined in the preparation phase of the specific audit you will be conducting. This granular scope defines the exact mapping of processes, products, and audit objectives. In this third phase we also decide on the corresponding audit activities.

Determination of the Development Processes
The first dimension we consider is the process dimension. Software development is not performed in a single monolithic process. There are sub-processes and associated processes outside the core software development process. We take a closer look at the different processes in Chap. 8. Nevertheless, here is a short list of corresponding processes or sub-process that could be subject to an audit:

- Customer engagement
- Requirements specification
- Architecture governance
- Requirements engineering and software design
- Secure software development
- Quality assurance and testing
- Reuse of software components incl. usage of open source components
- Developing usable and accessible software
- Ensuring legal compliance with export regulations

There are generic processes like architecture definition. Some processes focus on very specific aspects of software development, like the process of developing usable software. Ensuring compliance with export regulations is an example of a process going beyond the core software development process. We will look into this in more detail in the next chapter.

Creating an audit plan requires the identification of relevant processes that you want to audit. There might be obvious choices – like known deficiencies in a development process. For instance the company might have failed to deliver secure products in the past. You could select the corresponding processes to understand the root cause of the problem. Other processes might not be relevant at all – you do not deliver software outside your country so you are not subject to export regulations.

Core and Key Scopes

Each of the development-related processes mentioned above has a set of sub-processes and important artifacts. There are things like process descriptions, guidelines, or expected documents created during the process (e.g. a requirement specification). Each process should have an owner that is responsible for the process design and the artifacts. Most of these aspects remain stable over a longer period of time – there is no reason for frequent process changes. From an audit perspective it makes sense creating an inventory for the audit-relevant processes. This enables faster audit implementations through standardized audit scopes. These audit scopes cover aspects relevant for the audit function.

For each development process a *core scope* definition is created. The core scope itself is divided into smaller *key scopes* covering the sub-processes. Take the architecture governance process as example. This process can be sub-divided into an architecture strategy process, architecture guideline creation, architecture definition, etc.

Each key scope consists of a context and a content section. The context gives a short definition of the key scope, the goal or business objective (why does the key scope exist), and the associated risk (what happens if the affected sub-process fails?). An example for the architecture governance process can be found in Table 7.2 below.

The second part of a core scope definition is the content. The content provides more details on the individual key scopes with regard to the processes. It defines the required input for a process, the expected output, and the organization or person executing the corresponding process step. For instance defining the architecture of a software product the responsible product architect requires the requirements specification and the relevant architecture guidelines as input. The content part of the architecture governance example is provided in Table 7.3.

Selecting Products

Now that we understand the process dimension required for the audit planning let us look at the product dimension. A software company typically has a portfolio of products in different stages of the product lifecycle. We have to assess the relevance of these products for audit planning. The relevance is determined by two factors – the company's strategy and the individual state of the products. The strategy part can be split into two aspects:

- *Market and Product Strategy*: The software company defines the markets it wants to address with its software products. The term market covers all the different dimensions like locality (selling to different countries), industries, business processes (e.g. financial software, product planning, etc.), or technologies (software-as-a-service, mobile business, etc.). The product portfolio has to match the market strategy, i.e. there is a definition of which market is addressed by which product.
- *Architecture Strategy*: Based on the market and product strategy, an architecture strategy has to be defined. The product architecture mainly covers the non-functional aspects of a product or a product portfolio. The architecture strategy

Table 7.2 Example core scope context definition for the architecture process

Key scope	Definition	Goal/objective	Risk
Architecture strategy	Determine architectural strategy consistent with business strategy. Define framework to measure results. The strategy can either be company-wide, or product group specific	Establish comprehensive, consistent architecture strategy across the product portfolio, aligned with business strategy. Provide clear guidance for development	Low degree of customer adoption of products. Low profitability. Inconsistent and disruptive products resulting in high TCO for customers
Architecture guidelines	Definition, alignment, and roll-out of company-wide and product group-specific architecture guidelines	Align all development units with architecture strategy as well as with each other. Provide actionable directives and guidelines for teams developing products	Non-integrated products across product portfolio. Excessive heterogeneity and complex solutions. High cost for development, service and support. High TCO for customers
Architecture definition	Create architectural plans and artifacts for a specific product or a specific module, including non-functional aspects. Document technology risks and expected exceptions	Establish a working architecture, consistent with architecture guidelines, that fits the business requirements. Provide guidance for developers. Provide a basis for communication	Solutions riddled with stability and quality problems. Ineffective collaboration between teams. Requirements not fulfilled in consumer/ provider relationships. Timeline impact
Architecture feasibility check	Perform a feasibility check, and identify architectural risks based on initial concepts and capacity planning	Architecture that effectively supports functional and non-functional requirements. Enable accurate capacity planning	Solutions lacking non-functional attributes. Architecture issues identified late, resulting in wasted effort, high costs, and timeline impact
Architecture implementation	Realize architectural design as software artifacts/coding	Produce software that fits to the architecture definition. High quality software	Pieces of software do not fit together. Software with quality, stability, and supportability problems
Architecture validation	Review architecture in relation to business requirements, non-functional requirements, standards, and architecture guidelines. Test procedures	Ensure goals set by architecture definition are met	Desired quality of architecture is not achieved
Architecture training	Initial and continuous education of architects	Architects understand their role, the importance of non-functional requirements, and have the tools to define sustainable architectures	Architecture strategy not reflected in products. Architecturally flawed products

Table 7.3 Example core scope content definition for the architecture process

Key scope	Input	Output	Execution responsible
Architecture strategy	Product strategy document	Company-wide or product-specific architecture strategy document	CTO
Architecture guidelines	Company-wide or product-specific architecture strategy document	Architecture and programming guidelines	Central and local architecture governance boards
Architecture definition	Requirements specifications Respective architecture guidelines	Product architecture document	Product architect
Architecture feasibility check	Requirements specifications Respective architecture guidelines	Feasibility report Follow-up action items	Product architect
Architecture implementation	Product architecture document	Implemented product	Product architect, developers
Architecture validation	Requirements specifications Product architecture document Implemented product	Validation report Follow-up action items	Product architect, quality team
Architecture training	1. Training documents 2. Company-wide or product-specific architecture strategy document	1. Educated architects 2. Gap analysis of training requirements	CTO, Central architecture governance board

defines all these aspects relevant to address the strategic markets. Take as an example the mobile market. To address the mobile market you need an architecture strategy enabling the consumption of existing software applications through mobile devices. As another example, the operational costs and the seamless integration into existing customer landscapes might be important. The corresponding architecture strategy then has to focus on the harmonization of the product portfolio. This could be achieved by defining common standards the products have to fulfill.

The audit relevance of individual products is determined by the following factors:

- *Strategic Relevance*: Products in the portfolio have a differing relevance for the company. Some products are cash cows and generate the major part of the current revenue. Other products might be niche products. Others may not currently generate a lot of revenue, but are important for future growth.
- *Product Lifecycle*: The product lifecycle determines the investment and the amount of new development for a software product. In an early stage maybe only feasibility studies are performed and prototypes are built. This could result in a decision to continue or discontinue the investment. A new product receives high investments as major new functionality has to be covered. In this stage the core architecture is shaped and fixed with limited feasibility for later changes.

In advanced stages of the product lifecycle, the product becomes increasingly mature reducing the need for major functional enhancements. At some point in time the product might get out dated. A replacement with a new product is then required (for instance based on new technologies).

• *Product Issues*: Software products can face individual issues. This can be a high number of bugs, high operational costs, performance issues, limited scalability, etc. These technical issues might have led to a high number of customer escalations, or a low market adoption of the product.

Depending on the size of the portfolio it could make sense to create an inventory of all products. This inventory could contain the status of the products and their strategy relevance. The selection of products for an audit would then be based on this inventory. In addition to a list of individual products, also classes of applications – on demand application, mobile applications, etc. – might exist. This information should be part of the inventory. This allows planning your audits on product classes instead of individual products.

The Relation of Development Processes and Products

To audit a development process you need some samples where the process is actually executed. It is obvious in the case of software development processes you need development projects – software products – as samples. Otherwise you could not effectively assess the status of a process. The relation of products and processes may be less obvious in case of a product audit. It is practically impossible to assess all aspects – security, architecture, fit to customer expectations, performance, etc. – in a single audit. You have to define the most important aspects – based on risk exposure – to be covered in a product audit. Your priority could be the assessment of the core architecture of a product and the fit with customer expectations. Is the architecture suited to provide the expected performance and scalability, or other non-functional aspects? In any case, what you assess is the result of certain development-related processes. As an example, customer expectations should be documented as part of the requirements specification process. These specifications act as input for the architecture definition process leading to the product architecture. An audit could identify a mismatch between the architecture and these requirements. In this case it might not be sufficient just to document the pure fact. It would be desirable to identify the step where a process failed. This could have happened at different stages of the relevant processes. The requirements might not have been correctly documented or handed over to development. The requirements might have been ignored by development, or not correctly understood. Maybe the implementation was not feasible.

In this way, development processes and products are always linked together. To some extent they exchange their roles, switching from process to product audits. In a development process audit the products act as samples, while for a product audit, the processes act as the sample.

For the time being that should be sufficient to understand this topic in the context of audit planning.

Point in Time

The point in time is an important factor when looking at software development processes. We briefly explained the product lifecycle above. We would like add some comments on the relevance of the product lifecycle for scheduling audits accordingly.

Timing can be especially critical for scheduling for product audits. The reason is that a product is developed once – if you don't screw it up completely. A new product is developed in several waves or releases with the core functionality developed first. Over time the maturity of the product increases and only minor corrections and additions are made at later stages. Central architectural decisions are typically made during the early phase of the development lifecycle. This has to be taken into consideration for the audit planning. To unveil issues with regard to the general direction of the product or its core architecture an audit has to be scheduled early in the lifecycle. Changes to central elements of a software product at a later point in time might become practically impossible. But an audit should also not be scheduled too early in the lifecycle. As long as the direction and strategy for a product or the core architecture are not defined an audit will be ineffective.

For process audits the timing is less critical as processes are defined to be executed repeatedly. Although a single product is developed only once the corresponding development processes are executed for many different products. For process audits it is important to select products in their relevant phase of development. If the requirements engineering process is audited, but the selected project has not yet gone through this process, the audit will not be effective.

Unfortunately, it is not always possible to schedule the audit according to the best point in time. Limited audit resources, higher priorities of other topics, or limited availability of sample projects could impact the freedom of choice. Nevertheless, where ever possible the time aspect should be taken into consideration. If the audits have been selected for the upcoming year, it might be feasible to schedule them accordingly. Although one audit has higher priority than another, it could make sense to schedule it later in the year to align it from a timing aspect.

Required Effort

An important factor for planning Software Sustainability Audits is the effort required to implement an individual audit. Auditing a software development processes or software products are particularly challenging tasks. You will need time to understand products that now have inherent complexity after undergoing several years of development. The software development processes – especially in larger organizations – affect many people and roles. Software development requires product managers, development mangers, architects, developers, quality engineers, development process and standard owners, governance entities etc., often organized in multiple teams. Software Sustainability Audits take the different viewpoints and aspects of the different roles into account. To this end, a considerable number of interviews have to be conducted. Each interview requires corresponding preparation and post-processing. Audits also involve document analysis and other activities. All in all, experience has shown that the average amount of effort per audit is in the range of 50 person days. This effort is covered by two auditors in a timeframe of 3–4 month. Spending considerably less effort on these topics will not provide significant insight or value. Spending more effort or a longer timeline will be inefficient and ineffective. Today's software business is very dynamic, impacting the internal dynamics of software companies. Audits running too long might fail to create the necessary impact. Relevant findings could become obsolete in the meantime through organizational or strategic product changes. Too many findings caused by an extremely deep or broad analysis could be counterproductive as well. The affected development organizations have to respond to audit findings with changes in the processes or products. The ability to work on that kind of change is limited. Only a limited number of findings can be effectively "consumed". Either too many findings will lead to insufficient handling of all findings, or some findings will not be considered at all. Although it is highly recommended to carefully scope the audits to avoid an overload, no general recommendations can be given. Each audit team has to go through a learning process to find the appropriately sized scope. This scope depends on the size of the organization, the complexity of the processes, the product portfolio, and the experience and expertise of the auditors. Keep in mind – the number of audits is not the important success factor. It's the result and the positive impact that counts!

7.4.1.2 Annual Planning Cycle

Now we have all the necessary ingredients for a creating an audit plan. The goal for the annual planning is the creation of a schedule of audits. This plan defines the major scope of the audits – audited processes, products, and audit objectives depending on the priorities set for the audit function. Whether the planning cycle covers a full year, or maybe just 6 months is not important. The planning cycle is defined by the dynamics of the company. If the audit team faces a very dynamic environment, shorter planning cycles are appropriate. Otherwise the plans might become outdated and invalid before they are executed.

During the planning cycle not all slots in the schedule should be planned with predefined audits. Some slots should be reserved for ad hoc audits – audits not foreseen upfront. The assignment of auditors to dedicated audits is not part of the planning phase. This is done on an operational level during the year. The availability of auditors is not always foreseeable upfront, but the available audit resources and the required effort for audits needs to be factored into the audit plan.

While the creation of the process and product inventories is somewhat independent of the annual planning cycle, the inventories still require a regular update. The update can either be performed on a continuous basis or as part of the preparation for the planning cycle.

The audit plan has to be aligned with and approved by corresponding stakeholders like the audit committee, top management, or maybe the CIO. The specific stakeholders depend on the organizational assignment of the audit team – being the official internal audit team or some additional, product-specific team. In case the audit plan requires a change, it might be required to re-align and re-approve the plan accordingly.

Risk-Based Planning

The goal of an audit function should be maximizing the added value for the company by the delivered service. Roughly speaking, the added value of an audit is determined by two factors – the selection of relevant audit topics and the quality of the audit implementation. Even though both are challenging tasks, the focus is on the selection part, since we are currently discussing the planning phase. From a planning perspective the added value is the exposed risk covered by the audits. The exposed risk is defined as the probability of a negative event times the impact of this event. Most of the value comes through providing transparency on the status of certain affairs and by enabling corrective measures to prevent negative impacts on the company. While we have reserved Chap. 10 to cover risk-based planning and dealing with risk in general, we have re-emphasized the importance here.

7.4.2 Your Homework: The Preparation Phase

While the planning phase is concerned with setting up a complete schedule of audits for a specific period, the actual audit implementation starts with the preparation phase. During the preparation phase the detailed scope of the audit is defined. Furthermore the audited areas are informed about the audit activity. The auditors use the preparation phase to get into the topic at hand, and to start analyzing relevant documents.

7.4.2.1 Kick-Off

The preparation phase starts with a kick-off meeting where the audit manager and the assigned auditors meet. During the meeting the audit manager explains the scope to the auditors and clarifies open questions. If required, the audit manager can provide additional background information about the selected audit scope. For instance, the risk-based planning might have revealed that a product is exposed to a specific risk. This risk has to be closely assessed during the audit.

7.4.2.2 Work Program

The work program is a central element in the audit procedure. The work program maps the audit objectives to the audited topics. Also audit activities are assigned correspondingly. The table below provides a few examples of entries in an audit work program. The work program can contain more detailed information (Table 7.4).

The key purpose of the work program is fixing the scope of the audit. The scope defines what can be audited, but much more it defines what *has* to be audited. The work program establishes the duty for the auditors to cover the defined scope. At the end of the audit the auditors have to prove they have covered the complete scope. The defined scope together with the auditor's duty to cover this scope provides the foundation for an independent and fair assessment. This approach guarantees that auditors do not decide on their own what to cover during the audit. Auditors cannot change the scope and direction during the implementation of an audit. The work

Table 7.4 Example work program excerpt

Audit scope	Audit objective	Audit activity	Comment
Customer requirements management	Valid and effective results	Document analysis Sampling of requirements	Goal is to understand whether the requirements provided to the development team – especially non-functional ones – are suited to define a sustainable architecture
Architecture definition	Comprehensive and appropriate design	Document analysis Interviews	Assess architecture definition process with regard to support company-wide architecture goals
Software implementation	Consistent execution	Interviews	Assess consideration of architecture goals during scope changes
	Effective results	Code analysis	Assess compliance of the implemented code with defined guidelines

program is typically created by the auditors. Still it has to be approved by audit management to ensure consistency with the audit plan. The audit scope cannot be changed arbitrarily.

7.4.2.3 Announcement

After the scope has been clarified the audit areas have to be informed about the audit. The announcement is sent via email providing the responsible management insight into the audit scope and the associated timeline. This step enables the affected management to identify and inform required key personnel in their organization.

The announcement should be sent by top management – either the head of internal audit, or even the board. This approach demonstrates top management support for the audit activity. This is required to establish an effective audit function. This is even more important if the Software Sustainability Audits are not implemented by the internal audit team, but by an alternative team. In this case the natural authority coming with the official internal audit function is not given.

7.4.2.4 Audit Questionnaire

We do not recommend conducting interviews based on a completely structured approach going through a fixed set of questions. Still we highly advise gathering the most important questions for the audit in a central list or questionnaire. This does not mean that all answers have to come through interviews. Answers can be found while documents are analyzed during the audit. The questionnaire acts much more as a central theme for the audit allowing the auditors to check what is left open and still needs to be addressed. As preparation for an interview the questionnaire can be consulted to select a subset of questions relevant for the corresponding auditee.

7.4.2.5 Document Analysis

Above we already introduced document analysis as a key audit activity. In many cases relevant documents are available to the auditors even before the official start of the audit. Especially process descriptions, guidelines, or other standard documents are freely available. Project related documents might be subject to restricted access.

The document analysis should be started as early as possible. Even if not all documents are available, the early analysis supports a better preparation for the interviews during the following execution phase. Auditors can derive questions for the questionnaire or even identify first issues.

7.4.3 Gathering Evidence: The Execution Phase

The execution phase is the central part of the audit. During the execution phase the audit activities are implemented to gather evidence of potential issues. We discussed the different activities in Sect. 7.3 above and will not repeat them here. We focus on the framework aspects of the execution phase. This framework is required to make the activities most effective and to ensure transparency. The most important aspects for the execution phase are the involvement of the audited areas and the documentation of the audit activities.

7.4.3.1 Opening Meeting

The first step in the execution phase is the opening meeting. Participants from the audited area are invited – typically the management and identified key personnel. The opening meeting is used to present and explain the audit scope. Goal of the meeting is the clarification of all open questions with regard to the audit procedure. In addition, a qualified list of auditees has to be created to make the audit most effective. It is of utmost importance to keep transparency concerning the audit scope and procedure. This will support the building of trust and confidence in the audit function. Audits are most effective when actively supported by the audited areas, and when they see the added value created by the audit. Software Sustainability Audits are not conducted for their own sake or to blame people of making mistakes. They are performed to improve processes and products. And this increases the competitiveness of the company.

7.4.3.2 Documenting Audit Activities

An important goal of audits is creating transparency. Identified and reported issues need to be supported by sufficient evidence – provable facts. This requires the careful documentation of any activity conducted during the audit and any information obtained.

The following aspects have to be taken into account when documenting audits:
- *Central Storage*: Any relevant document or information received has to be stored in a central and audit-specific document store. Storing information on local stores – for instance on an auditors laptop – is not permitted as it does not allow for an independent assessment.
- *Complete Documentation*: All documents have to be stored. Although a document is not required to support a finding storing it is still required. This allows

proving which documents have been taken into account during the audit. Complete storage also documents the coverage of the defined scope.

- *Authorizations*: Access to audit documents has to be controlled by authorizations. Only auditors assigned to the corresponding audit are provided access. The document store has to support a corresponding authorization concept.
- *Document Indexing*: Each working document has to get a unique identifier allowing an index of all audit documents.
- *Interview Documentation*: Interviews do not have to be documented literally, for instance by recording them. Still it is important to document them in a way that findings can be based on the interview protocols. This requires that relevant statements made during an interview are documented in a clear and unambiguous way.

7.4.3.3 Documenting Observations and Raw Findings

The formal audit approach ensures traceable and sufficient evidence about existing issues. During the execution auditors are exposed to a lot of information. Documents have to be analyzed, interviews are conducted, etc. In many cases it is not possible to immediately assess information with regard to its audit relevance. Is it information really a fact of what you heard during an interview, or just the personal opinion of the auditee? Is an objective just not documented, or has is not been defined? Over the course of an audit certain patterns emerge. The picture becomes clearer. But it is based on a lot of details. Ensuring that the different details do not get lost along the way is important. It makes sense to document all these little observations – or raw findings as we call them – continuously during the audit. These artifacts can be identified issues, or something the auditors wants to follow-up on later. During the execution phase of an audit the raw findings are just entered into a list. This list can grow up to a few 100 entries per audit. Later in the reporting phase a systematic analysis and consolidation of the raw findings is performed. The result of the consolidation builds the essence of the audit. These are the important findings that will make it into the audit report. The list of raw findings is meant as an audit internal tool. It is only used and accessed by the auditors.

The following Table 7.5 provides an example of a raw finding list. The information put into the list should enable a discussion without constantly going back to the source documents. Basing the discussion on the source documents is very inefficient. Each raw finding should be documented with

- A unique number to identify the raw finding later on during the discussion.
- A short descriptive text.
- A reference to the working document (source documents, interview protocols, etc.).
- A short description of the source.
- *The Note Taking Auditor*: The note taker might remember what he or she had in mind when adding the raw finding in case the descriptive text is not self-explanatory.

Table 7.5 Example raw finding list

Number	Raw finding/observation	Reference	Source	Note taker
C_1_10#1	Business objectives not documented	C_1_10_120	Strategy document	Sam
C_1_20#2	"Recent reorganization impacted product development"	C_1_20_101	Interview with Carl Meier	Sam
C_1_10#2	"Developers are not trained on the new technology"	C_1_10_122	Interview with Greg	Peter
...	...	...	...	...

The raw finding list is a very effective and efficient tool to ensure nothing gets lost along the way. But it needs to be constantly maintained during the audit execution. This list of raw findings builds the bridge between the audit sources – documents, interview protocols, etc. – and the findings presented in the audit report. The consolidation of the findings is the first step of the reporting phase and will be discussed in Sect. 7.4.4.1.

7.4.3.4 Staying on Track

We emphasized the scoping of an audit as an important task. The scope – represented by the work program – is a plan created during the preparation phase. This plan has to come to life during the execution phase. As discussed in Sect. 7.4.2.2 the work program does not only delineate what *can* be audited, it also defines what *has* to be audited. This has to be taken into account during the execution phase. To be more explicit the auditors have the duty of:

- *Completely Covering the Defined Scope*: At first sight this requirement looks easy to fulfill. Just go through the defined activities and cover the full scope. The issue is that it is not easy to correctly estimate the effort required to cover the scope. More interviews than expected might be required, or a code analysis takes longer than planned. While there might be some flexibility in the timeline of an audit, it does not make sense to significantly exceed the timeline. In such cases it is difficult meeting the full scope and it might be required adjusting it. But the decision about the required adjustment must not be made by the auditors. Scope adjustments have to be made by audit management, maybe in alignment with affected audit stakeholders. In any case the impression of a random scope change has to be avoided. The decision about reducing the scope has to be clearly documented and communicated.
- *Not Going Beyond the Defined Scope*: The first requirement was somewhat straight forward. The requirement not to go beyond the defined scope is to some extent demanding and requires even more discipline of the auditors. During an audit you are exposed to a lot of information and often you see issues that are at the border of the defined scope. It could also be that the root cause of an issue is outside the defined scope. As an example, you are implementing a product audit but an identified product issue goes back to a deeper issue in a corresponding development process. Or maybe an issue closely outside the scope seems more

severe than what was identified within the scope. By extending the scope the audit could provide more value. It would also be much more satisfying for the auditors to find the real cause of an issue. Auditors are constantly exposed to the temptation of going beyond the scope – the dreaded *scope creep*. In most cases the auditors have to stick to the scope. But sometimes at least a minor enhancement to the scope can be justified. As above, this decision is not made by the auditors, but by audit management in alignment with affected stakeholders.

In many cases auditors need guidance and help staying on track. The mentoring described in the Chap. 5 is a very effective and successful method of supporting auditors. It provides the auditors with a platform to discuss required scope changes, but also to remind them of their duties.

7.4.4 The Essence of the Audit: The Reporting Phase

The reporting phase has two main goals. First, issues have to be identified and documented in an acceptable way by the audited areas. This includes a fact-based description of the situation, an estimate of the risk exposure associated with the identified issues, and some recommendation of how to respond to the situation. Second, the findings and issues have to be aligned with and accepted by the audited areas. To this end owners are assigned to each finding. The alignment process is comprised of coming to an agreement on the situation, clarifying the ownership, defining corrective measures, and agreeing on a timeline.

Let us look at the different activities of the reporting phase in detail.

7.4.4.1 What We Can Prove: Consolidating Raw Findings

We recommended in Sect. 7.4.3.3 to document raw findings and observations during the execution phase. This approach acts as a kind of initial filter to the information received during the audit. This filter could be labeled "potential issues". The task in the reporting phase is structuring these filtered raw findings in several waves or iterations to distill the actual and provable issues.

The process of consolidating the raw findings requires different steps. These steps can be divided into three phases. The first phase focuses on intense discussions of the raw findings and comprises the following steps:

- *Coarse Granular Grouping*: The first step of the consolidation process is defining a coarse granular structure to which the raw findings are assigned. There is no fixed structure and it is up to the auditors to decide on an appropriate one. For instance, as a first approach the scope items defined in the work program could be used. Another approach could be structuring the information according to the audit objectives. But the structure could even be freely defined. The structure has no impact on the final audit findings. It merely serves as a tool for the consolidation process. It could be that the structure evolves from the discussion between the auditors. After defining the structure, all raw findings are assigned to a particular category of the structure.

- *Fine Granular Grouping*: After the first round of assignments, the raw findings are structured according to further commonalities. Raw findings addressing the same or similar issues are grouped together with the intention to identify more fundamental issues.
- *Discussion, Discussion, and Discussion*: As you see from the two points above the description of the process is kind of vague. The reason is that there is no silver bullet for the best approach. Only a rough approach can be sketched. Getting to the results requires a lot of intense discussion between the auditors. Different people have different understandings and perceptions. The discussion is required to separate the facts from mere feelings, perceptions, or opinions. This highly depends on the audited topic. So the interactive character of this phase of the audit cannot be over emphasized.
- *Dropping Raw Findings*: As described above raw findings may only reflect the idea of a potential issue without clear evidence. Consequently raw findings can turn out to be of no relevance for the audit. Either there is no real issue or there is not sufficient evidence for an issue. First – if there is no clear evidence of an issue – it is easy to drop raw findings. The second case it is a little more difficult. In such a case raw findings must not be simply dropped. If auditors are still under the impression of potential issues but cannot prove it, this has to be mentioned in the audit report. For instance an additional audit with a dedicated focus on the potential issues might be recommended. The final decision about uncertain cases can be made later in the process, but always needs to be clearly documented.

The first phase might require several iterations until the right structure and granularity is found. It requires some experience to be efficient and to find the shortest path to the correct results. Our experience shows that the initial consolidation phase can take up to 2 weeks. At the end you have clusters of raw findings representing (potential) issues.

The second phase steps away from the individual raw findings. The focus is shifted to the clusters of raw findings. At this stage it still might be uncertain if each cluster reflects a real issue.

- *Finding Headlines*: The first step in this phase focuses on finding headlines for each cluster or group of raw findings. This task reflects the attempt of the auditors to get their head around the real issues. As this is still an purely internal phase only affecting the auditors, the headlines do not yet need to fulfill an adequate language requirement. They have to align on the issues. And this step is the main part of the auditor's alignment. At the end of the discussion all involved auditors need to have a common understanding of the different clusters expressed by the corresponding headlines.
- *Finding Root Causes, Symptoms, and Examples*: The most difficult task with regard to identifying audit findings is determining root causes of issues. Even though addressing and resolving the root cause of an issue is the most effective contribution and highest value an audit can deliver, it is not always possible to finally decide whether the root cause to an issue has been found. Other factors – maybe beyond the scope of the audit – could be the real root cause. Nevertheless,

the aim should always be to go as deep as – in the context of the current audit – possible. When communicating issues to (potential) owners and stakeholders of an audit it is very valuable to support the finding by corresponding examples. Assessment of raw findings includes judging whether they reflect (at least parts of) the root cause, are symptoms for something else, or simply represent examples that can be used making the issue more tangible for readers of the audit report.

The last phase in this consolidation process is the adequate formulation and documentation of the audit findings. An audit finding comprises three main aspects – the facts concerning the creation of the issue (including examples), the associated risk, and a recommendation how to resolve the issue.

- *Formulating Findings*: The most important and demanding task is the formulation of the findings correctly. The description has to be based solely on facts, not reflecting any opinion or judgment of the auditors. The finding has to exactly describe the situation creating the issue. Something like "the architecture is not adequate" or "the process does not work" is not valid as a finding statement. The facts are missing. Fact-based findings have to be presented like "The product requires supporting 1,000 concurrent users. Tests have only proven stability of the product up to 500 concurrent users." The finding must not convey the impression of a biased assessment based on the auditor's opinion. As formulation of the findings is such an important topic we will specifically focus on this topic in Chap. 13 about communication.

- *Identifying the Risk*: The next step is the identification and documentation of the risk associated with the issue. Only the associated risk makes the finding an issue for the company and allows the classification of the different findings according to their importance. The risk comprises the risk condition – a scenario in which the identified deficit is of importance –, the risk probability (i.e. the probability that the situation will occur), and the risk impact – the consequence resulting if the situation occurs. While the finding is strictly fact-based the associated risk requires the auditor's judgment and experience. The risk covers potential events in the future. Consequently, it requires judgment and experience of what could happen based on current facts. Nevertheless it is important to make the risk assessment comprehensible.

- *Formulating Recommendations*: The last step is providing recommendations of how to resolve an identified issue. This step depends highly on the philosophy followed by the audit function. If the mere idea is to identify issues, recommendations are given in a very limited manner, without specific guidance. If a more consulting oriented approach is followed, the audit team tries to give very specific guidance on potential resolutions. This often requires a lot of expertise and experience, but can add a lot of value. The drawback of the latter approach is that finding owners might feel limited in their freedom to decide about the best resolution. This reaction could negatively impact the perception of the audit function. In the end, the finding owner is responsible for the resolution of an issue and the approach taken, and the recommendation from the auditors is not binding for the owner.

This closes the discussion about identifying and documenting issues as audit findings.

7.4.4.2 Handling of Positive Aspects

In the discussion above we focused on the negative aspects – issues – within an audit scope. Sometimes you will also encounter positive examples during an audit, an audit might only reveal minor issues, or possibly no issues at all. Another aspect we would like to discuss is auditing as a certification. Let us look at these three aspects. How would we deal with them in the context of auditing?

- *Positive Examples*: From time to time you will encounter audited areas that perform a certain job better than others. Maybe their approach could act as a blueprint or archetype – a good or best practice – for other groups. For the audited area this is clearly no issue and thus cannot enter the audit report as such. There may be other areas where the identified practice might be of importance, but has not been in the scope of the audit. So, what are the options to appreciate these positive examples? A first option would be a memorandum that is added to the audit report, explicitly explaining the positive aspects. There are also two options to create a higher awareness of these aspects in the context of auditing. The auditors could assign a finding to the process owner. The process owner could take the positive example and consider it for generalization in the context of the affected process. The other option is not making it a finding, but still informs the process owner about the positive example. Typically the audited area where the positive example was identified will not object to such an approach.
- *No Findings*: Sometimes an audit ending with no or no major findings will cause some discussion between auditors and audit management. Has the scope been defined thoroughly? Have the auditors really assessed the situation with the required diligence? While this could be the case, the simple answer is: it can happen! Sometimes there is simply nothing to discover and people should be happy about it. There is no quorum for severe issues or similar circumstances. It makes life easier for the auditors as there is less work for documenting and following up on issues. In the third aspect we will cover the interpretation of a *non-resultant audit*.
- *An Audit as a Certification*: Having found nothing severe during an audit is very positive for the audited areas. This sometimes leads to a discussion concerning a certification of the audited area, like the statement "Proven by the audit team." This is understandable from their perspective, but from audit perspective it is a tricky discussion to undertake. The reason lies in the audit approach. Having *found* nothing does not mean there *is* nothing. Auditing complex topics always requires a sampling approach. It is basically impossible to *completely* cover a topic, especially in software development. For instance assessing the quality of an interface implementation you will take a few samples, assess them and draw your conclusions. Even though you have diligently selected the samples, it is always possible to have missed hitting an important aspect during the audit. All the analyzed interfaces might be fine, but selecting one more sample might

uncover an interface flaw. Imagine you allow the audited areas to promote their product with reference to your audit. What kind of impact would it have on the audit function if a customer escalation would occur resulting from issues outside your assessed sample? Audits can add a lot of value, but there are limits, and using an audit as a certification – especially when based on samples – are clearly outside these limits.

7.4.4.3 The Closing Meeting

After you have identified the main issues and findings it is time to get back in touch with the audited areas. The first step is the closing meeting. All participants and auditees of the audit are invited to this meeting. The auditors first give an overview of the audit results during the meeting and present the findings. The goal of the meeting is getting initial feedback about the correctness of the findings. Moreover the meeting can help in identifying potential finding owners that will be responsible for resolving the issues.

The closing meeting does not require presenting the findings in their final form. They have to be understandable and provided in a non-offensive style. There must be room for integrating feedback from auditees. The auditors have to be open minded towards possible mistakes they have made with their findings. Misunderstandings during interviews could have happened, or a wrong document version might have been analyzed. This could lead to wrong findings and conclusions. Identifying this kind of error is one of the main aims of the closing meeting and the subsequent alignment with the finding owners. During this phase the importance of a strict and consistent documentation of the audit becomes evident.

It is not required to conduct a single (maybe quite large) closing meeting. Much more might be gained by splitting the closing into several smaller meetings. Too many people in a meeting can be quite inefficient when discussions are required. A natural split by audited areas or responsibilities might be possible to ensure more focused meetings. In the best case the findings can be split accordingly, i.e. only a subset of the findings needs to be discussed in each meeting. In addition to this size-oriented split there is another type of closing meeting that has a specific character. Sometimes it is advisable to have a dedicated closing meeting with some top managers or stakeholders. In case the audit has revealed major issues in one area it is fair to brief the responsible manager upfront in a separate meeting about the results. This avoids showing up the manager in front of his or her team. It also gives the manager time to prepare for the discussion during the larger closing meeting. For instance, the manager could make a decision on the corrective measures. The idea is not to remove some unfavorable findings from the audit report to make it look nicer. It is about generating impact with the audit by getting the buy-in from finding owners and stakeholders. Put yourself into the shoes of such a manager. You might have the feeling that your area is mainly okay and you do not expect the audit to reveal anything severe. The last thing you want to happen is to be exposed to bad results in front of your team. As an auditor, always take the situation of your stakeholders into account.

Let us extend the latter point a little bit specifically for Software Sustainability Audits. Whoever has developed a software product knows that personal identification with this code can be quite high – it's your baby. Take this into account when presenting negative findings about a software product as an auditor. A well-founded assessment has to be complemented by a fair and open communication approach. Be prepared for discussions with the mommies and daddies of the software. They are probably the better experts than you.

7.4.4.4 The Draft Report

The next step after the closing meeting(s) is the compilation of the draft audit report. The report comprises a management summary, some technical details like dates etc., the list of findings, and the audited areas. If some findings or observations require a more detailed explanation, a dedicated memorandum can be included into the report. For internal audits it is typically not required to document all implemented activities as part of the report. It is rather sufficient to store all relevant documents according to the audit standards in a central place, and to be able to prove the correctness of findings and implemented activities on request (for instance by external auditors).

There are some aspects of the draft report we would like to emphasize here without going into too much detail.

Findings

Findings should be documented in a standardized format and governance of the finding content is of utmost importance. The value of the audit is imbedded in the findings. Most of the work has been put into revealing and identifying issues. But this effort and value can easily be destroyed by bad communication – so to speak on the "last mile". The communication of audit findings has formal as well as content-related aspects. We discussed the structure of audit findings in Sect. 7.4.4.1. This structure of findings as proven valuable and should be used in the audit report:

Headline
Finding description
Risk
Recommendation

Memoranda

Sometimes it is required to provide more context information as part of an audit report than suitable for an individual finding. In this case a typically free-form memorandum can be added to the report. Here are some examples in which a memo might be the proper approach:

- *Explain Findings*: Sometimes a finding needs more explanation and more context information to make it understandable. Any shortening of this context could lead to misinterpretation or simply would not effectively and truthfully describe the situation.

- *Lack of Clarity*: More often we face unclear situations. As we explained in Sect. 7.4.3.4 it is not always possible to get to the root cause of an issue or it might be unclear whether a real issue exists. The reason might be that the root cause or issue is outside the scope of the current audit, or there has not been sufficient time for further analysis. In such cases it is required to document this status in a memorandum to keep transparency and enable affected management to take further actions (like additional audits).
- *Concepts*: In some cases auditors want to provide more profound concepts as part of their recommendations. This could be anything from proposals for process improvements, to specific proposals for architectural concepts of the software product.
- *Special Events*: In some audits it is required to document certain unusual events. For instance it might have been required to reduce the scope or stop a project subject during the audit. In other cases the attempt to interview some person(s) might have failed – for instance by their not reacting to emails, invitations, or phone calls. These events need to be made transparent.

7.4.4.5 Getting to Yes: The Alignment Process

The first part of the reporting phase after the audit has been focusing on consolidating, documenting, and communicating the findings. The second – and equally important part is the alignment of the findings with corresponding owners. It is important to understand what *alignment* exactly means. First of all a responsible person has to be identified who will own a finding. This owner is responsible for deciding and implementing corrective measures. In most cases the responsible person might be clear, but there are also cases where some discussion is required. If there is an identified owner, auditors need to get to an agreement on the finding with that owner. Agreement means confirmation of the factual correctness of the finding, and the situation described by the finding is confirmed to be correct. This agreement with the owner does not necessarily extend to the risk or the recommendation. As explained in Sect. 7.4.3.3, both the risk and the recommendation are based on the auditor's judgment. The owner can assess the situation differently. For example, an owner can agree to a finding, but will not take any action as other issues have higher priority. The best case is clearly a full agreement to finding, risk, and recommendation. The formal agreement only spans the factual correctness. Any disagreement with the risk or recommendation should be documented accordingly. Still there is also the option of a disagreement with the finding itself. There can be cases where the factual basis requires some interpretation leading to different results for the auditors and the owner. For instance, a development guideline might not be precise enough leading to different interpretations (a product might be or might not be compliant with the guideline). Such a disagreement with the finding – for whatever reason – has to be documented in the audit report.

Besides understanding what alignment means, it also has to be clear what it does *not* mean. Alignment does not include any kind of bargain or tuning of findings to make it look nicer. There is no "I agree to this finding if you remove this other one from the report." There is no necessity to always get to an agreement. If there is disagreement between the auditors and an owner – so be it. As long as auditors can independently prove factual correctness of their findings the audit standards are fulfilled. Still, auditors are required to openly listen to complaints or concerns and to make corrections if required. Use of non-violent and non-offensive language is obligatory (see Chap. 13 for details). Also disagreements have to be documented in a non-offensive way, focusing on the facts.

The result of the alignment process is documented in the final report. To this end specific fields need to be included for each finding:

- *Responsible/Owner*: As discussed, a dedicated owner per finding needs to be assigned. Sometimes a finding affects multiple areas or requires action from different persons. In this case there are two options. The finding and responsibility can be split into corresponding sections assigning a responsible person per section, or an overall responsible person is assigned to coordinate all contributions of the finding. The latter approach is clearly favorable from an audit point of view.
- *Agreement*: A field that clearly indicates the agreement (or disagreement) with the finding itself.
- *Owner's Comment*: Owners have to be able to provide comments with regard to the finding. These comments could be initiated or actions already taken, as well as disagreements with the finding, risk, or recommendation.
- *Due Date*: Every finding requires a due date when the issue has to be resolved. The due date limits the time for the resolution, reflecting its importance. The due date also indicates when follow-up activities from an audit perspective are suitable.
- *Status from Owner*: The owner has to provide a status of the finding. The natural status directly after the audit is "new", but depending on already initiated or corrections already made, the status could be "in process" or "completed".
- *Status from Audit Team*: Similar to the owner the auditors have to assess the status of a finding. While the owner's assessment has the character of an opinion in the context of auditing, the auditor's status assessment requires an independent assessment. This kind of assessment is performed during a follow-up audit. Until then the status is "open". But there are also cases where auditors can confirm tangible actions even before issuing of the final report.

Similar to all other audit activities, the alignment needs to be carefully documented. All agreements or disagreements need to be received in written format (e.g. via email) to ensure owners cannot repudiate agreement/disagreement later on.

7.4.4.6 All Is Done: The Final Report

After the alignment process the final report of the audit is compiled, comprised of all the information described above. The final report is the basis for any follow-up activity and is a binding document. It is recommended to allow the owners to review the final version of the report before it is officially released.

With the release of the final report the audit is officially closed.

7.4.4.7 Can We Do Better?: The Audit Survey

With Software Sustainability Audits we intend to improve the overall situation of software products and processes, but this should also apply to the audit process itself. We should constantly seek for improving our own work as auditors. To this end we recommend conducting an audit survey at the end of each audit. Participants in the audit should have the chance to give feedback about their experience and expectations with regard to the audit. Did they feel well informed about the audit scope? Have they been treated fairly? Do they expect an impact from the audit?

A short survey of about 8–10 questions is absolutely sufficient. The more convenient the survey, the more the auditees are willing to participate. The survey is sent to all participants to get a broad spectrum of feedback.

Audit management should discuss the survey results with the auditors. In case negative feedback is received in the survey, the auditors should have a chance to clarify their point of view, or to comment on specific events during the audit. The discussion should focus on ways of improving the audit process, taking the feedback into account.

7.4.5 Follow-Up Activities

The audit framework provides two different follow-up activities; these are the status check and the follow-up audit. The intention of the follow-up activities is ensuring audit findings get effectively resolved. An important factor for the effectiveness of the follow-up activities is timing. Finding owners need to have a fair chance to react to findings and to resolve them. In software development this can easily take 1 or 2 years. Code or architectural changes are usually bound to new releases of software products. Process changes not only need to be defined, but also rolled-out to the development teams. This needs to be taken into account when scheduling follow-ups.

7.4.5.1 Status Check

A status check is a very short and efficient audit procedure. A suitable time after an audit – typically 12–15 month in case of software related audits – the owners are contacted. The idea is to get the status of findings resolution from their perspective. No independent assessment of the status is performed by the auditors. The status check has two main functions:

- *Reminder*: Requesting the status from an owner acts as a kind of reminder – in case the owner has not worked on the issue so far. The status check also conveys the message that the topics are still on the radar screen of the audit team.
- *Reassignment*: Especially in large organization there is a certain likelihood that responsibilities have changed between the audit and the status check. During these reorganizations it is possible that audit findings are not handed over to the new responsible person accordingly. In such a case, the status check provides the platform for officially reassigning a finding to a new owner. This requires a

meeting with the new owner to give the context of the audit and setting the expectations from audit perspective. This process is similar to the initial alignment process with the original owner.

The status – as always – has to be provided in written form and is documented in a corresponding status check report. The report is based on the final audit report, changing the status from owner's perspective, adding comments, and changing responsibilities if required.

7.4.5.2 Follow-Up Audit

In contrast to the status check, the follow-up audit aims to assess the status of finding resolutions independently. A follow-up audit is conducted in the standard audit fashion. This time the scope is limiting to the findings of the initial audit. Whether a follow-up audit has to be conducted depends on the severity of the findings from the initial audit. If only minor issues had been identified, it can be sufficient to rely on the owners to resolve the issues. In other cases an independent assessment might be required.

As pointed out, a follow-up audit is implemented like any other audit. All the requirements of diligent documentation apply. Depending on the outcome of the follow-up audit, even a second follow-up audit might be required. In most software development-related cases, scheduling follow-up audits should take place about 18 month after closing the initial audit. This best point in time has to be decided based on the due dates agreed upon in the initial audit.

7.5   What Else?

There are additional aspects we have to cover in the audit framework besides the audit process and its phases described above. These topics affect multiple phases of the process in general. This is why we have listed them in a separate section.

7.5.1   Audit Charter

In the example at the beginning of this chapter we have seen that it is important to have clarity about the authority of the audit function. Typically this is documented in an audit charter. The charter describes the general tasks, duties, and authority of the audit team and the auditors. This charter is signed by the board or the audit committee of a company to document management support and empowerment. In the example the authority of the auditors to assess specific aspects was questioned. Auditors will face this situation from time to time. The audit charter can help in getting clarity in such a situation.

7.5.2   Documenting the Audit Process

It is essential to have transparency on the audit process. The audit process itself has to fulfill the expectations set by the audit objectives described in Chap. 6. The goals for the audit function itself have to be clear, and a comprehensive design and description of the audit process is required. Any important aspect – process phases, tasks, procedures, roles, etc. – has to be documented. The documentation has to be updated accordingly when changes are applied to the process.

The process description is the basis for a consistent audit approach. Auditors can only act consistently if the different tasks and procedures are clearly defined and documented. This is the prerequisite to a unified appearance to the outside – *one voice*. As explained in Chap. 5, a one voice approach supports establishing trust in the audit function and the reliability of the results. Documenting the audit process is not done for its own sake of fulfilling formal requirements. The purpose is to create consistency.

7.5.3   Checklists

Sam, our auditor, is also responsible for the audit operations in the organization. In this role he owns the audit process description which he has to update if there are changes to the process. In addition he has to ensure that changes are actually applied during the audit implementation, i.e. that auditors follow the defined changes. The process description is a text document of about 40 pages covering all major aspects of the process, like process steps and tasks, responsibilities, and relevant templates. After changes have been applied to the document, he sends out a mail to all auditors, making them aware of the changes. Furthermore, important changes are presented to the auditors during the weekly team meeting.

Even with all the communication to the auditors, Sam constantly faces situations during audits where changes are not applied as described and communicated. To get a better understanding why this happens, he schedules 1:1 meetings with each auditor. Sam wants to get feedback why changes to the process are not applied and how he could improve the situation. Besides the auditors' individual aspects, he receives consistent feedback about the practical limitations of the lengthy and detailed process document. One proposal that was mentioned by many auditors is to have an audit checklist. Based on this feedback he creates a set of checklists for the different audit phases reflecting the important steps and tasks auditors have to follow. In addition, as the checklist is created in electronic form, each item on the checklist is linked to the corresponding section in the process description document. Where relevant, a link to the relevant templates with a description is attached to the task items. From now on, important process changes are included into the checklists, providing a handy tool to the auditors.

It is very annoying for audit management if the auditors do not follow the audit process as documented in the process description. Auditors should focus their creativity on audit content, not on the invention of an individual audit process. It is not only a matter of efficiency to follow a harmonized process; it creates a consistent picture of the audit team to the outside. Auditing requires a solid and serious reputation based on an independent and reliable assessment. A consistent approach – one voice – supports that kind of reputation.

Table 7.6 Example checklist for preparation phase

Checklist for preparation phase	
Create and update contact list	☐
Study available material (e.g. from intranet, wiki, etc.)	☐
Develop a questionnaire for the interviews	☐
Align travel plans for audit	☐
Prepare for continuous communication to auditees	☐
Put all preparation material on the audit share!	☐
Identify responsible managers of audited areas	☐
Prepare audit announcement	☐
Send out audit announcement	☐
Map audit objectives to work program	☐
Define and document test procedures	☐
Get approval for work program from audit management	☐
Identify participants for opening meeting	☐
Organize facility for opening meeting	☐
Send invitation for opening meeting to participants	☐
Prepare opening meeting presentation	☐

Table 7.7 Example checklist for execution phase

Checklist for execution phase	
Conduct opening meeting	☐
Create meeting minutes for opening meeting	☐
Update contact list	☐
Get a solution overview	☐
Prepare short presentation for interviews	☐
Prepare, conduct, and document interviews	☐
Document raw findings and observations	☐
Check whether next steps or delays need to be communicated to auditees	☐
Put all working papers on the audit share	☐
Send invitation for opening meeting to participants	☐
Prepare opening meeting presentation	☐

Ensuring a consistent implementation is a key success factor. A very helpful tool for the auditors (also for audit management) to achieve a consistent implementation is a set of checklists reflecting the audit process. We have given examples of an audit checklist in the tables below. They are not intended to be complete or to be used out-of-the-box, but rather to get a glimpse of the core idea. In the end, each audit team has to create its individual checklists reflecting their own process. The checklists are not only handy for the auditors. It enables audit management to introduce changes to the process much easier, especially if the checklist is linked to the process description (Tables 7.6, 7.7, 7.8).

Table 7.8 Example checklist for reporting phase

Checklist for reporting phase	
Consolidate raw findings to indentify audit findings	☐
Review audit findings with audit management	☐
Create presentation for closing meeting	☐
Invite participants to closing meeting	☐
Conduct closing meeting	☐
Create meeting minutes for closing meeting	☐
Create draft report including feedback from closing meeting	☐
Create management summary	☐
Send draft report to all auditees	☐
Align findings with responsible persons	☐
Request written acceptance from responsible persons	☐
Check whether next steps or delays need to be communicated to auditees	☐
Create final report including feedback from auditees	☐
Send final report to senior management of audited areas	☐
Trigger audit survey	☐
Conduct audit survey review meeting with audit management	☐

7.6 Summary

Efficient and effective audit work requires a solid framework. We stared by looking at different audit activities required in the context of Software Sustainability Audits. We introduce the audit roadmap defining the core phases of auditing – planning, preparation, execution, reporting, and follow-up. The discussion of the different audit phases was based on the author's experience gained through Software Sustainability Audits in the context of large scale software development projects. We emphasized the practical and relevant aspects in the specific context of software development. The discussion of the audit framework was complemented by additional aspects like process documentation, and checklists.

Reference

1. Kagermann, H., Kinney, W., Küting, K., & Weber, C. P. (2008). Internal audit handbook, management with SAP®-audit roadmap. Berlin/Heidelberg: Springer. ISBN 978-3-540-70886-5.

The Process Audit: Not Just for the Auditor

8

What's In It for Me?

Software Sustainability Audits comprise process as well as product audits. In this chapter we focus on the process aspects of software development. We explain the relation of development processes and the sustainability of resulting products.

CIO/CTO

From an executive perspective it is important to understand how the development processes can impact the sustainability of the final solution. To this end we recommend focusing on the initial Sects. 8.1 and 8.2 that provide the corresponding insight. The concept of process validation audits introduced in Sect. 8.3.1 is the backbone of Software Sustainability Audits. Processes are assessed whether they effectively assure strategic objectives given are achieved. We highly recommend also looking at this concept. The remainder of the chapter contains more details and discusses the sustainability aspects of different development (sub-) processes. It is up to you taking a look at this.

Software Architect

As a software architect you take the development processes as they are defined. You might see there is a need for improvement in these processes. But systematically assessing the quality of development processes is probably not your business. It is important for you to read this chapter carefully. Although you are not implementing a formal audit approach, the ideas can help to sharpen a mindset required for delivering sustainable software. Section 8.4 can be used to understand the impact of different development processes.

Auditor

Auditing processes should be familiar to you. Nevertheless, auditing software development processes has its specific aspects. The idea of process validation

(continued)

R. Gutbrod and C. Wiele, *The Software Dilemma*, Management for Professionals,
DOI 10.1007/978-3-642-27236-3_8, © Springer-Verlag Berlin Heidelberg 2012

audits introduced in Sect. 8.3.1 will be of interest to you. Compared to other IT processes, software development is and cannot be standardized to an extent where pure compliance audits are effective. This understanding is essential. Auditing software development processes requires continuously challenging their validity and effectiveness. The impact of the process on product sustainability will be helpful for you to understand. Take a look at Sect. 8.4 for explicit examples.

8.1   The Key to Sustainable Software: Development Processes

Our company has acquired a new product to complement the offering, and closing a gap in the portfolio. Early after the acquisition our CIO Kai calls his principal architect Greg:
Kai: "Greg, I need your help."
Greg: "Okay, what's up?"
Kai: "Well, you know we have acquired this new company and we are at the early stage of integrating them. We have looked at their customer base and figured out that customers seem to be very reluctant to move to the latest product release. This fact really puzzles me as they have otherwise been quite successful with this product. I need to understand the reason and you have to help me. Without transparency I will not be able to take corrective measures."
Greg: "So, whom can I contact in the acquired company?"
Kai: "Well, that's the issue. You know the situation is still a little political, and we have to be careful. Right now, I don't want to involve them because I need an independent assessment. As you know we have no access to their source code; we only have a demo installation."
Greg: "Wow, that's not much to work with but I will try my very best."
Kai: "That's why I assigned my best guy to this mission."
Back at his desk, Greg (still wondering about the arguable honor of this undercover mission) starts his analysis with no real clue how to attack the beast. "Well let's see what we have. The product only runs on a single operating system and database system. That makes life easier. Still I have no experience with this technology. Let's look at the executables and libraries in the product's directory. Wow, there are quite a lot of libraries. Hmm, there is no way understanding all the functionality. I need to get deeper into the structure of the product."
Greg starts to reverse engineer the product. He decompiles the binaries, and tries finding communication paths between the components and the database. He visualizes all the identified connections in an architecture diagram. After he gained a rough overview Greg calls Kai.
Greg: "Kai, I reverse engineered the product to the extent possible in the given time frame and I gained some interesting insights."
Kai: "Sounds great. What have you found?"
Greg: "Well, the most interesting result is that this product does not have a designed architecture."
Kai: "What do you mean?"
Greg: "First of all, the product is built with three different versions of the programming language. There seems to be an old core product that has been extended, but the old core is still implemented in the old technology. Basically any component calls any other component. There is no hierarchy or any other structure I could identify, and more than half of the components directly open connections to the database. There is no abstraction layer."

Kai: "This sounds like the product has been grown organically without a clear direction. This could also explain the issues. The product might have reached an unstable state where any bug fix introduces more bugs. Changes to the code cause unpredictable behaviors."
Sometime later, Kai and Greg have a chance to speak to Steph D'Alosusi, a manager of the acquired company about their development process.
Kai: "Steph can you give us some insight about your development process?"
Steph: "You know, we are a rather small software company. We have developed the core application centrally, but what we delivered was not enough to keep the customers happy. So, consultants had to extend the solution on a project basis. Whenever this happened, we rolled the new code back into the standard solution."

Sustainable software and development processes, how do they relate? Let us look at the story above. We can learn two things. First of all, reverse engineering in a forensic analysis can help reveal the core structure of a product. In this case it helped reveal the status quo of the product – a non-sustainable architecture. Typically this is the scope for a product audit which is discussed in the next chapter. Nevertheless, some path – certain development processes – has led to this status quo. And this is the central point to make here. The example shows how the development processes and the products – and especially its architecture – are closely linked. In the above case, the development approach of having a central development team, plus consultants extending the product in a decentralized manner, was reflected in a 1:1 ratio in the final product architecture. This was a direct consequence of a missing sustainable development approach and corresponding governance.

The understanding that software products are intrinsically tied to the corresponding development processes is essential for Software Sustainability Audits. Auditing development processes will always have product aspects. And product audits will always have to take process aspects into account. How this is achieved is the content of this chapter and the next chapter. But before we start our discussion about auditing development processes we will need some deeper understanding of these processes.

8.2   Become an Insider: The Software Development Process

Before you can audit a development process you have to understand the expectation towards such a process. First of all there is not just a single monolithic software development process. There are different sub-processes focusing on a variety of software aspects. Requirements engineering, security, architecture definition, design and implementation, or quality assurance are all different sub-processes in software development. Each of these sub-processes has a dedicated purpose and goal. Still, they are interconnected and depend on each other. There is one thing that makes auditing software especially challenging: There is no single best practice for the different sub-processes. Yes, there are different models for software development – waterfall or agile development – well described and lively discussed in the software community. But as we explained, processes and products are inseparably connected. So there is always a high dependency to the concrete context in which a product is developed. Whether a software product is developed standalone for separate usage or whether it has to fit into a dedicated landscape makes a huge difference for the development process. Similarly, other common factors that affect software development are the size of the development organization or the target markets. Let us take a closer look at this.

8.2.1 Keep Growing: The Evolution of Development Processes

The situation in the example previously presented in this chapter – even made up – is quite typical for smaller software companies growing over time. Imagine a small software company with only a few customers. In the extreme case maybe even just a single customer. The ultimate goal is to make your customers happy. Without the next paycheck there will be no future for you. In this situation short term delivery is often much more important than sustainable software. It does not mean that you intentionally compromise on sustainability. The short term pressure is simply too high. The result is often – as in the example – a software product with many custom "enhancements". You may have different code lines for each customer. There is nothing objectionable about the approach to make your customers happy. But issues easily arise when your company grows. At some point in time it might not be feasible to handle each customer individually. The proliferation of code lines and the requirement for patching them continuously overloads your development team and kills your ability to innovate. The increased size of your development team makes it indispensable to improve the development process. Several products might have to be developed in different locations based on different technologies. And after all you want to satisfy your customers by providing required functionality – assuring your next paycheck.

Responding to this challenge requires three different types of measures – (formal) development processes, governance, and (internal) controls. Governance and controls can be seen as sub-processes or aspects of the overall development process. But all three have their individual purpose. Only the right choice and combination of all three will lead to sustainable software.

8.2.1.1 Reason to Exist: The Purpose of a (Formal) Development Process

Being a small software company or having just a few developers can result in very efficient and effective software development. The result can be great products. Colleagues are co-located discussing and deciding about necessary topics. There is a moderate level of specialization – everyone might do a combination of development, product management, and quality assurance work – ensuring a unified understanding of the goals. The size of the team allows for relatively good direct interaction with customers. In a nutshell, (highly) formal development processes are not considered as required in such a situation. Missing documentation of requirements and architecture concepts is compensated by knowledge and expertise of individuals. The small number of customers allows for individual patches, maybe sent via email. Customer issues and escalations can be handled by sending developers onsite.

But with increasing size of the company and the development team the informal structure of a small company becomes inefficient and ineffective. At one point of time you have to formalize your development processes to sustain further growth. You need to keep control over your product development. A segregation of duties is required. The number of customer requirements is too big to implement them all. Dedicated product managers have to select and validate a subset of requirements that are implemented. The complexity of the product requires a componentization and alignment between the components. Individual developers might not be able to have oversight of the complete product anymore but only their respective component. Dedicated architects define the core structure of the product to reflect the non-functional requirements. Dedicated security experts define, implement, and test the corresponding features required through the increased expectations of customers. An increased market reach might require dedicated people working on internationalization aspects like translation, or localization of different legal requirements.

Each of the different aspects is covered by dedicated sub-processes with corresponding roles. The purpose of each sub-process is reliably and repeatedly assuring the achievement of specific goals and objectives. All of this has to work across different development projects. The security process has to ensure that secure products are effectively and efficiently delivered (whatever this concretely means). Without the security process you might assume your products are secure. This could result in harm to your customer and to your company.

Let us come back to our small company. The absence of formal development processes does not mean the delivered products are bad, insecure, or unsustainable. Formal processes are just required to scale your development with increased size. From the discussion it should be clear how the development processes relate to the sustainability of the software products. Processes have to be reliable and valid to assure the achievement of corresponding goals and objectives. This also includes sustainability objectives. A main focus for the process audits in the context of Software Sustainability Audits is the reliability of the processes. We will discuss this in detail in Sect. 8.3.1.

8.2.1.2 Never Without: The Need for Governance

The next thing to look at is governance. We restrict our discussion to the aspects of sustainability. Getting to sustainable software always requires directing the software development and corresponding teams. In other words you need guidelines and rules to harmonize technology, to align different products, or to enforce certain architectural concepts. This is nothing more than governance. There can be no sustainable software without governance. Still it does not require formal development processes. This might sound a little irritating. Imagine again a small software company without too formal development processes. The development process is based mainly on a self-organized approach. In this situation it is still possible to have governance. The development manager could enforce certain rules informally, or the architect might apply certain rules intrinsically. Some people simply know what to do, preventing future damages and creating sustainable products. The decision to stick to a single technology might be a natural one for small teams. It is much harder to enforce technology harmonization in a large organization. Nevertheless, similar to other development processes the requirement to formalize the governance approach grows with the size of the organization. Informal governance or governance depending on individual experience, expertise, and influence does not work anymore in a large organization. This is where governance and development processes meet.

Governance is not separable and independent from the other development processes. Although you have a separate process defining governance rules and guidelines; they have to be applied in other sub-processes. This can affect the validation of customer requirements, the architecture definition and technology selection. It could also affect each and every developer for instance through guidelines for developing harmonized user interfaces.

As governance and sustainable software are intrinsically tied to each other, it is obvious that the governance related processes play an essential role in Software Sustainability Audits.

8.2.1.3 Assuring Product Qualities: Internal Controls

We now look at the third element in this discussion – the controls. Development processes define how something is to be performed or implemented, and governance defines additional rules and guidelines. Controls are measures ensuring intended actions are enforced and rules are followed. Controls can be a variety of things – quality gates, review meetings, or code scans to name a few. Even development guidelines or the definition of a process can be seen as controls. Looking at controls from your business objectives is the most comprehensive approach. Anything that assures the achievement of these goals can be viewed as a control.

Controls are defined as part of the development and governance processes. Since they play such an important role in auditing, it is worthwhile looking at them separately. Selecting and implementing effective controls is a crucial step on the way to sustainable software. Only the controls ensure corresponding rules and guidelines are effectively applied. To this end we have reserved Chap. 11 to discuss the effectiveness of controls in great detail.

8.3   Raising the Value: Auditing Development Processes

We are now well prepared for attacking the beast called process audit. Process audits in the context of a Software Sustainability Audit typically have a very different character than a process audit in the context of an IT audit. The main difference is the critical view on the validity of the processes. We are assessing the processes in the context of defined business objectives and the outcome – the final software product. Only valid development processes in combination with effective governance and controls will yield sustainable software. This is the reason for a dedicated audit type – the process validation audit. Beside this a rather classical process execution audit is discussed. We will introduce both types next.

8.3.1 Never Invalid: The Process Validation Audit

We have repeatedly emphasized the importance of valid and reliable processes. What does this mean exactly? A valid process can be characterized by two aspects:
- *Appropriate and Comprehensive Process Design*: By following the process as it has been defined, the achievement of corresponding business objectives is assured. For instance the secure development process ensures that the final product meets corresponding security standards, the requirements engineering process ensures that the product meets customer expectations, and so on.
- *Effective Controls*: Effective controls ensure the process is actually implemented as defined. Deviations are detected and corrected. This could be code scans to detect security breaches, customer review meetings to validate requirements, or other types of controls.

8.3.1.1 What to Look for: The Audit Objectives

Assessing the validity of a process with an audit, the above requirements have to be mapped to our audit objectives. There are three objectives directly affected building the core of a process validation audit – clear business objectives, and a comprehensive and appropriate process design. Let us look at these aspects a little closer.

What do we have to assess with regard to clear business objectives? Only if it is clear what we want to achieve with a process is it possible to define the process effectively. For instance what level of security do we want to achieve? Do we need to pass an independent security certification or is a lower level of security sufficient? To how many different countries do we want to sell the software? Do we need bi-directional support for the user interface (UI)? Auditors have to have a dedicated focus on these types of questions. If you ever have participated in such an audit you will recognize that few software development processes have clear and crisp objectives. Software has fewer tangible objectives than other products. In manufacturing the quality objectives can be defined with a very fine granularity. Corresponding production processes can be controlled with a respective precision. In the software business, one has to accept limitations in the ability to define precise objectives. The assessment of the objectives requires auditors with considerable experience. Is the defined objective really appropriate to define a corresponding process? The objective "We want to harmonize the architecture of our products" is clearly not sufficient. Although everyone easily agrees to such a goal, it is not obvious what makes a "harmonized architecture". Is it a common technological basis, a design pattern, or just common interfaces? Questioning the goals and objectives in such a way is very uncommon in software development. This approach requires a specific mind set. In every audit text book it is written to start with the business objectives when assessing a process. Still the auditor is typically not urged to challenge the objectives themselves. Challenging does not mean to necessarily question them in general. It is about two specific aspects. Are the objectives clear enough to define a process correspondingly? And much more, is it possible to assess whether the objectives have been achieved?

The second and third audit objectives relevant for process validation audits are a comprehensive and appropriate process design. We explained in Chap. 6 that the process design has to be comprehensive, i.e. all roles, responsibilities, process steps, etc. need to be defined and documented. While this is rather easy to assess, the appropriateness is tricky. Can we assess whether a process is suited to achieve an objective without looking at the implementation of the process? No, we cannot. You have to look at sample projects implementing the process. In other words the scope of a process validation audit does not only comprise the three main audit objectives but *all* audit objectives. Let us understand why.

Remember, we want to understand whether the process – followed as designed – will assure achieving our business objectives. Let us start with the output of the process. Depending on the process the result can be anything – a piece of code, an interface definition, a test result, a design document, or other artifacts. Imagine the result is available for an assessment by the auditors. There can be two different outcomes – the business objectives have been achieved or they have not. A software product fulfills the security requirements or it does not, a specification has been thoroughly reviewed with customers or not, the architecture concept is in synch with the non-functional requirements or it is not, and so on. If the objectives have been clearly defined, there shouldn't be ambiguous cases (reality might not be as ideal as assumed here . . .). But we are not done yet. Let us understand what the two possible outcomes mean:

- *The Result Meets the Business Objectives*: Okay, this is what we wanted to have. Does it mean the process design is appropriate? No, not necessarily. So far we have not looked at the execution part. The people in the development project might know that the process design is flawed and instinctively compensated for the short comings. Teams with less experience following the process as designed might fail. Even a positive assessment of the results requires us looking into the execution of the process.

- *The Results Do Not Meet the Business Objectives:* Now the other case. If the objectives are not met, can we directly conclude that the process design is flawed? Again, not necessarily. The development team might not have followed the process as designed (i.e. the project has not been compliant to the process definition). Or the process is basically okay, but some effective control is missing to identify deviations. In any case a pure statement about whether the process is appropriate or not is not sufficient. If the design is flawed we need to understand at which point exactly we have an issue.

We always have to include execution into our audit assessment. Assessing whether the process design is appropriate requires following the process step by step. This does not mean that the audit will take as long as the audited development project runs. It is only required that we gather evidence about the implementation of the process. This evidence can be protocols, meeting minutes, statements from the development team, or something other item.

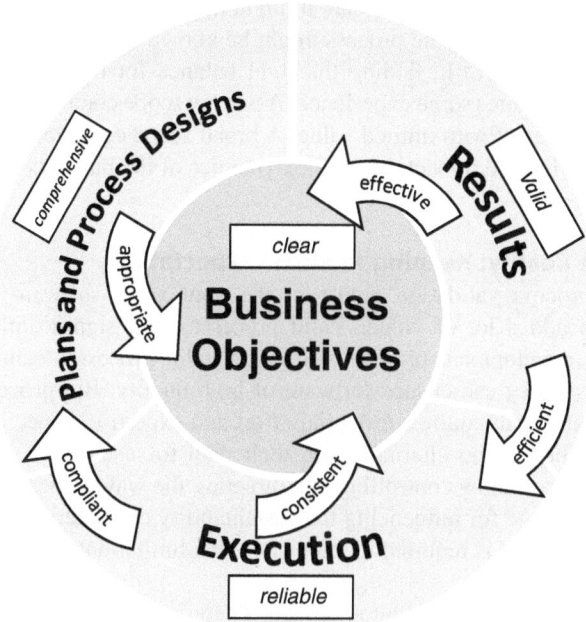

Fig. 8.1 Audit objectives for software sustainability audits

Summarizing the above, a process validation audit has as its primary audit objectives of assessing the clarity of the business objectives, and the comprehensiveness and appropriateness of the process design. The appropriateness can only be assessed by extending the scope to include *all* other objectives defined in the context of Software Sustainability Audits. The extended audit objectives can be viewed as secondary or supporting objectives as they are required to assess the primary ones (Fig. 8.1).

8.3.1.2 360°: The Overall Scope

We have seen that the nature of the process validation audit requires including the complete set of audit objectives. Assessing the execution of the process requires selecting sample areas implementing the process. To provide ample coverage in a typical Software Sustainability Audit at least two sample areas should be selected. This sampling requires extra effort and it is advisable to limit the overall scope of such a process validation audit. Keep in mind you need to assess whether the audited areas have made decisions consistent with the priority of the business objectives, whether the acting people have the required skills, and other influencing factors. Finally the output or result of the process has to be assessed against the business objectives.

The set of audit objectives is fixed and not less than two sample areas should be audited. The only variable is the audited process itself. You do not necessarily have to audit a complete process end-to-end. It might make sense to validate only certain aspects. Some elements of the process might be known to be valid already or they might be less critical. Still, finding the right balance for the scope of a process validation audit requires some experience. A narrow scope could be implemented in a short time frame but with limited value. A broad scope could require a long time for an audit but limited impact due to the dynamics of the business as explained in Chap. 7.

8.3.1.3 Face Reality: Keeping Realistic Expectations

Conducting process validation audits in the context of software development processes can add a lot of value. Valid processes will significantly reduce the risk of failed development projects. Although valid processes cannot guarantee market success, they can ensure software of high quality. But process validation audits are painful and require substantial effort and expertise. Especially for larger organizations there is no alternative on their path to sustainable software. Only validated processes allow controlling and directing the way software is developed. This is a prerequisite for influencing the sustainability characteristics of the developed products. Still it is required to understand the limitations of such a validation approach.

Auditing is always a sampling approach. There is no option of auditing everything. You can carefully select the sample areas for a validation audit. Still it does not guarantee that the actual issues of a process will show up in these areas. This is called the audit risk. Besides this audit specific aspect, the optimization of processes requires, in particular, management support. Issues revealed by the audit have to be effectively resolved. Processes concern all areas and teams implementing the corresponding process. Finally, process validation is an iterative business. An audit reveals issues, the issues need to be fixed, and the process has to be re-assessed. In the re-assessment the fixes might turn out not to be as effective as expected. Maybe additional issues may be identified due to organizational changes. In other words, process validation is a suitable tool in the context of continuous improvement. Auditing is not a one-time activity.

There is another aspect of a different character that should be considered, innovation of great ideas and solutions. So far one could have been under the impression that there might be a kind of optimal process or a set of processes for software development. If objectives are sufficiently documented and followed correspondingly, they are fully achieved. Unfortunately, software development (and probably any development process) does not exactly work like this. Even with defined processes, software development remains a creative process. Great ideas and intelligent solutions cannot be boxed into a strict process. It requires some freedom for the development teams to independently choose the right approach for their development project. We will discuss this in detail in a Chap. 11 when we look at the effectiveness of different controls. Just to give you a hint. Think about the optimal way to interact with customers for gathering requirements, and to validate specifications, prototypes, or products. There are a lot of influencing factors making it impossible to define the single best approach. Is it a new product, or an extension to an existing one? Do I have existing customers or only prospects? Does the product have to fit into some landscape? Is it a custom or standard solution? As response to situations where no single best approach exists we will introduce the concept of Control Self-Assessment (CSA) in Chap. 12. This is an alternative approach to strict process definitions. From an audit perspective it has to be considered that "appropriate" can also mean a less strict defined process supported by additional controls like the CSA.

Setting the right expectations, embracing a continuous improvement approach, and proving the necessary management support will gain you a lot of value from process validation audits.

8.3.2 Where Things Get Done: The Process Execution Audit

Besides the process validation audit, the process execution audit is the second class of process audits in the context of Software Sustainability Audits. Compared to the validation approach the execution audits have a more traditional character. Nevertheless, there is a significant difference to the popular class of compliance audits often conducted in IT. We will start with a critical assessment of compliance audits in the context of software development.

8.3.2.1 Limited Use: Compliance Audits

Compliance audits have the charm of being relatively easy to implement. Take the process definition and check whether it is applied accordingly by the audited areas. Maybe some checklists make the audit even more efficient. A couple days and you have the result. But what have you accomplished? You might be able to certify a defined process was followed. But did you really add a lot of value to your company? Did it help identifying or avoiding risk related to the delivery of software products? Probably not. We know this is a very unpopular answer. The reason is twofold. First of all compliance audits only make sense with regard to an already validated processes. With any given process, business objectives have to be accomplished without doubt. Otherwise compliance to the process definition has no meaning. You can be compliant and still completely fail with your product.

The second aspect is even more serious. When discussing the process validation audits we touched on the point of creativity as an essential ingredient for software development. On the one hand, there are development processes that cannot be strictly defined (which are a prerequisite for meaningful compliance audits). On the other hand, assessing the status of a software development project requires the assessment of the content and not just the formal aspects. For example, the requirements specification process might enforce the creation of specific specification documents. Maybe this is even required in a dedicated format. The existence of that document – even formally correct – will say nothing about the content. The specification could be completely meaningless because the responsible product manager had no clue about the business. The specification might not effectively be validated with corresponding customers or prospects. A compliance audit would probably not detect such kind of issues.

Compliance audits, originating in the financials area, might be very effective. In the context of software development they are of very limited use. There are surely some sub-processes in software development where compliance audits can be effective. But unfortunately, compliance audits are not effective for relevant parts of development, like customer interaction, requirements engineering or architecture definition. These are the areas where the highest value is generated and the essential decisions with regard to the sustainability are made.

8.3.2.2 Audit Objectives and Scope

After reviewing the approach of a pure compliance audit we now turn to the process execution audit. The goal of process execution audits is the adherence to the defined processes and the achievement of corresponding business objectives. The core assumption and prerequisite is that the affected processes have been subject to a process validation audit in the past. This does not mean that necessarily all identified issues from the process validation audit have been resolved. Auditors can take known issues into account when implementing a process execution audit. But at least the status of the overall process needs to be available.

While process validation audits have a rather broad scope process execution audits typically have a more specific scope. They focus on dedicated aspects. For example, an audit could focus on the reliable execution of a process. This audit would assess how well the developers are trained in a new technology, or what they know about secure development. Other audits could focus on aspects where a strict process cannot be applied. An example would be customer interaction. But this shows that it is not always possible to clearly separate validation and execution audits. You have to look into the execution for validating a process, and you might find issues in the process definition during an execution audit. An additional option is using an execution audit as a regular control. This could be the case when a process (like customer interaction) cannot be strictly defined and thus completely validated.

As for any process audit, the audit areas only act as a sample. We already know that it is required to assess product aspects when auditing software development processes. Process validation audits have a very distinct character. Process execution audits in contrary are rather close relatives of the product audits discussed in detail in the next chapter. Both have a focus on the execution and result (always assessed against the business objectives) and thus cover process and product aspects. The difference is that a process execution audit will focus on a single process only. A product audit can have multiple aspects – for instance security and architecture – in scope. A product audit will typically assess the product in more depth. Nevertheless, the borderline between process execution audits and product audits is to some extent fuzzy. There is nothing wrong about this. The development processes and products in software development are intrinsically tied to each other. This is the reason why the process and process audits have been combined under the umbrella of Software Sustainability Audits. There are audits with clear process character as well as with clear product character. Conversely, exposing both characteristics is possible and required as well.

8.3.3   This and That: Some Additional Aspects

8.3.3.1 We Need Them: The Role of Audited Areas

As explained, process audits in software development always need to audit sample areas or development projects. Still the main focus is the process, not the audited product. The audited areas and products are a kind of tool or vehicle for assessing the process. Performing process audits will not only reveal process related issues addressed to the corresponding process owner (typically also in scope of a process audit), but you will also discover issues in the product or in the behavior of the audited areas and people. As with any other finding these issues have to be addressed in the audit report accompanied with corresponding assignment of responsibility and recommendations.

It is not the intention of a process audit identifying individual misbehavior or blaming people accordingly. "Misbehavior" in this context does not necessarily mean intentional misbehavior. It is rather any behavior not in synch with the actual process definition or with the intention of the process. The main focus is identifying systematic issues, i.e. things that affect all development projects. Furthermore, if individual misbehavior is identified the question is rather why it was not detected in the course of the normal process operation. The question would be how misbehavior could be avoided or at least detected by an optimized process in the future.

Finally, process related findings might lead to several required actions. Imagine you perform a security process audit. You identify a security issue in a software product which results from a flawed security process. It should be obvious that the process – identified as the root cause of the issue – needs to be improved. But in addition, the issue in the product also needs to be fixed independently from the process issue.

8.3.3.2 Seek to Understand: Mind Set for Process Audits

Conducting process audits, especially process validation audits in the context of software development requires a specific mind set as well as a lot of experience. An adequate mind set seeks to understand the mechanics behind things. A process on paper might look convincing and might even work in another context. But the process has to fit to the acting people and the company culture. If people instinctively do the right thing, it might not be required to implement additional controls. The experience of auditors will not only help asking the right question and detecting issues efficiently. It also helps anticipating changes and thus making valuable proposals and recommendations.

But the central mind set is really looking for the root cause of issues. Process issues in software development often materialize in the resulting products. Identifying the product issue comes often first (and could even be the trigger for the audit). Identifying the real root cause is often much more difficult. Is it just an issue in the corresponding development team, or is it further up in the process itself? Even worse it could be a combination of different process issues leading to the final product issues. This requires patience and diligence from auditors, but also continuous challenging of your own assumptions. A helpful and valuable tool is the coaching approach introduced in Chap. 5. The ability to discuss findings and challenge them before addressing them to the responsible people is very helpful in getting to the actual root cause.

8.4   Creating Impact: The Audit-Relevant Processes

After having understood the general approach for process audits we will now take a closer look at the processes having an impact on the sustainability of the software. For each process a short description, the impact on sustainability, as well as challenges in the audit context will be given. As already elaborated, these processes do not stand alone but are embedded into a larger framework. Some processes might be organized as a hierarchy of sub-processes. This is not too important for us as the focus is the content and the impact on the software.

8.4.1   Customer Engagement and Requirement Engineering

Customer engagement and requirement engineering is one of the central aspects in software development. As any other product, software is built to be used by somebody – the customer – at the end of the day. The term "customer" does not necessarily mean that somebody is actually purchasing the software, i.e. customers can be internal or external to the provider of the software. A customer is to be understood in a broader sense. Customer in the context of software development comprises the entity (e.g. company) acquiring the software as well as the individual user. This is very important to understand as both can have very different requirements and expectations with regard to the software.

The process of customer engagement and requirements engineering comprises all necessary steps interacting with customers to gather, prioritize, clarify, document, and validate requirements. Even beyond the pure requirements engineering, we include steps to validate the implemented software by customers or other ways of gathering feedback. In the current context of software development, selling the software and rolling it out to customers is not part of our discussion. Nevertheless, established customer contacts through sales or support can be utilized in our context.

The overall goal is building software products meeting customer requirements. The activities covered by this process comprise the selection of customers for gathering requirements, customer workshops, site visits, customer reviews, or customer validations. This scope is beyond the classical requirements engineering process. But as requirements engineering and customer engagement are so tightly coupled we decided to treat them together.

8.4.1.1 Impact on Sustainability

There is one very obvious impact on the future of a software product if the customer engagement is not effective – there might be no future. A lack of customer interaction results in a product not meeting customer expectations. The software product might not be sold or used at all. In this case the effort spent on the development is to a large extent lost. This might not even be the worst case. If the software is not used there is no legacy in case you decide to re-develop the product (this time maybe caring about customers). If the product is adopted by customers the impact might be much higher. On the one hand, customers could escalate issues resulting in a loss of reputation. This could impact future sales. On the other hand the resolution of issues might require a complete re-implementation. In this case, customers have to migrate to the new solution. Deficiencies with regard to non-functional requirements cannot be resolved without massive changes to the product. This comprises areas like performance and scalability affecting the overall architecture.

8.4.1.2 Audit Aspects

Customer engagement cannot be covered by a single strict process. This is the main challenge in auditing. Requirement engineering itself can be embedded with strict formality. The best approach for customer engagement and the appropriate activities in this engagement is highly dependent on the context of the actual software product. There are many aspects influencing the right approach. Is a new product developed or just an extension to an existing product? Do we already have customers? Which market is addressed? What is the development location? It is relevant to assess whether a process exists and development teams actually follow it. It is much more relevant to assess whether the process and the boundary conditions for customer engagement are appropriate. Only this allows building customer-centric products. This requires a rather individual assessment of the customer engagement process based on the concrete situation of the company and the respective development teams.

8.4.2   Architecture, Design, and Implementation

The requirements engineering process is followed by the actual implementation of the code. This is a process typically approached in waves of defining a high-level architecture, design of modules and interfaces, and the actual coding. There are different core concepts like the waterfall or the agile approach – typically also affecting the requirements engineering process. It is not our ambition to discuss all the pros and cons of the different approaches. Rather we assume the reader having some basic understanding of the core software development process. We focus on the sustainability and audit aspects.

8.4.2.1 Impact on Sustainability

The aspect with the highest impact on the sustainability is the architecture definition process. Selecting an inappropriate technology for the implementation, or choosing architecture concepts not suited to meet the (non-functional) requirements can make a later correction hard to impossible. Less fundamental but still important is the design and the quality of the code itself. These aspects to a large extent determine the supportability of the software. This goes beyond the pure number of bugs to be fixed. A flawed design in combination with bad code quality can lead to an unstable state where the impact of a bug fix cannot be controlled, i.e. each bug fix will introduce further bug fixes.

8.4.2.2 Audit Aspects

The first step in the process is the adequate documentation of requirements. Furthermore the requirements have to be communicated to the development teams. In larger organizations requirements are gathered by dedicated product managers. The subsequent development is performed by developers and architects. This requires an exchange of information between the two groups. This implies the risk of losing relevant aspects. The first focus has to be on this communication channel. This includes the alignment of the requirements ensuring a common understanding. The alignment is not a one-way communication but requires discussion. It is of special interest how it is ensured that each developer has the appropriate understanding of requirements he or she has to implement.

When auditing the architecture definition the most relevant aspect is the consideration of non-functional requirements. These requirements need to be explicitly documented. Our experience has shown that functional aspects often dominate the discussion. Functional requirements are more tangible and at first sight seem to provide the actual value of the product. Non-functional requirements might be things a customer expects but will not explicitly mention. On the other hand, the architects have to take the non-functional aspects effectively into account. The process must ensure architectural concepts are capable of supporting the non-functional aspects. This could either be existing products based on these concepts, or dedicated prototypes and feasibility studies with corresponding reviews. In any case, the sustainability of the architecture has to be validated before the actual coding starts.

The focus of an audit in this context has to include the reliability of the execution part. The developers need to have the required programming and development skills. Expertise in the corresponding technology is a prerequisite for an effective and efficient implementation. But they also need to have a good understanding of the business context in which the software is developed. From a process perspective the development teams need to be empowered to find the best solution to the given problems. Any software development project is under time pressure. This often leads to scope additions or reductions. It is important that these changes are consistent with the priorities set for the product.

8.4.3 Architecture and Technology Governance

The first two processes covered the core software development process. The focus of these processes is an individual software product. As soon as several products are developed by a company or products have to adhere to legal regulations, some kind of governance is required. The governance process ensures that products are aligned with regard to architecture and technology, or that legal requirements are met.

Compliance with legal requirements is mandatory. Any further architectural or technological alignment solely depends on the strategy of the company, the market, and customer demand. The governance process comprises the operational aspects and also includes the definition of an architecture strategy. The required governance structure depends on the size and organization of the company. Typically the strategy is cascaded down. More specific guidelines the product teams have to follow are derived from the higher-level strategy. The development teams have to apply the guidelines and rules during product development. The governance structure has to ensure this is actually done. For instance, the governance process could enforce certain deliverables. Still, the process has to be flexible enough to allow for exceptions to the rules. Otherwise it would not be possible to react to specific market and customer requirements.

8.4.3.1 Impact on Sustainability

Non-compliance with legal regulations can have obvious impact on your product or company. You are either not able to sell the product at all, or you might be sued by customers. In either case, you will have to ensure legal compliance.

Lack of governance across products will lead to the proliferation of technologies used in your products. Inconsistent architectures will make it hard and expensive integrating different products and operating them. Having to support many different technologies impacts your bottom line. Each software technology requires specific skills and infrastructures for support. Different development environments, debuggers, loggings tools, and patch mechanisms are required. Consequently the cost for support increases with each additional technology. Synergies between products become harder to achieve.

Customers begin to suffer from increasing operational costs. Each software technology requires its own operational concept and corresponding skills. Integrating different systems requires expensive projects. Increasing complexity of the system landscape negatively impacts the customer's flexibility. He loses the ability to react to changing market conditions. Changes to the landscape become dangerous. They could lead to unpredictable behavior. As a result many customers are very restrictive with regard to changes. Installation of support packages, patches, or even upgrades to new releases are rarely applied. As a software provider it becomes harder to get customers off old releases and to sell additional products.

8.4.3.2 Audit Aspects

Architecture and technology governance is a tricky thing. Weak or lack of governance can lead to the effects described above. Too strong governance can impact the ability of the development teams to effectively meet the customer and market requirements.

Key to successful and effective governance is a clear strategy accompanied by corresponding objectives which results in a clear understanding of where you want to go with your product. Achieving these goals requires appropriate governance processes effectively enforcing the strategy. Architecture and technology governance necessarily restricts the choice for the development teams. This type of governance needs to be well explained and carefully rolled out. Otherwise this harmonization aspiration will lack the required support and buy-in from the development teams. A corresponding audit has to focus on the execution of the governance process and the adherence to guidelines and rules.

An audit aspect of a different kind is the following. Software Sustainability Audits are themselves part of the architecture and technology governance. Depending on the organizational setup one has to ensure that this audit function is sufficiently independent. If there is any doubt there is sufficient independence, the audit is better performed by a different audit team. Nevertheless, finding the right governance structure requires an independent assessment. This even might require several iterations of audits and subsequent changes to find the right balance between governance and the required flexibility of the development teams.

8.4.4   Secure Development

Software products have to be secure. A corresponding process has to ensure that a certain level of security is ensured. This process comprises development guidelines, code scans and reviews, testing, and education. But it also has to cover how the company responds to identified security breaches in products already productively used by customers.

Security in software has gained significantly increasing importance and awareness over time. We just briefly touch this process as our intention is not a comprehensive coverage of this topic.

8.4.4.1 Impact on Sustainability

The direct impact of security vulnerabilities can be seen almost every day in the news. Besides the direct impact like stolen or compromised data, the main impact caused by security breaches is a loss in reputation and trust. This can lead to complete market disruptions like many examples of internet browser vulnerabilities. Trust is not only impacted by the raw number of severe security breaches in a product, but is also influenced by the way a software provider reacts to such security incidents.

8.4.4.2 Audit Aspects

As security is such an important topic it is not the question whether or not to deal with it. There are two other central aspects to be assessed by an audit. The first aspect is the right level of security required for the product portfolio. For everyone in the security business it is obvious that absolute security cannot be achieved. By applying different means like code scans the level can be increased. But the effort spent also has to be balanced with the actual risk to which a product is exposed.

The second aspect is a holistic security approach. Security has many facets and requires different means and technologies to effectively address the topic. The different measures have to fit and complement each other. A typical example is the handling of security issues in open source components. Using open source components can be very efficient to quickly develop software. But it has to be ensured that security issues in these components are as effectively tackled as in the company's own code.

8.4.5 Reuse and Open Source

The idea of reuse is that certain problems are only solved once and then the solution is reused many times in the same or different software products. A typical example of reuse in business software is the currency conversion function. Another very popular approach of reuse is the idea of open source software. Effective reuse of any software, whether open source or internally developed allows for faster development with more focus on the actual business problems to be solved. At the same time reuse helps in harmonizing the architecture.

The reuse process requires covering the identification and provisioning of potentially reusable components. Transparency of available components to development teams has to be ensured. Furthermore, contracts between provider and consumers about the stability of and adherence to standard interfaces, the patching procedure, and the provisioning of new features have to be included. For open source components the adherence to corresponding license agreements has to be ensured.

8.4.5.1 Impact on Sustainability

The idea of reuse embraces the idea of sustainability as necessary work is only done once. Lack of reuse can lead to architectural incoherence. On the other hand, flawed reuse can lead to severe impact and unwanted side effects. This flawed reuse is a typical problem of the extension of existing reuse components.

As an example, a software application requires a new feature from a component to solve a business problem. If the application does not get the required functionality, a direct impact to the success of the product can be the result. By reusing an immature or flawed function to solve this business objective, you have enforced adding a problem to your product.

Non-compliance to open source license agreements can cause severe impact. Some licenses require making the complete software product open source if it includes corresponding components. In other cases the company might be sued for misusing open source components. From a technical point of view, open source requires a critical assessment. It is easy to select and download an open source component. Still, in case of problems with such a component it has to be ensured that a fix or update to the component can be provided.

8.4.5.2 Audit Aspects

The focus in the context of Software Sustainability Audits is clearly the use of open source components. The entry barrier to open source usage is very low. If no corresponding governance is established a proliferation of open source usage can be the consequence. This might be in the interest of the open source community. It is not necessarily in the interest of the company using the components. Our experience has shown that most companies struggle keeping transparence on open source usage in their products. Without transparency there can be no conscious and informed decision, especially with regard to the different open source license models. In addition, a clear strategy for supporting open source components has to be assessed by a corresponding audit.

For internal reuse of code of all types the focus of an audit has to be the right balance between architectural coherence and the flexibility of the development teams. Providing reusable components requires a higher investment which needs to be balanced with the expected benefits.

8.4.6   Export Control

There is an aspect of software development that is not too well known. Software products are subject to export regulations when sold or shipped to foreign countries. This affects mainly two types of software products – products that have been developed for military usage, and software containing cryptographic algorithms. Companies providing software in the first context know about the issues. But cryptographic algorithms are pervasive and affect all software providers. We will limit the discussion to this aspect. The legal implications of this topic are quite complex and we will not elaborate on them. Nevertheless, the combination of complex legal requirements and the technical implications makes export control a very specific process.

The export control process requires keeping transparency on the used cryptographic algorithms. Depending on the usage, export to a country might be generally allowed (for instance within the European Union), might require a dedicated export license, or is generally forbidden.

8.4.6.1 Impact on Sustainability

There are several issues related to export control. The most severe one is that you might be banned from some markets if you export software illegally, i.e. without a required license. You as a software provider will be put on a black list together with terrorist organizations and other criminals. Handling of export regulations and requesting of corresponding licenses is outside the core development process. But other entities can only act accordingly if the development teams ensure transparency on components subject to export regulations.

The above sketched scenario might be possible, but not too likely. There is another more operational impact. In some cases a dedicated export license is required. Requesting this license is required any time the (cryptographic) software is shipped. This might affect shipments of patches and support packages. The use of cryptographic algorithms does not prevent the shipment of the software. Requesting export licenses is just time consuming and overhead that should be avoided. The optimal solution is one where the cryptographic component can be installed and patched independently. The rest of the software is not subject to export regulations and can be freely shipped and patched. In the best case the cryptographic part is stable and does not require further patches. Then only once an export license is required.

You see that the export regulations have a direct impact to the architecture and design of the software.

8.4.6.2 Audit Aspects

The main objective for handling export control in software development is creating transparency about the used cryptographic algorithms. Also ensuring optimal product architectures for the handling of export licenses is important. These aspects are natural candidates for corresponding audits. Another aspect is the interpretation of export regulations and translation of them into development guidelines. The interface between the legal world (and terminology) and the technical one is critical. The translation requires education and experience on both sides to bridge the rather big gap.

8.4.7   Extending Enterprise Resource Planning (ERP) Systems

The last example is a process of a different kind. The examples discussed so far concerned the initial development of a software product either by a vendor or maybe the IT department of a company. Now we look at the extension of an ERP system. This concerns customers operating the system or partners providing add-ons to the ERP system. The extension of such a system is required to close functional gaps or to adapt the system for a specific industry.

8.4.7.1 Impact on Sustainability

There is one main difference in this example compared to the others. Here the software lifecycle of the original product is not owned by the development team performing the extension. This adds an additional level of dependency. There might be other dependencies stemming from the underlying operating or database system, or further technologies. This dependency implies that extensions have to be developed in a way consistent with the lifecycle of the underlying ERP product. If this is not the case upgrades or patches to the core ERP system might become more expensive or even impossible. For example, ERP interfaces called by the extension have to be released for external usage. Other Application Programming Interfaces (APIs) could be changed by the vendor without further notice. Extensions using unreleased APIs would in the best case produce errors upon such changes. In the worst case the API would still be called syntactically correct, but a changed semantic could lead to corrupted or inconsistent data.

Another typical mistake extending ERP is the lack of knowledge about existing functionality. Required functionality (at least partly) exists but is not used. Instead the functionality gets re-implemented but usually less optimal. This adds unnecessary costs, and might even hamper and impact system operations.

In other cases the extension might focus on missing functionality, but the gap is closed later on by the ERP vendor. In such cases a migration from the extension to the new standard functionality is required for optimizing system usage and operational costs.

8.4.7.2 Audit Aspects

Software Sustainability Audits in the context of ERP extensions have to focus on the following major aspects:

- *Alignment with Existing Functionality*: Is it ensured that the required functionality does not already exist?
- *Alignment With ERP Roadmap*: Is the extension aligned with the roadmap of the vendor? Has it been assessed whether the required functionality will be provided in the foreseeable future as part of the standard package?
- *Adherence to Guidelines*: Are there published guidelines from the ERP vendor about extending the system? Have they been followed?
- *Skills*: Does the development team have the required skills and experience to provide a reliable extension?

From a technical perspective the adherence to the guidelines is the most important and tangible aspect. Nevertheless, the other aspects must be regarded as well.

8.5   Summary

Software Sustainability Audits comprise product as well as development process audits. In this chapter we focused on auditing software development processes. It is important to understand how the development processes impact the sustainability of a software product. We explicitly focused on this aspect. The concept of process validation audits was introduced as a core element and backbone of Software

Sustainability Audits. To make the impact of processes on the sustainability of the solution we assessed different and relevant development (sub-) processes. For each process we explained the impact and addressed aspects to be taken into account for corresponding audits.

The Product Audit: Look at This, Architect! 9

What's In It for Me?

Product and process audits are significant functions within the Software Sustainability Audit. We will explain in this chapter the uniqueness of product audits.

CIO/CTO

In the last chapters you already learned the concepts of Software Sustainability Audits and process audits as a specific variant. With the two Sects. 9.2 and 9.4 you will get a fair view of the different flavor of a product audits. While Sect. 9.2 explains very briefly the essentials of product audits and how they relate to process audits, Sect. 9.4 highlights the importance of different perspectives that need to be considered.

Software Architect

The introductory story in 9.1 provides motivation on why a product audit is necessary, while 9.2 further elaborates that product audit is more than assessing architecture. In 9.3 we define the main procedure of a product audit and in 9.4 we emphasize the different perspectives which should be considered. Section 9.5 provides you with a toolbox of questions that can be easily used in product audits.

Auditor

You are already familiar with process audits as they do not differ too much from your internal audits. What is the challenge that you will encounter with product audits? Sect. 9.2 compares these two audit variants and how product audits relate to process audits. Sections 9.3 and 9.4 show some specifics of auditing software. First, in 9.3, the procedure of assessing software products is described. And then, in 9.4, the most important perspectives for a product audit are introduced. The toolbox in Sect. 9.5 will be valuable to you as well.

R. Gutbrod and C. Wiele, *The Software Dilemma*, Management for Professionals, DOI 10.1007/978-3-642-27236-3_9, © Springer-Verlag Berlin Heidelberg 2012

9.1   Request for Aid: the Introductory Story

Gregory has gathered quite a lot of experience with Software Sustainability Audits. He is now well known for his Software Sustainability Audit responsibility. And yet, the difference between process and product audit has not been recognized.

Knowing about Greg's Software Sustainability Audit responsibility, Felix approached Greg. Felix was a software architect of a new application development team. He had been asked by his manager to do an audit for a recently designed architecture, on which all future applications should be based. His manager wanted to verify this decision before any major investment on this new architecture is done.

When Felix asked Greg about his audit experiences, Greg started to elaborate broadly and deeply about the architecture framework. He was about to explain every detail from audit scope, touching audit objectives, and dug deep into the architecture relevant processes.

"Hold on! Wait a minute!" Felix was overwhelmed. He could not follow Greg at all. "There might be a misunderstanding" Felix interrupted Greg. "I don't want to turn the company inside out. It's just about an architecture assessment. What should I look at? What should I verify? I don't think that I need to check the processes. I am not concerned with improving the development processes for activities that have already happened. I just need an answer about the quality and reliability of the architecture. Have you conducted Software Sustainability Audits?" Felix was really puzzled. He felt uncomfortable because he got the impression that he and Greg were talking about two different things while both are calling them Software Sustainability Audits.

Greg smiled. "It's all right. I understand that you might be puzzled. Why I am talking about all our audit processes when you are only interested in questions to ask and criteria that can prove your architecture sustainability."

"Yes, that's what I am looking for" Felix was delighted by this surprising turn.

"What is the reason for you to do a Software Sustainability Audit?" Greg tried to fuel the thinking process with Felix.

"Well, our future development should use this new architecture as a foundation. My manager would like to know, whether that will be a good decision", Felix repeated his instructions given him by his manager.

"How will you and your manager know that this is a good decision?" Greg tossed the discussion back to Felix.

"Ah, a good question." Felix now deliberated on the right rationale. "We will have some new requirements when we start development. The architecture foundation needs to be flexible enough to support future requirements." Felix found an important architecture property.

"Good" said Greg. "Let's assume that you will figure out that the architecture is flexible enough for your purposes. How do you know that the architecture will not finally break by adding new enhancements?" Greg silently drilled into the Software Sustainability Audit framework.

"I have to rely on the architects' experiences", Felix admitted. "Yes, and also interesting, how do I know those experiences for building an architecture foundation were used?"

Greg was fascinated at how the discussion was proceeding. "Where can you see the experience of someone? When you have experience on a topic, you ask the right questions, you consider important aspects in your design. The reliability of the architecture depends on the completeness of architectural questions which have been asked and answered." Greg furthered the discussion.

"Ah, I understand. You mean I should not only look at the given architecture, but also how architecture was designed. I should ..." Felix was surprised about this turn again. "The process execution of architecture definition will tell me something about the reliability of the architecture, won't it?"

"Look! That is what I was going to explain at the beginning." Greg summarized the results. *"First, you need to understand your audit objective – you mentioned the flexibility of the architecture. Then, you also need to understand the reliability of your audit results – you said a check of the architecture execution process will support you. Summarized, you need to do both an architecture assessment and a process validation."*

"Thanks, Greg. I got it." Felix understood the advantage of the audit framework, now.

9.2 Approaching the Beast

9.2.1 Take the Framework from Process Audits

It happens that product audits and process audits are seen as very different. When processes are going to be investigated, a strict and formal framework for the procedure is accepted. When architecture is reviewed, the first question that comes to mind concerns a check list for architectural properties to be considered. The basic framework [1] for the architecture review procedure is relevant too. For instance, your audit results are more reliable if they answer expected audit objectives. A framework for an audit increases the level of quality of the outcome. That is true for both process audits and product audits. We propose to use a common framework for both process and product audits. This commonality will make it easy to follow and your results will meet expectations.

9.2.2 Combining the Process and Product View

One special aspect of the audit framework is the process view. It is important to include the process assessment in a product audit. Sure, the product architecture is the center of gravity in a product audit and is indentified as most important. But by accepting this top priority of the product architecture, the process aspect should be given the next priority in the audit hierarchy. The architectural properties show you the current situation. The process quality adds answers to the reliability of your view and indicates the future quality for both product and architecture.

So, what is different from process audits, you might ask. Auditing processes have two views. You can look at a process and validate its definition. Is a process defined such that it delivers results as expected? You can also look at the implementation of a process. How is the process executed? Can you assume reliable results from how the process steps are done? While process audits primarily look at the first part, the definition of the process, product audits review the process execution.

The question remains, which processes should be considered in product audits? Of course, not all architecture relevant processes can be taken into account. Priorities need to be set.

9.2.3   Selection of Processes

There are two very prominent processes: The architecture definition process and the requirement identification process. These are the core processes for each software development. Reliability and sustainability depend heavily on these two processes. Let's have a closer look at them to better understand this dependency.

The first process, the architecture definition process, gives the answer to the reliability of the current and future architecture. Is, what you have seen concerning the architecture, well-thought out and does it cope with all requirements? Will the next implemented feature make the architecture tumble down? Experienced architects will say, "I will recognize it by inspecting the architecture and the software." And they are right. That is the purpose in validating the architecture. You can and should find indications for stability or for any points where the design will break. But are you sure that you have found all the significant factors? Is there any guarantee that the next version will be stable like this one? The architecture process wraps your architecture findings with a certification of reliability and a view into the future.

Root cause analysis means asking why something occurred. It means to explore one step or more back. And that is what we do, when we consider the requirement identification process. The architecture might be okay. But is the architecture stable enough to cope with future requirements? What happens, if the requirements were not exactly understood? What happens, if a change request arrives? Will the architecture withstand those changes? Or are major redesigns required? The manager, who asked for a Software Sustainability Audit, typically expects an answer about the sustainability of the architecture. He wants to know, whether further developments are easily added without any architecture redesign. Redesign is a horror from business perspective; but is very different for architects, who like it. This kind of sustainability in architecture is like tossing the dice for your manager. What we need is a crystal ball that we can use to glance into the future, the crystal ball called the requirement identification process. Similar to a crystal ball, you will not get 100% surely that the architecture will not break. But you would see further defects or risks that should be considered.

While these two processes, architecture definition process and requirement identification process, are always highly recommended to be considered in product audits, there might be others which are essential for the product. Like with architecture and requirements, a good idea is to proceed like a root cause analysis. Take the crucial properties of the product or the architecture and ask how they have been solved and why.

One process that is used from time to time by peers from a product audit is the reuse process. Like in the example above, the architect Felix needed to check whether a given architecture is stable and flexible enough to be used as the foundation for a new development. He and his team want to use or reuse other software. Felix would like to be able to recommend building on this foundation. And later, during the development of the first version, other team members might find out that there is other software which could be used. The other software is similar to the one currently being used, but this new software fits much better to the requirements. Felix was not involved in the selection process of the respective foundation software. However, questions will arise why this new software was not identified in the Software Sustainability Audit. Now, you can argue back and forth whether Felix should have found this new software during his Software Sustainability Audit. Remember, there is limited time for a Software Sustainability Audit. It is difficult to assess the given foundation software and also identify and validate other software at the same time. That is almost impossible for reasons of time. But it is palpable that software reuse identification has happened or should have happened before now. Somehow this foundation must have been selected. So, there is a certain risk that the foundation identification procedure used was not perfect. An option would have been to have the reuse identification process as part of Felix's audit objectives. There he could have challenged the colleagues with the question of comprehensiveness of their investigation to find the right foundation. The reuse process is another good process candidate for product audits.

A similar process that we find in a large amount of product audits is the technology selection process. For instance, you want to develop a modern user interface. Many UI technologies are on the market. Sometimes the selection process is based just on preferences or outdated knowledge. Does the technology match with the requirements? Is a good infrastructure available to allow the technology to be used easily? Is the technology already supported by the current development infrastructure? Which criteria have been considered when the technology was decided? Particularly when a brand new product development has started, the process of how the technology was selected should be on your audit objective menu.

9.3   Let's Return to the Start: Procedure at a Glance

Every product audit has characteristics which need to be considered. Every product will have its own natural aspects and special treatment in Software Sustainability Audits. There is a proven cook book on procedure, but this guidance from best practices does not replace the architecture framework we have introduced, instead it fills the framework with content.

We propose seven steps from which to create your content for audit objectives.
1. Clarify the purpose of the audit.
2. Identify relevant processes for your product audit.
3. Understand business and technical requirements.
4. Figure out, what the architecture drivers are.
5. Assess the architecture using results from 1 to 4.
6. Verify the architecture by looking into its implementation.
7. Iterate, when necessary.

9.3.1 Clarify the Purpose of the Audit

From the reasons why a product audit is requested, audit objectives and audit scope are derived very easily. There will always be a lot of audit objectives. It is always a fight between breadth and depth of audit themes. The purpose of an audit may be betrayed within the product secrets or possible priorities of the requestor.

Are there any suspicious facts? e.g. Are there any complaints about quality? What types of quality issues are mentioned? Have there been concerns about performance reported? Any hint you receive can be used to add an audit theme or increase its priority. Those facts tell you how deeply you should look into the architecture.

In addition, the reasons for the product audit show which architecture aspect is most relevant. There is a bunch of architecture criteria, which are interesting in general. Towards the end of this chapter, in Sect. 9.5, we provide a check list for those architecture criteria. You need to be and stay focused on your audit objectives. The purpose and potential of suspicious facts define the architecture criteria which are essential for this audit.

Moreover, the audit rationale tells you something about the processes. It reveals what processes are crucial for this product architecture, at which processes you better have a closer look.

9.3.2 Relevant Processes

The process audit part is used as additional verification of the good architecture shape you might have found or as root cause analysis for weak points you may have identified. There are two standard candidates: the architecture and the requirement identification process. The nature of the product or the purpose of the requested audit may lead to other processes worth-while to look at. A typical set of processes will also contain the reuse process. The next portion of Software Sustainability Audit description covers these three architectural relevant processes. We leave it to the interested reader to extend the product audit work plan similarly by other processes as appropriate to their Software Sustainability Audits.

Architecture Process: While inspecting the architecture you could assess a relevant processes quality assurance, quality assurance as it pertains to the architecture you reviewed and the quality assurance of your own findings. In particular we recommend three processes:
- Architecture definition process
- Architecture validation process
- Architecture implementation process

Usual *proof points* are: How is the architecture defined? Who participated in the architecture definition? Which requirements influenced the architecture? Who validated the architecture? What experience from developer or architect community was available to define and validate the architecture? How has the architecture been documented and communicated? How good do the developers understand the architecture? How is the architecture supported and applied by the developers? In case of an existing architecture governance process, the question of dealing with deviations from common architecture or design rules gives illustrative insight.

Relevant *audit objectives,* as introduced in Chap. 6, are
- Reliable implementation
- Compliant implementation
- Effective results
- Valid results

How does the architecture and design fit into the business requirements and business objective? Does the developed software match with the designed architecture? Do the software and the product efficiently cope with the business objective and the product goals? Are the architecture and product valid? With this type of audit objective question it is important to use your own architecture experience and knowledge about good architectures and design patterns.

Requirement Process: While trying to understand the rationale for the provided architecture design, you could challenge the business requirement process. The requirement process can indicate further weak points of the architecture, which typically will be visible in later versions of the software. Main aspects of the requirement process are
- Customer requirement management
- Market requirement management

Usual *proof points* are: How are the requirements identified? How were the requirements documented and communicated? How are the requirements understood? How were potential customers of the software (often called "the business") involved in requirement engineering? The market requirement management looks even further into the future. It clarifies the view of extending the software for other users or businesses. Common questions are: How many customers have been involved? How diverse were the business sources from where the requirements have been gathered? Which flexibility requirements have been derived and addressed in the architecture?

Relevant *audit objectives* are
- Reliable implementation
- Effective results
- Valid results

How does requirement engineering support the architecture? How is the architecture involved in requirement process? How is stability and sustainability of the requirements ensured? How comprehensive and reliable are the non-functional requirements? Are all architectural questions addressed by the collection of requirements? Do the requirements cope with the business scope of the product?

Reuse process: Particularly in audits of products, where major parts of other software are supposed to be reused or major parts of developed software should be offered for reuse; the reuse process is advised to be put on the audit menu. Crucial processes hereby are:
- Identification process
- Provisioning process

– Consumption process
– Commitment process

Usual *proof points* are: How has the reusable component been identified? Which criteria were used to identify the reusable software? How is the reuse characteristics of the reusable software addressed in the provisioning process? How are the customers of the reusable component involved in the requirement process? Which guidance is given to apply the reuse software properly? How is sustainability of the reuse software guaranteed? Which commitments to the applicants are granted? How reliable are the commitments?

While we aligned the audit objectives with the main stream processes of architecture and requirements, we recommend rather broadening the audit objective view for special selected processes. This underlines and emphasizes the importance of the process in the given product. Focus audit objectives for reuse process could be:

– Reliable implementation
– Consistent implementation
– Effective results
– Valid results

If it is the first time, however, that the reuse process is a focus theme of an audit, the product audit can be extended with particular process aspects of the reuse process. The audit objectives can be extended by:

– Comprehensive design
– Appropriate design
– Compliant implementation

How is the reuse process designed? How is the relationship between reuse providers and consumers modeled? Which commitments are requested for both

Core Scope	Key Scopes			
Architecture Process	Architecture definition	Architecture Validation	Architecture Implementation	
Requirement Process	Customer Requirements Management		Market Requirement Management	
Reuse Process	Identification	Provisioning	Consumption	Commitments

	Core Scope Relevance		
Audit Objective	Architecture Process	Requirement Process	Reuse Process
Clear Goal Comprehensive Design Reliable Implementation Appropriate Design Compliant Implementation Consistent Implementation Efficient Implementation Effective Results Valid Results	Product Audit & Process Implementation		Process Design & Implementation

Fig. 9.1 Product audit example with relevant processes and audit objectives. *Highlighted cells* in the lower matrix (audit objective) mean audit objective is relevant for the respective process

roles? Does the reuse process guarantee robust, flexible and reliable offering? Is the reuse processes adopted as described? How is the reuse process and obligations herein communicated? Do the consumers know about the release strategy of the provider? Does the provider know the requirements the consumer have for next releases?

Figure 9.1 shows an overview of audit objectives and relevant processes.

9.3.3   Understand Requirements

One day Greg was contacted by a young architect Robert, who proudly presented his first master piece of architecture. He was very happy that he could successfully design a complex architecture for a new product. He already invited experts to an architecture review. His work was very well received. "Sound architecture" was one remark he received. Robert knew Greg and his experience in Software Sustainability Audits. He wanted an additional certification for his first major architecture.

"Hi Greg! You are well known for your experience with good architecture. I would like to get your opinion about this architecture design." said Robert and laid the architecture diagram on the table. "What do you think? Do you see any flaws in it? Do you recommend any change?" Robert was very convinced about his master piece.

"Before we look at the architecture, could you please explain to me the business requirements?" Greg replied rather unconventionally. Symbolically, Greg moved the architecture diagram aside showing that he wants to concentrate on business requirements first.

Robert was unprepared for this reaction. "Yes, I could. But could we just focus on the architecture? I can refer to the business while explaining the architecture." Robert moved his diagram again back into the middle of the table and started to explain the building blocks.

Greg interrupted Robert's speech. "Robert, I understand that you are very proud of your architecture. And I agree, at first glance, your architecture shows high degree of symmetry and looks well organized. And I also see with your first explanations that you perfectly understand the business requirements. However, I still insist on first understanding the business requirements, the business objective, and independent from the architecture. If you explain both to me at the same time, I could get detracted from your architecture. I already see a solution in front of me. That prevents me from analyzing the requirements. If I understand the business first, I may come to quite different questions related to your architecture."

Robert nodded, moved his diagram aside, and started to elaborate on the pure business.

We have frequently seen the attitude such as Roberts toward architecture analysis. "Please tell me whether the architecture is good or bad!" Unfortunately, architecture seldom is good or bad. Yes, there are badly used design patterns or other typical architecture mistakes that you can notice with a first glance. Some flaws can be identified by pure architecture review. But in a detailed analysis the better questions are "Is the architecture appropriate to the business requirements? Does the architecture meet the business objectives?"

We highly recommend you to understand the requirements, to listen to the business requirements and the business objectives first. Be architectural unbiased. Looking at the architecture at the same time you learn the requirements leads you to the architecture solution as provided. It narrows your view and cuts off important questions you should have asked. It is like common puzzles which give the impression of a certain bandwidth of solutions. But the real solution is actually beyond the first glance. You need to think outside the box. One of the most common puzzles for this approach is the following example: Draw four joined lines which touch all nine of the given points (Fig. 9.2).

Most people are detracted by the given "architecture". Many try to add into the mix some undefined criteria like lines are supposed to start and end at points, all lines are supposed to be within the dotted box. But none of these rules are given actually. The obvious but not stated conditions make it difficult to find the solution (Fig. 9.3).

There is a similar behavior in the relationship between requirements and architecture. If you stare at a given architecture while listening to business requirements, you see the given architecture as the one and only option. Better separate the business and requirement perspective. Look at them independently from the architecture offering.

From the requirements you can learn important features and properties for the architecture. All the characteristics from performance to usability can be derived from the requirements and the business objectives. Collect these aspects. They build another part of your Software Sustainability Audit work plan. Alternatively, you can use these insights to prioritize your audit objectives.

Summarized, the task of understanding the requirements is twofold. First, understand the business. That enables you to later compare the architecture with the understood requirements. Second, derive architecture drivers from the requirements. Architecture drivers are requirements or constraints, which have essential impact on architecture. All architecture drivers need to be actively addressed, when reviewing the architecture.

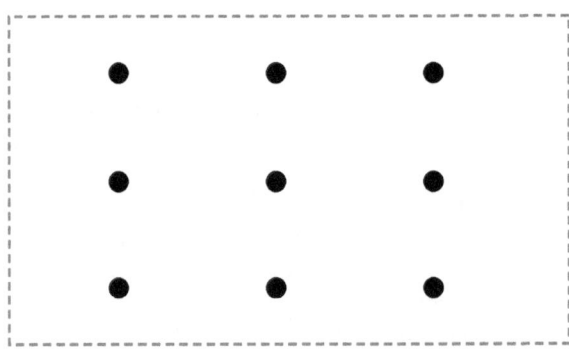

Fig. 9.2 Think out of the box puzzle

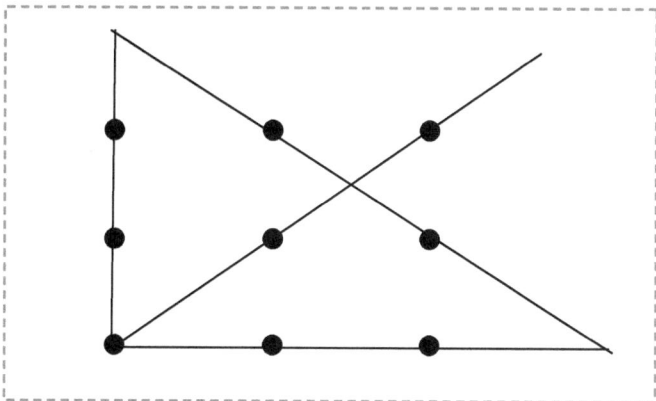

Fig. 9.3 Think out of the box solution

9.3.4   Figure Out Architecture Drivers

After listening to the business requirements you are ready to collect architecture drivers. Architecture drivers are important influencing factors for the architecture. They can be boundary conditions, limitations or just specific requests. For instance, you can learn from the business that business rules vary and need to be changed frequently. However, all business process steps depend on the same set of business rules. Once the business rules are decided, the whole process must be compliant with these rules until the business rules are redefined again. Such requirements will affect architecture decisions. A definition and usage of those business rules must be envisaged in the architecture. Also a versioning concept might be required to allow the business to validate the compliance with a valid set of business rules at any time.

Compatibility with other software could be a business objective, which you will not learn from the business requirements. You need to look at the overall strategy of your company and consider related business objectives. One such company strategy could be consistency of all software solutions provided by the company. This has many impacts on the software architecture, starting with the reuse aspect and other subjects like configuration and the common usability experience.

Strategic technology or rapid market entry are other examples of architecture drivers. These may lead to either; being bound to a certain technology with a limitation of using better options, or it may lead to intensive usage of open source programming.

All the architecture drivers are important to be retained, not only for your architecture assessment, but also for your final reporting. Whatever you find out in your assessment, it is often valuable to refer your findings and recommendations to the architecture drivers. The architecture drivers yield the rationales for observed architecture decisions. Your recommendations can offer alternatives, which take the architecture drivers into consideration. Since architecture drivers are sometimes derived or even assumed, but not officially requested, these can be questioned while stating alternative recommendations.

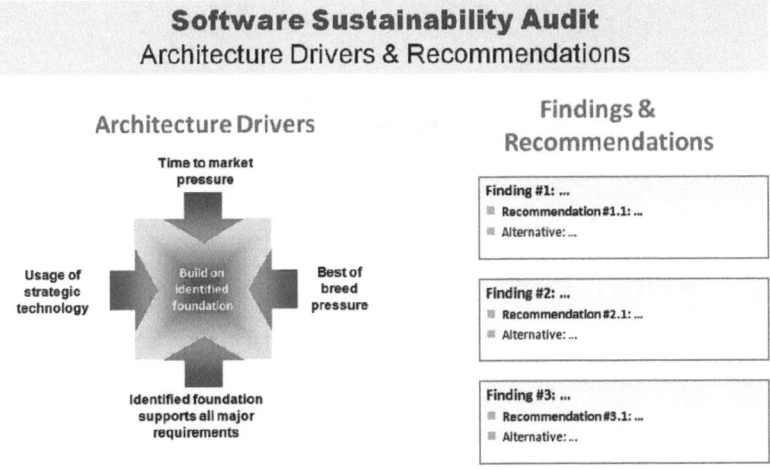

Fig. 9.4 Architecture drivers with findings and recommendations

Example: Figure 9.4 shows an example, which depicts the architecture drivers ("time to market pressure", etc.) which lead to the architecture decision "build new application on the identified foundation". The negative consequences of this decision are listed as audit findings. The recommendations with optional alternatives are provided to improve the architectural situation.

9.3.5 Assess Architecture

There are many architecture properties which are worth-while to challenge. We often call them non-functional requirements. That is because these properties do not cope with functional features, but describe behaviors such as scalability or performance. In the next chapter we will learn about many of these non-functional properties.

In addition, we need to judge to what extent the architecture is self-explanatory. How easy it is to understand the architecture design determines how easy it is to communicate the architecture. This relates directly to how good the architecture and its essential properties are understood by the developers.

Many criteria which we expect from good software are relevant for architecture as well. Is the architecture well structured? Are exceptions caught? Are common functionality separated and reused? And so on.

Before we look into the details, let's have first a look at the big picture. How does the architecture fit into a larger architecture schema? Is there any integration into other products needed? Are there common features the product should share with other products? The big picture of architecture, as we call it, should be considered, too. Or, as we elaborated on before, look outside the box, and take it literally this time.

9.3.6   Look in Implementation of Architecture

Greg was already at the end of a Software Sustainability Audit. Everything looked very good. The architecture was in excellent shape. Actually, the architecture drivers were precisely documented in the architecture paper. This document explained in detail how these architecture drivers were addressed. All major architecture decisions were captured. It was just fun to read this documentation. "This architecture is really easy to understand" thought Greg.

He met a developer to make some further deep dives to verify the architecture's implementation. Tim, the expert, explained to Greg which part of the architecture he was responsible for.

"This is what I have developed" Tim proudly pointed to some components of the architecture.

Greg was curious what the implementation looked like. "Certainly I will find the same clear structure in the software" he thought. Greg pointed to a software component. The architecture diagram showed two interfaces to other components.

"Tim, this component looks interesting. Could you please show me some samples in the coding which implements this component? I would also be interested in the implementation of these two interfaces."

Tim started to elaborate on the implementation. "Look!" he said. "I have developed several classes for the implementation of this component." And Tim continued to show more than 100 classes in the class library which seemed to be relevant.

Greg paused. "Tim, I notice that the prefixes used in naming the classes are quite different. Some prefixes match with the component name. Others differ quite a lot. What rules for defining prefixes did you use?"

And Tim again had a prompt answer. "You're right, Greg. We have a naming convention to use the component name as the prefix. But there are classes that are used by several of the architecture components. We had to decide to use only one component as the prefix, didn't we?"

Architecture design is as good as its implementation. We cannot judge the architecture by assessing the software: too many details, too complex. So we look at architecture pictures to understand the design. Architecture pictures are not necessarily based on reality. The real architecture is in the code. So, how do we solve this dilemma? We need to verify the architecture by looking into its implementation. But architecture verification is just one reason to have a look into the source code. We can also validate how good the architecture is communicated. We can check how good the architecture is understood. Even more importantly, we can see how the crucial properties of the architecture were acknowledged. Furthermore, we get an impression of the code structure and code quality, other essential aspects of robust software.

9.3.7   Plan Iteration

It is like a waterfall model for project management that competes with scrum projects. The outlined sequence of steps is not sufficient in many cases. You learn some facts from the architecture where you need to know more about the corresponding business requirements. You notice something in the coding which you cannot properly assign to the architecture based on your current understanding. You suddenly identify a new architecture driver, where you would like to know more. You should now adjust your plan to go back one or more steps in the current sequence of planned steps.

There is one risk that we should mention at this point. When you carefully analyze all the information you get, and if you follow the recommendation to iterate, you can end up in an endless loop. Before you start iterating, you should be aware of the given priorities. A helpful method is to divide the scope in two parts, one part where you plan to dive deep into details, and one part where you want to stay at the surface. The most important parts, those where you expect highest risk, should be taken for the deep dives. When you identify major issues for those parts, where you planned to stay at surface, it is hard to resist going into details. If you still have time, you can follow those tracks. Otherwise, you can capture those facts. A further risk assessment can lead you to decisions to live with an observation or propose an additional, separate Software Sustainability Audit. However you decide, be aware of your scope, your priorities and your time.

9.4   Change Your Seat: Always Look from different Perspectives

We already came across architecture properties as very relevant audit objectives. But what are the architecture properties, or non-functional requirements as they are often called. And even more interesting, how can we judge those architecture properties?

There is certainly an architecture opinion, the usage or omittance of fitting design patterns. That is a valid view. And though we recommend you not restrict the assessment to a pure architecture view, you can add value by changing your seat. Change seats with a stakeholder of your architecture and look at the architecture through his eyes. A different perspective shows a shadow you may not have seen before. Or an illuminated side shows up and you wonder why. We propose you take up three to four positions. Start with your pure architecture view, look from the developers' perspective, understand impact for customers, and learn what partners or other stakeholders might see.

9.4.1   Architecture View

One could argue that whatever we find out should have an impact for at least one of our stakeholders. So, why don't we just look at the architecture with our stakeholders' views? The first assumption is true. Yes, all important aspects of the architecture will have an impact for one or another of the stakeholders. However, this may not be directly visible in all cases, and some of the aspects found might not be requested by them.

Let's take an example from the architecture of a house. You can find supporting walls in a house. In a larger building a supporting wall could be a pillar. Supporting walls are planned with the architecture for the sole sake of preventing a collapse of the building. Gregory once travelled to a foreign country on his vacation. He visited a historic building and spying a particular pillar placement asked his tour guide why the hell they placed this pillar at this particular spot. It looked both ugly, placed incorrectly, and hid view from many of the spectacular historic points of interest. The answer was, it was needed as a supporting pillar.

This was an important request for the customer, the owner of the building. His implicit request is that the building will not collapse. As that is such a natural requirement, the building owner would never have had to ask for it. He would not have asked for the details of supporting elements, since he knows there needs to be supporting walls or other elements needed to support the general design of the building.

So, the architecture view is important to understand the needs from an architectural stand point. From most of these criteria you can easily derive impacts for the stakeholders (independent from whether they like them or need them).

Typically, architecture criteria from an architecture view determine the overall robustness of the architecture. They shall prevent the software from a collapse upon usage or after minor changes.

9.4.2 Development View

The development view describes the internal software complexity with which we burden our software developers. We also use the term Total Cost of Development (TCD) to describe this complexity. The more complex the architecture is, the more complicated is it to produce clear and clean code, the higher the costs to develop software according to this architecture.

It is like the architecture of a house. A bricklayer needs to understand the architecture to lay bricks where they are planned, and to leave holes in the walls for windows and doors. During the building of a new house, a wall was constructed without the planned opening for a large window.

The house owner recognized that mistake and asked the bricklayers "Why haven't you left a hole for the window?"

"What window?" was the craftsman's reply.

The house owner showed the architecture plan as provided by the architect.

"I have never seen this plan with that window. This must be a different version."

In the telling of this story, correct communication of architecture is one aspect of the development view. Developers can only understand an architecture that has been clearly communicated. That is the starting point and prerequisite. Easy to understand and easy to implement are other architectural properties of development view.

9.4.3 Customer View

At the end of the software production chain is the customer. A good architecture is hidden for end users. A bad architecture is an architecture that is (annoying) visible and even worse, if the architecture has to be understood by end users. Consistency is just one example. Consistency is a shape of the overall architecture where the different architectural styles of the delivered software are not readily visible to the end user. On the contrary, inconsistencies are when different architecture styles are visible to the end user.

Architectural impacts for customers are typically measured within Total Cost of Ownership (TCO), the costs to implement and run the software. Contribution to TCO starts with costs for IT departments (installation, hardware, implementation projects and so forth), and continues with necessary training for end-users. Costs that arise through errors in imbedded in the software also are additive to TCO. Hence, things like usability should be considered in architecture assessments as well.

9.4.4   Partner View/View of Other Stakeholders

Another stakeholder may be a partner, whose perspective could add additional value. If a software vendor is supposed to enhance software products delivered to a customer, and (implementation) partners are used to adapt software to the customers' needs, further non-functional requirements should be considered by the architecture. Extensibility by partners while still guaranteeing software upgrades and bug fixes, is just one prominent property.

9.4.5   Other Views

There are many other views. But we want to keep the checklist simple and restrict it to these prominent views. A few more are used but selectively only.

There is a legal view for open source treatment and there is also a support view. In most cases the support view is equal to development view. Although in many cases we could use the development perspective or conversely the support perspective, we will introduce support as own architectural property where we need to mention the support view explicitly.

9.5   Stripping It Down: The Tools You Always Should Carry

Let's now start to list the architectural properties, which are worth-while to assess. The next few pages can be used as a check list to identify your priorities in your architecture assessment, to define your audit scope and objectives, and to verify what architectural aspect you have considered.

9.5.1 Process Check List

9.5.1.1 P.1 Architecture Process

How relevant is the architecture process from architecture definition, architecture communication, to the implementation of designed architecture?
- *Architecture View*: Is the architecture considered to be robust and sustainable?
- *Development View*: Is the architecture easy to understand?
- *Customer View*: Is the architecture hidden to customers?
- *Partner View*: Are partners' non-functional requirements considered?

9.5.1.2 P.2 Requirement Process

How important is it to look at the process of how customer and market requirements have been collected and considered in architecture?
- *Architecture View*: Are non-functional and functional requirements considered in the architecture?
- *Customer View*: How complete are the functions covered by the architecture?

9.5.1.3 P.3 Technology Selection Process

What is the impact of the selected technology on the architecture and the product?
- *Architecture View*: How is the architecture influenced by the selected technology?
- *Developer View*: Have the developers had experience with the selected technology?
- *Partner View*: How will the partners be enabled to use the selected technology?
- *Customer View*: Is state-of-the-art technology used? Does the used technology fit into the customer's IT seamlessly?

9.5.1.4 P4. Reuse Process

Will the designed software be used by other products? Will other software components be used in the product development?
- *Architecture View*: Which commitments are given? How long will the reused software be supported and enhanced? How will new requirements be incorporated in the reused software? What dependencies have to be considered?
- *Developer View*: Does a developer need to know the details of the reused software? What is the effort to get familiarized with the reused software?

9.5.1.5 P5. Open Source Process

How are foreign Intellectual Property (IP) rights considered when using open source software?
- *Architecture View*: How is the open source product selected? What are the criteria used to decide when to use open source or to develop your own software?
- *Support View*: How can the open source product be maintained?
- *Legal View*: How do the IP licenses affect the ownership rights?

9.5.1.6 P6. Security Process

What is the security relevance of the developed application? Which data is stored that needs special security treatment? Which data is stored that needs to be protected?

– *Architecture View*: How is security considered by the architecture?
– *Development View*: What security treatment needs to be considered by developers?
– *Customer View*: Which data needs to be protected?
– *Partner View*: What measures are required to avoid the extensions by partners adding to security leaks?

9.5.1.7 P7. Development Process

Which development model (SCRUM, XP, agile, waterfall) is used? Where are the development teams located? Which roles are defined in the development process? How does the communication between teams and different roles work? How many internal and external developers are involved? How does the know-how flow to the development teams?

– *Architecture View*: How is the architecture definition embedded between requirement analysis and coding?
– *Development View*: How do tools support the development process?
– *Customer View*: How are customers involved in the development process? How are customer requirements considered?
– *Partner View*: Which development relevant information is available for development partners? Which tools are available for partners?

9.5.2 Architecture Check List

9.5.2.1 A1. Technology

Is the technology appropriate for the planned solution? How many different tools or technologies are used?

– *Architecture View*: How is the architecture influenced by the selection of the technologies?
  Development View: How much effort is it to get familiar with the required technologies?
– *Customer View*: How visible are the used technologies to customer? How does the technology impact the customer's TCO?
– *Partner View*: How easy is it to use the necessary technologies?

9.5.2.2 A2. Platform Fit

Which platforms like databases, operation systems, hardware, frontend devices (PC, mobile) are supported by the architecture and software?

– *Architecture View*: How is platform enablement addressed by the architecture?
– *Development View*: How many specific details must developers know about the supported platforms?

- *Customer View*: How do the supported and not supported platforms affect the customer's TCO?
- *Partner View*: How are ISVs affected by the supported platforms?

9.5.2.3 A3. Scalability

What scalability is foreseen by the architecture? How does performance scale by adding servers?
- *Architecture View*: How is scalability addressed by architecture?
- *Development View*: Which rules have to be obeyed by developers to support scalability?
- *Customer View*: How easy can the infrastructure extended to allow more access for the users?

9.5.2.4 A4. Performance

What performance is guaranteed by architecture?
- *Architecture View*: Which performance requirements have been considered by architecture?
- *Development View*: Which guidelines exist for developers to allow for optimal performance?
- *Customer View*: What response time requirement is supported by the architecture?

9.5.2.5 A5. Sustainability/Maintainability

How easy can the software be enhanced with further requirements?
- *Architecture View*: How are future requirements considered by the architecture? How is the architecture prepared for enhancements and continuous innovation?
- *Development View*: How does the architecture support maintenance of the software? What kind of dynamic programming is allowed or restricted? How fine is the granularity of objects and classes? How good are the responsibilities of classes defined and separated? What programming guidelines exist?
- *Customer View*: What is the effort to receive and install new versions?

9.5.2.6 A6. Extensibility

How are extensions supported?
- *Architecture View*: What are the architecture features for extensibility?
- *Development View*: How easy can developers add optional components?
- *Customer View*: What is the effort to enable and disable optional components?
- *Partner View*: How are add-on components from partners supported?

9.5.2.7 A7. Stability

How stable does the software run supported by architecture?
- *Architecture View*: What are the stability characteristics of the architecture?
- *Development View*: What have developers considered in order to avoid the destruction of the software's stability?
- *Customer View*: What is the minimal downtime guaranteed by the architecture?

9.5.2.8 A8. Robustness

How robust is architecture with respect to future extensions? How much of the architecture needs to be changed with the addition of new features?
– *Architecture View*: How decoupled are the architecture components?

9.5.2.9 A9. Consistency

How consistent is the look and feel of the software product?
– *Architecture View*: How does architecture contribute to this consistency?
– *Development View*: Which guidelines and cookbooks exist for developers to guarantee consistency?
– *Customer View*: How consistent is the user interface through all software products? How consistent is configuration?
– *Partner View*: How are partners enabled to support the delivered consistency?

9.5.2.10 A10. Flexibility

How flexible to use is the software? How easy can the software be adopted to users' needs?
– *Architecture View*: How is the architecture designed to support flexible usage?
– *Customer View*: What flexibility is supported?

9.5.2.11 A11. Language Support

How are different languages supported?
– *Architecture View*: How does the architecture enable translation?
– *Development View*: What do developers have to consider to allow translations?
– *Customer View*: What language versions are available?

9.5.2.12 A12. Country Versions

How are country product versions supported?
– *Architecture View*: How does the architecture support separate and differentiate features for different countries?
– *Development View*: How easy can be country-specific features be added?
– *Customer View*: How simple can a customer version be activated?

9.5.2.13 A13. Configuration

How is the technical and business configuration supported?
– *Architecture View*: Which tools and infrastructure are provided to support configuration?
– *Development View*: How easy can be configuration be attached to the software?
– *Customer View*: How complex is the configuration?

9.5.2.14 A14. Easy to Understand

How easy is the software to understand?
– *Architecture View*: How easy or complex is the architecture design?
– *Development View*: How easy is the architecture to understand and to implement?

– *Customer View*: How easy is the software product to use? How good is the architectural complexity hidden from the end users?

9.5.2.15 A15. Deployment/System Landscape

How complex is the required system landscape?

– *Architecture View*: How homogeneous is the architecture design? How many different resources are required by architecture?
– *Customer View*: How high is the TCO due to deployment?

9.5.2.16 A16. Open Source/IP

Which foreign intellectual property (IP) is used?

– *Architecture View*: What architectural consequences are assumed by using of open source?

9.5.2.17 A17. Security

How is security built into the architecture?

– *Architecture View*: Which security model has been designed and considered by the architecture? Which authorization concepts are incorporated in the architecture?
– *Development View*: How easy is secure programming supported by the architecture?
– *Customer View*: How secure is the delivered software? How easy are security levels enabled?

9.5.2.18 A18. Supportability

How easy can traces be enabled and analyzed? How easy is the support of bug fixes?

– *Architecture View*: Which tools and infrastructures are offered by the architecture to enable traces?
– *Development View*: How easy can bug fixes be implemented by the underlying architecture?

9.5.2.19 A19. Cloud Enabling

How is cloud enabling supported?

– *Architecture View*: How is hosting or service offering (Saas/Paas) supported by the architecture?
– *Development View*: To what extent is cloud infrastructure hidden to developers (by an abstraction layer)?
– *Customer View*: How easy can a hosted infrastructure be used to run the software?

9.5.2.20 A20. Accessibility

How accessible is the software?

– *Architecture View*: How does the architecture and infrastructure enable the application software to be accessible?

- *Development View*: How easy is it to provide accessible software?
- *Customer View*: How is the degree of accessibility support documented?

9.5.2.21 A21. Product Maturity

How mature is the software and the architecture?
- *Architecture View*: Do old architecture fragments still exist? Which re-architectures were planned in the past? What were the reasons for planned or completed redesigns?
- *Development View*: How are old architecture pieces wrapped and non-transparent/ made untouchable for developers?
- *Support View*: How many active versions of the architectures exist? What is the frequency of new versions creation? How many customers exist per version?

9.5.2.22 A22. Design Patterns

Which design patterns are used?
- *Architecture View*: How does a design pattern support the architecture and make the architecture homogeneous and easy to understand?
- *Developer View*: How familiar are the developers with the applied design patterns?

9.5.2.23 A23. Architecture Structure

How clear is the architecture structure?
- *Architecture View*: Does a target architecture exist? How has the target architecture evolved? What are the gaps between the actual and target architectures?
- *Development View*: Which structure does the software show? How structured are the building blocks? How large or small are the classes? How is the principle "separation of concerns" considered? How are technical aspects separated from the business aspects?
- *Customer View*: To what extent is the architecture unnecessarily visible to customers?

9.5.2.24 A24. Abstraction Layers

What abstraction layers exist or are expected and missing?
- *Architecture View*: What abstraction layers are foreseen in architecture?
- *Development View*: Is the abstraction layer too abstract to understand it easily?
- *Customer View*: Is the abstraction visible to the customers (in terms of adding unnecessary complexity in usage)?
- *Partner View*: Does the abstraction layer support partner development or make their add-ons even more complicated?

9.5.2.25 A25. Documentation

How is the software and architecture documented?
- *Architecture View*: Which development artifacts like specification, requirements, architecture and design documentation exist?

– *Development View*: How is coding documented? Which overview of the business objects is provided? How easy can the architecture documentation be used and make development easier?

9.5.2.26 A26. Test Support
How is testing the software supported?
– *Architecture View*: What infrastructure exists to document test plans?
– *Development View*: What evidence exist that there are accumulations of issues in specific components?

9.5.2.27 A27. Reuse
How much reuse is offered and used?
– *Architecture View*: How is reuse supported by the architecture? What reuse library exists?
– *Development View*: What overview of the business objects exist?
– *Customer View*: Are duplicates of the business objects visible to customers?

9.5.2.28 A28. Standardization
How standardized is the solution?
– *Architecture View*: What is specific in the architecture? What deviations exist compared to known standards? Is the architecture a standard or a special solution?
– *Customer View*: What industry standard if any has to be supported?

9.5.2.29 A29. Strategy Orientation
How does the architecture match with the business strategy?
– *Architecture View*: What is the comprehensive target architecture? How does the actual architecture fit to the target architecture?

9.5.2.30 A30. Restrictions and Limitations
What restrictions and limitations are caused by architecture?
– *Architecture View*: What are the architectural drivers for those limitations?
– *Development View*: How is development affected by these limitations?
– *Customer View*: How are those restrictions visible to customers?

9.6 Summary

Product Audits and Process Audits are two shapes of Software Sustainability Audits. In this chapter you have learned, how the process audit approach can be taken also for product audits. You have seen a typical procedure for a product audit, which you can easily apply. You have learned how different perspectives make a product audit even more valuable. The chapter was completed by a checklist of characteristics, which are worth-while to consider in a product audit.

Reference

1. Kagermann, H., Kinney, W., Küting, K., & Weber, C. P. (2008). *Internal audit handbook, management with SAP®-audit roadmap*. Berlin/Heidelberg: Springer. ISBN 978-3-540-70886-5.

Do You Know the Risk?

10

What's in It for Me?

Risk is an important element in Software Sustainability Audits. Audits should be based on risk with each risk impact weighted appropriately. In this chapter we illuminate risk from two sides. First, we introduce the concept of a Software Sustainability Audit portfolio based on risk assessment. Second, we describe how risk assessment can be used in audit reporting.

CIO/CTO

The risk based planning in Sect. 10.1 gives you many ideas about how you can pro-actively tackle your risk. From this section you can derive guiding principles for your own risk planning and adapt ideas to your own needs. You can leave Sect. 10.2 mainly to your Software Sustainability Audit team to create valuable business oriented reports. Just have a look at the end of Sect. 10.2.4, where you get some idea how to treat findings fairly by considering the materiality principle.

Software Architect

You conduct a Software Sustainability Audit and you are curious about the rationale. You may ask "Why exactly is this audit theme and objective planned?" The proposal of a proper risk based planning in Sect. 10.1 provides you a fair understanding of the complexity of risk treatments and might give you a first answer to your question. Section 10.2 then offers very practical guidance. It introduces risk as an element to deliver business oriented audit reports.

Auditor

How have you collected your audit themes in your department? Compare your methodology with the proposal in Sect. 10.1. Besides many commonalities, as we hope, you will find ideas for adjustments. You can skip Sect. 10.2, as this should be common practice in you audit workaday life.

R. Gutbrod and C. Wiele, *The Software Dilemma*, Management for Professionals, DOI 10.1007/978-3-642-27236-3_10, © Springer-Verlag Berlin Heidelberg 2012

10.1   Risk-Based Planning

Risk is a fundamental element in each business. Risks can be allowed, watched, mitigated or eliminated. Whatever you do, however you decide, you at least should be aware of your risk portfolio.

We start with an introductory story again, to illuminate a situation, which everybody likes to avoid.

> *Kai, the CIO, asked Gregory to conduct another audit. "Your Software Sustainability Audits have always been very valuable. There is a new development project currently underway that I think would be interesting if we look at the planned architecture from the beginning", Kai explained.*
> *"Is there anything in particular you are interested in?" asked Greg.*
> *"This is a new business application which we are building. Please identify the risks for our business when we introduce this new application. For instance, can you identify any risk for business disruption?" Kai highlighted the audit theme.*
> *Greg started as requested. After a few weeks, he could finalize the audit results. He identified the risks with potential impacts for the business. He was proudly going to present his audit report. He found Kai in a bad mood. At the same time Greg was conducting his audit, a very strategic project failed. A project that was actually not a new development project, but still very crucial for the company's success.*
> *"We should have looked at the other project instead", Kai murmured.*

As long as you are not a prophet you never know what project will succeed and which one will fail. Actually, Software Sustainability Audits should help to give some confidence in development projects. They help to let developments with low risk run, and advise with actions for those projects with higher risk. But what risk is important enough to take action? There are always risks. Where there is no risk there is no business. So, one important question is to identify and measure risks.

However, identifying the risks starts with the right selection of Software Sustainability Audits. Where should you look first? Yes, a new project certainly bears a high risk of failure. But is the potential impact important enough to assess it? Sometimes it is a good idea to just let a new development project run. The lessons you can learn from this project might be worth more than the product risk. So, it all ends up in the question, how to figure out proper Software Sustainability Audits to cope the appropriate risks of your company.

In software development, like in other industries, we typically have two categories of risk: The risk that current business fails and the risk that your strategies cannot be realized. The first risk is an imminent risk. The impact will occur immediately. You endanger your current success and your current business. This can lead to catastrophic short-term business results, but there may remain a chance for a business saving correction in your midterm planning.

The second risk is a mid-term or long-term risk. Your running business will neither notice these risks nor the impacts. Business continues as usual. But this risk could lead to business disruption in the future. These mostly veiled risks can be dangerous for the company as well. The business will report good figures, but the company could be out of business in future due to strategic or investment failures. The company will not be competitive any longer.

In valid risk-based planning both aspects, the short term business success as well as the long term strategic aspects are covered. Since the methods though are the same, we will concentrate on only one aspect, the strategic long term aspect.

Several theories about risk and risk based planning exist. In [1] there are a few listed and assessed with the goal of adaptability for Software Sustainability Audits. Our approach is based on the recommendation you find there. It is enriched with experience from practiced planning. Lessons learned from performed Software Sustainability Audits are incorporated. While the following approach is the combination of theory and best practices, we still keep it as an open framework that can and should be adapted to individual needs.

10.1.1 Basics About Risk

Before we start how we can use risk in Software Sustainability Audits, let us first introduce plain definitions and basics about risk.

In contrast to facts, a risk is the probability that an event can occur and the accompanied potential damage if the event happens. A fact is given and the damage happened. The risk is a foresight estimating that something could happen.

We want to use the element of risk to properly deal with business impact and materiality. Therefore, we need to calculate risks as we calculate factual damages. To this end, we need some definitions and information borrowed from statistics.

We define *risk* as a potential event that can happen with a probability of less than 100% caused by a fact and with a potential damage, if the potential event occurs.

We divide a risk into two parts, the risk condition and the risk consequence. The *risk condition* is the fact that exists and can cause the potential event. The *risk consequence* is the potential event that might happen and might cause some damage.

Figure 10.1 shows these definitions as relationship of the basic risk elements.

Example 10.1.1 from security of software products
If the possible security threat of a software product is unknown, then there is a (higher) risk of security vulnerabilities. The risk condition is "security threat is unknown". The risk consequence is "there may be security vulnerabilities". The potential damages and risk impacts are loss of reputation, escalations from customers or the business, and claims for damages.

In Software Sustainability Audits the risk conditions are less factual, but more assumptions of facts with close to 100% probability. There the risk condition is derived from the findings, the actual facts. Figure 10.2 depicts the audit situation.

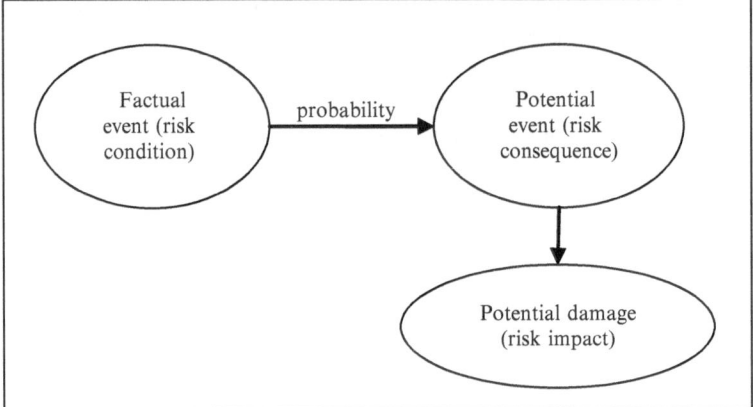

Fig. 10.1 Risk and its elements

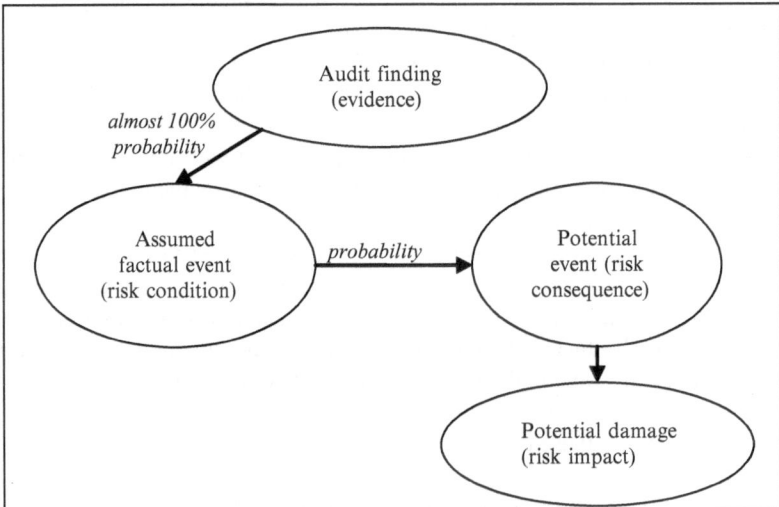

Fig. 10.2 Risk derived from Software Sustainability Audit finding

Example 10.1.2 from security of software products (10.1.1 continued)
The Software Sustainability Auditors have evidence that no threat modeling for a certain product exists. From the finding "there is no threat model" they can assume the risk condition "security threat of the audited software product is unknown" with the consequences and potential damages as described in Example 10.1.1 above.

Since you usually find more risk than existing business impacts, the risk as defined here is used in Software Sustainability Audits as a substitute for business impacts. However, still open is the question of materiality. How essential is the risk? Colloquially we talk about high, medium, and low risk. But what is a high risk? Is a risk high, if the potential event (risk consequence) will most probably occur? Or is a risk high, if the potential damage is high? To answer this question, we will borrow from mathematics, statistics to be precise. Let us assume that we identify a risk condition in Software Sustainability Audits of many software products or software components. Statistically the average damage will be the probability of the risk consequence multiplied with the damage size. Statisticians call this risk exposure.

A *risk exposure* is the average damage of a given risk. It is calculated by

$$\text{Risk Exposure} = \text{probability (of risk consequence)} * \text{risk impact}$$

Now we can answer the question above. What is a high risk? The risk exposure is the proper figure to estimate the business relevance of a Software Sustainability Audit and the materiality of an audit finding.

10.1.2 Dimensions of Risk Planning

In our risk based planning we recommend three dimensions for evaluation. Each dimension represents a source of information that can be used to estimate your business risk. Thus these dimensions determine your risk based audit plan at the end.

The first two dimensions answer the question, what aspects of your planned software development projects could harm the business? In other words, they describe the risk drivers of your software development.

First, there is a strategic component. We certainly should cover strategic projects, strategic themes, strategic game changers, or however the strategic topics are called in your company. The first dimension should cover all the company's strategies which are relevant in software development projects.

Second, there is the architecture component. The architecture view can be represented by architectural properties like security or usability. In addition, processes in software development, which impact architecture, can be used to determine your risk. Or you may take a combination of properties and processes for the architecture dimension.

The last dimension deals with the source of information: Who can give you the proper input to estimate the risk? This dimension takes care of your stakeholders.

10.1.3 Keep It Simple

We could easily add more dimensions. Development locations could be another one. Even at this stage, we recommend to keep the risk planning simple. You could easily end up with quite a complex system, if you want to consider everything that can influence the planning result. In the end stakeholders need to be involved. Your approach must be simple to explain it to your stakeholders. And you yourself must be able to understand the results of your risk based planning. You should be able to explain how your audit portfolio is derived from the planning process. Your planning must be reliable and auditable.

Hence: Hide complexity! Accept missing details! And keep your approach simple!

10.1.4 Two-Dimensional Matrix of Risk Factors

In order to keep it simple, we propose a two-dimensional matrix of risk factors. Such a matrix can be used for both collecting input from your stakeholders and evaluation of your overall risks that should be considered by Software Sustainability Audits.

Example 10.1.3
The first dimension comprises company strategies. These could be business strategies, which are relevant for Software Sustainability Audits. For instance, there could be a strategy to address new markets. This will impact architecture and influence the risk of new development projects. Other company strategies could be architecture strategies. Let's assume the following (architecture) strategies.
1. *Infrastructure*: Defining a new Service Oriented Architecture (SOA) based foundation for future applications
2. *Mobility*: Supporting new mobile devices
3. *Technology*: Definition of a new technology for building modern applications
4. *Apps*: New state-of-the-art applications, leveraging the given infrastructure and technology.

The second dimension covers all architecture relevant processes as well as essential architectural properties.
(a) *Architecture definition process*: The process to define the architecture of new software.
(b) *Requirement engineering process*: The process to define the business requirements.
(c) *Third party process*: The process of third party involvement in software development.

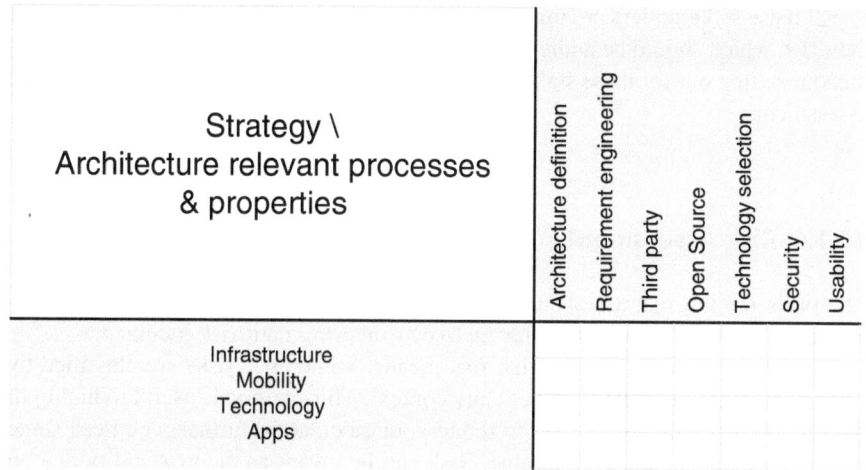

Fig. 10.3 Risk identification matrix

(d) *Open Source process*: The process of open source handling (which covers IP related questions) and influenced architecture property (which covers questions like supportability, adaptability, and so on).

(e) *Technology selection process*. The process of how to select the proper technology for new applications.

(f) *Security property*: The security property of the software architecture.

(g) *Usability property*: The software property related to the question how usable the software is. This can include aspects like ease-of-use and also aspects like how accessible it is for handicapped persons.

Figure 10.3 shows these two dimensions as risk identification matrix.

10.1.5 Identification of Stakeholders

For the risk identification the right selection of stakeholders is important. There are three kinds of stakeholders.

First, there is the group of senior managers, who contribute with their teams and departments to the selected strategies.

Second, there are managers, who define or own the architecture relevant processes, or take care of the architecture relevant attributes. These responsibilities can be centrally or de-centrally set up.

And finally, there are central teams, who do not necessarily have responsibilities for the strategy deliveries or the identified processes. But they know the risks of them quite well. Those teams can be central risk management teams, internal audit teams, or any other controlling team.

There might be even a fourth group of stakeholders, namely expert teams. For example there could be a central team who takes care of security of the developed products.

All these stakeholders are important and necessary to achieve a precise image of the risks, which should be addressed by Software Sustainability Audits. We recommend reaching out for these stakeholders and ask them to provide input to your risk assessment.

10.1.6 Risk Assessment

The basis for the risk assessment is the risk factor matrix. The stakeholders are supposed to fill all elements of this matrix by entering their risk judgment.

At first, we need to clarify what risk means. Sometimes risks are classified by 'high', 'medium' and 'low' without any context. This method is useful to highlight the severity of risks briefly. But to refine your calculation further, you need some context to understand the risk value. Risk can be meant as the probability that an event occurs. Risk can be the potential damage if the risk actually happens. Or risk might be meant as risk exposure, the probability multiplied by the potential impact. We recommend using risk exposures. The risk exposure is a fair value of the company's real danger. The sole probability can be high, but the potential impact harmless. The potential damage could be catastrophic, but the event is quite uncertain. The risk exposure gives you the mathematical or statistical value of the company's damage as an average.

It would certainly be best if stakeholders could enter their estimates of risk exposures. But that would be rather complicated in reality. To figure out the exact risk exposure, means to calculate values of the probability and the potential damage. That is certainly possible but takes time. And your stakeholders do not have time. As stated earlier: Keep it simple!

A good approach is to work with classifications.

Example 10.1.4
Use classification 0–3.
- 0 = almost no risk exposure.
- 1 = low risk exposure (<1 million US$).
- 2 = medium risk exposure (about 10 million US$).
- 3 = high risk exposure (>100 million US$).

These figures certainly vary and depend heavily on your company's size and revenue. A classification is easy to estimate. First, managers are used to dealing with money and have some gut-feeling about the magnitude of amounts. When they can compare the risks easily – 2 is a higher risk exposure than 1 – then this attempt of risk assessment is an easy task for them.

When you ask your stakeholders to return their estimates on the risks, don't forget to precisely explain the risk value you expect. If you miss this information, you will find many puzzled colleagues, who ask for guidance. Or the stakeholders

Strategy \ Architecture relevant processes & properties	Architecture definition	Requirement engineering	Third party	Open Source	Technology selection	Security	Usability
Infrastructure	3	0	1	1	2	3	0
Mobility	2	3	2	0	2	3	3
Technology	3	2	0	2	0	2	1
Apps	1	3	1	2	2	1	3

Fig. 10.4 Returned values from a stakeholder

do not dare to fill out your sheet and valuable input is missing. In worst case you will receive values with different meanings which falsify the total results.

Figure 10.4 shows an example of a filled out risk matrix.

10.1.7 Stakeholder Weights

Before you aggregate all incoming results, another question needs to be answered. Do you expect that every stakeholders vote will be treated the same? It is a good idea to group the stakeholders (as we have done before) and assign a certain weight to each group.

Example 10.1.5
You ask 20 development managers and just one central controlling group to participate in your risk evaluation. The controlling group could have quite some reliable risk information compared to the development managers. However, the number of development managers would easily outweigh the controlling manager. This approach would end up in unreliable risk values.

Weights again could be difficult to identify. The simplest and most pragmatic way is to just group the stakeholders and assign an equal weight to the groups.

Example 10.1.6
Take the four stakeholder groups: The development heads, expert teams, process owners and the central controlling teams. Calculate the average values for each team. Then, calculate the average value of these team values again.

Figure 10.5 shows an example of return values from stakeholders. Figure 10.6 aggregated these numbers assuming equal weights.

Strategy \ Architecture relevant processes & properties	Teams	Architecture definition	Requirement engineering	Third party	Open Source	Technology selection	Security	Usability
Infrastructure	development heads	2,8	1,0	1,0	1,0	2,0	3,0	0,0
Mobility		2,0	3,0	2,0	0,0	2,0	3,0	3,0
Technology		3,0	2,0	0,0	2,5	0,0	2,5	1,0
Apps		1,0	3,0	1,0	2,0	2,0	1,0	3,0
Infrastructure	experts	3,0	2,0	1,5	2,0	2,5	3,0	1,0
Mobility		3,0	2,5	2,0	1,0	3,0	3,0	3,0
Technology		2,0	1,5	0,5	3,0	2,0	3,0	0,0
Apps		3,0	3,0	2,0	1,0	0,0	1,5	2,5
Infrastructure	process owners	2,0	2,0	0,0	0,0	1,0	1,0	0,0
Mobility		0,0	2,0	1,0	0,0	1,0	2,0	2,0
Technology		1,0	1,0	0,0	2,5	0,0	3,0	0,0
Apps		1,0	2,0	0,0	1,0	0,0	2,0	3,0
Infrastructure	controlling	1,0	0,0	0,0	0,5	2,5	1,5	0,5
Mobility		2,5	2,0	3,0	0,0	1,0	2,8	2,0
Technology		0,0	0,5	0,0	3,0	2,5	2,0	0,5
Apps		3,0	2,5	0,0	2,5	0,0	2,8	2,0

Fig. 10.5   Risk assessment results from each stakeholder group

Strategy \ Architecture relevant processes & properties	Architecture definition	Requirement engineering	Third party	Open Source	Technology selection	Security	Usability
Infrastructure	2,2	1,3	0,6	0,9	2,0	2,1	0,4
Mobility	1,9	2,4	2,0	0,3	1,8	2,7	2,5
Technology	1,5	1,3	0,1	2,8	1,1	2,6	0,4
Apps	2,0	2,6	0,8	1,6	0,5	1,8	2,6

Fig. 10.6   Aggregated risk assessment

10.1.8 Collecting the Risk Input: Some More Variants of Risk Assessment

It is a matter of company culture how to collect the risk input. One option is to invite the stakeholders to a joint meeting. The discussion about possible risks during the meeting inspires the stakeholders to identify new risks through this fruitful exchange of thoughts. In particular, such a brainstorming session is helpful, when you start Software Sustainability Audits, or when you need initial risk input. In further risk assessments you can leverage previous risk assessment results and iterate on them. Some risks may have vanished or declined. Other new risks appear. Many, however, are still valid and can be reused with a slight reassessment.

This stakeholder team session also changes the procedure of risk evaluation. Instead of aggregation of individual values, the team can be asked to align their risk judgment and offer just one result. The advantage of this approach is obvious. From the perspective of others, everyone makes iterations on his own risk judgment. You can expect a more precise result.

However, the stakeholders are typically those in the company who have less time for this type of activity. It is a challenge, may be even impossible, to get all of them for a joint meeting. New technologies can be used to take care of this challenge. Web collaboration tools like a wiki could substitute for a meeting. Stakeholders can make their assessment in such a web collaboration tool, exchange with others their ideas about their rating. And they can vote for an aligned and common risk value in the web collaboration tool. This procedure keeps the advantage of the team approach and minimizes the given limitation of stakeholder availability.

There is another factor which might need to be considered. Risk assessment can also be a task your stakeholder would like to delegate to another person, e.g. to his Chief Operations Officer COO. Even though the task has been delegated to another person, the delegator reserves the right to adjust the proposed results and approve them. Moreover, risk is a delicate matter. There might be risks or underlying facts, which are not supposed to be unveiled to others. Risk and facts, which are strictly confidential, will hardly be mentioned in a team approach. Least of all will those confidential details be captured in a collaboration room. Those pieces of information can only be collected in one to one interview sessions. There are particular stakeholders, like risk managers, which should receive special treatment.

There are certainly many other variants on how to collect risk input. It depends on the company cultures and the individual roles of your stakeholders, which treatment is the best one, which balances best the advantages with fewest limitations. A combination of several approaches might be a wise approach to get the most reliable results.

10.1.9 Algorithm for Analysis of the Risk Assessment

With the approach described you get some valuable input for your Software Sustainability Audit planning. Still one question is open. How do you analyze the results? Which Software Sustainability Audit do you plan? We introduced two kinds of Software Sustainability Audits: Process audits and product audits. Actually you can find both types in the risk matrix. In the rows we find the products, the columns describe processes.

If we build the average for both columns and rows, we can easily rank processes and products according to their associated risks. By calculating just the average, we ignore the characteristics of the risk categories. Typically, risk categories are exponential; e.g. 1 means an average damage of 100 thousand dollar, 2 means 1 million, and 3 means 10 million. In order to consider this exponential function and still keep the calculation simple, we calculate the averages from the squares of each entry.

$$\text{Average} = \text{sqrt}(\,(\text{sqr}\,(\text{entry}\,1) + \text{sqr}\,(\text{entry}\,2) + \ldots)\,/\,n), \ n = \text{number entries}$$

Figure 10.7 shows an example of such an analysis. The result the analysis ranks a product audit for strategic topic mobility as number 1, the highest ranking process audits are security and requirement management.

There is another valid input you can retrieve from this analysis. When we take the highest values of the cells for the selected rows and columns, we can easily identify the most significant causes for the calculated risks. The associated counterpart rows and columns for these cells can be used as a focus theme for the identified Software Sustainability Audits. In Fig. 10.7 we highlighted these pivot cells.

> **Example 10.1.7**
> For the product audit in mobility, security should be a focus theme. Or for the process audit of requirement engineering, a sample from apps would be appropriate.

This algorithm helps to easily identify candidates for product audits and process audits according to their risks. Be aware there could be other audit themes which are not captured by this algorithm. In the example of Fig. 10.7 we marked such a special situation. The cell, which is the intersection of row "technology" and column "open source", is the one with the highest risk value of

Strategy \ Architecture relevant processes & properties	Architecture definition	Requirement engineering	Third party	Open Source	Technology selection	Security	Usability	average	rank
Infrastructure	2,2	1,3	0,6	0,9	2,0	2,1	0,4	1,5	4
Mobility	1,9	2,4	2,0	0,3	1,8	2,7	2,5	2,1	1
Technology	1,5	1,3	0,1	2,8	1,1	2,6	0,4	1,7	3
Apps	2,0	2,6	0,8	1,6	0,5	1,8	2,6	1,9	2
average	1,9	2,0	1,1	1,7	1,5	2,3	1,8	1,8	
rank	3	2	7	5	6	1	4		

Fig. 10.7 Analysis of risk assessment

all cells. We marked this cell. The corresponding semantic is that open source process for the strategic topic technology shows significant risk. Hence, it would be worth-while to capture this specific topic by a Software Sustainability Audit. Unfortunately, this topic is neither covered by the selected process audits nor by the selected product audits. This specific theme should be added as further Software Sustainability Audit.

10.1.10 Change of Risk Values

The risk values as calculated by the algorithm from 9.1.9 can be invalidated by certain factors. One influencing factor is time. Over time processes might get more mature or even more immature. For instance, when a process is redesigned, the associated risk can be higher. Also the strategic themes will mature over time or may even vanish after successful execution. Thus, the calculated risks need to be recalculated from time to time. The period of risk validity depends on the volatility of strategy and process changes.

Another invalidation factor is the existence of Software Sustainability Audits themselves. If a selected audit theme has already been covered by a Software Sustainability Audit, the risk should already be decreased. At least, the topic will be covered by follow-up audits. Those selected topics can be excluded by the Software Sustainability Audits plan.

10.1.11 Audit Requests During Risk Assessment

We described an algorithm to programmatically identify Software Sustainability Audits according to the associated risks. However, this does not guarantee a complete coverage of all high risk topics. There still might be unscreened risks. Why not tap your sources for other risks? When the stakeholders fill out the risk assessment template, they are already thinking about potential risks. Just allow them to further add Software Sustainability Audit candidates where they see value. Ask them to estimate the associated business risk. This enables you to compare the additionally gathered audit requests with the calculated ones. You can use these audit requests in your Software Sustainability Audit plan, when they show appropriate associated risk.

10.2 Risk-Based Reporting

"IS auditors should also understand the concept of materiality. i.e., the relative importance of findings based on business impact." [2]

In every Software Sustainability Audit the auditors collect many evidential artifacts. Evidence may lead an auditor to an extremely significant conclusion. The auditor may state a finding of utter relevance for the company. Or the evidence may be irrelevant. It has no important impact to the business. With the words from CISA ®, "auditors should understand the concept of materiality". They should differentiate the levels of materiality and apply them in their audits accordingly.

But what is the business impact? In cases like fraud or violation of laws the damage is almost obvious. You can estimate the financial damage of the fraud or the fines from respective authorities. And still, that does not comprise the complete business impact. As a potential damage that could result is the impact on a good company reputation. An involvement in such a case could tie up key resources and thus hamstring your business for some time. The real financial damage is embraced by many "could" statements indicating accompanied additional risks. The potential damage from a risk could be much higher than the original loss. A reputational damage could impact a sales and revenue loss in the magnitude of the primary fine payment.

In other cases you will not identify an occurred damage at all. It is just a potential damage, a risk.

Thus it is essential to describe the risks properly. Then finally, the risks will decide on the business impact and will describe the level of materiality.

In this section, we outline how a risk approach can be used in audit reporting. We walk through an audit risk assessment, starting with identification, continued by the question how to describe the risk properly. We add some ideas of risk calculation and finish with inspirations about your risk response in the audit report.

10.2.1 Identifying Risks

It is the Software Sustainability Auditors duties to consider business relevance of their findings. We take the risk approach to define and estimate the business impact and thus the relevance for the company. The first step of the risk approach is to identify the risks. Risks, which we derive from our audit findings, already define the severity. Risks are valuable and helpful already for the purpose of convincing management in taking proper actions.

Now, how can we identify proper risks of our findings? As we just have learned, a risk consists of two parts: the risk condition and the risk consequence. So, we can make use of both risk components to identify proper and relevant risks.

10.2.1.1 The Assumption Approach

We can take the risk condition for our risk identification. The main identification question is: "What can we easily assume from the identified facts?" Here, the auditors can bring in their software development and architecture experience. They can brainstorm what situation – based on their experiences – they can most certainly assume. They can even use identified risks conditions and validate them in the Software Sustainability Audits.

Example 10.2.1

Finding: an architecture document does not exist. As software architect you can assume (risk condition) that without an architecture document non-functional requirements are not reflected in the software. You can also assume that not all necessary integrations between software components are known by the developers. As (risk) a consequence, the architecture could not be as robust as needed with (risk impact) higher support costs than calculated. And there is a risk consequence that some integration is missing and (risk impact) the business or customers will escalate the missing integration, because that will lead to cumbersome manual steps or even data inconsistencies.

10.2.1.2 The Result Approach

While the assumption approach is the natural approach, we can identify the risk from the end result as well. Highly experienced software architects often skip the assumption part and compare given findings with results they have experienced. If you have a lot of experience in software development, you have established patterns for "what happens, if . . .?" Hence, it can be valuable to first ignore all assumptions and brainstorm potential results. The leading question is: "Have you experienced such a situation several times? What was the typical result in those situations?" You first look at the business impact. Then you can "reverse engineer" the risk conditions and try to validate them.

Example 10.2.2

Finding: Customers (or the business) were not involved in the software development process. From your diverse and vast experience you have often seen (and judge) that there is a risk consequence of invalid or incomplete functional coverage. A further software release is needed to fill those gaps and repair the invalid business functions. Why has this happened according to your experiences in the past? You can derive the assumption (the risk condition) that the business requirements were not understood by all developers.

10.2.2 Specifying Risks

Both identification approaches, as introduced in the previous section, are valid. Most of the time a combination of both approaches results in even more risks, which are worth being mentioned in your audit report. However, there are two important rules: First, clearly separate the risk description from the findings. Second, describe complete risks with all risk components.

You might sometimes feel a smooth transition between finding and risk. You may find it difficult to clearly extract the risks from the finding (or the finding from the risk). However, separation of findings from risks is essential, because there is a sharp dividing line: A finding is a fact, a risk is an assumption. For findings you must have evidence which proves your findings. Risk can be derived from your experience. Thus, you must clearly separate facts from probabilities. If you combine both without the needed separation, you will end up in discussions about your finding. A probable consequence is easy to debate, a fact remains a fact.

The risk description is your business card for showing business expertise. The risk description is the bridge from accepting facts to being motivated to take actions. In the end it is a business decision, how to deal with the risks. A risk can be accepted ("the risk is manageable"), a risk can be mitigated to lower the probability or to decrease the potential impact, and a risk can be remedied by resolving the issue as described in the finding. Complete risk descriptions help to convince on the last risk response type: it supports that actions are accepted which resolves the issues and risks. The gap between the noticed facts and the potential damage can be huge. A complete risk description makes the real risk more tangible.

With the risk condition, you show your architecture experience and depict deficiencies. It is always a judgment beyond pure facts, and a first step to understand the possible consequences of the current situation.

The risk consequences usually describe the internal impact. It typically explains what potential impact you can expect within your software development including software support. It is often a first business impact with respect to the software development and support costs. But still these are internal costs and as such not too relevant for business.

The risk impact is the tangible impact for the business. Those impacts are visible and should be avoided.

A complete risk description acts as a chain from pure fact (finding) to visible business impacts.

Example 10.2.3 (10.2.1 continued)
Let us take the example from the assumption approach in Sect. 10.2.1. The finding is "an architecture document does not exist." The risk consequence "no robust architecture" and "missing integration" could be seen as the CTO's problem. He has to fix it with the available resources. That still seems to be no damage for the company and the business. It is an internal damage. However, the risk impacts "customer escalations", "disrupted business" or "higher support costs" are external impacts as those directly and visibly affect the profit.

10.2.3 Weighing the Risks

We have learned from the risk basics to use risk exposure in order to calculate the risk value. Risk exposures are difficult to calculate, and can be too complex to compare. What does an isolated (without context) risk exposure value of $100,000 mean? Is that an acceptable or unacceptable risk? And how can we calculate the customer escalation costs at all?

10.2.3.1 Risk Classification

We want to provide you with two hints for weighing the risks. The first hint is regarding comparability of risk exposures. In order to reduce complexity, it is common to still use risk classifications. A risk value "high" is just easier to handle than an exact risk exposure value. Typically, there are classifications of "high", "medium" and "low" risk. In most cases this is just a synonym for a range of risk exposures.

Example 10.2.4
High risk = risk exposure > US $1,000,000
Medium risk = risk exposure between US $100,000 and US $1,000,000
Low risk = risk exposure < US $100,000

We know other, more complex risk classifications, where the classification range is the same (high, medium, low), but the evaluation is different. For instance, you can consider the pair, risk exposure and risk impact, for your classification. In such a classification system, you can express that a catastrophic impact still means a high risk, even if due to extremely low probability the risk exposure is low.

We do not want to elaborate on the risk classification systems we know. It is more important to understand the purpose and proper usages of such risk classification systems in the context of Software Sustainability Audits. In the end, the risk impact should lead to an agreement on appropriate measures. A classification of your risks can be used to also classify the measures and the reporting.

Example 10.2.5
High risk is essential for the company to understand and know about, thus this type of risk should always be reported to top management.
Medium risk is important for the company, but can be managed by mid management.
Low risk can be fully treated within the responsibility of the respective manager.

10.2.3.2 Risk Calculation

One of the most discussed questions in Software Sustainability Audits is: "How can we calculate the risk exposure?" In fact, that is not an easy task. We started with a mathematical equation to introduce an exact equation for risk exposure. And we will almost complete this chapter with heuristic approaches to find the estimated risk exposure value.

One valid attempt of retrieving a risk exposure value uses reference values from experiences in the past. This is like an extrapolation from historic events and values.

Example 10.2.6 (10.2.1 continued)
We continue the Example 10.2.1 above. We had the audit finding: "An architecture document does not exist." That led us to risk impacts of "higher support costs" and "customer escalations". The burning question now is: "How to estimate the financial damage of both impacts?" For both impacts – we assumed experience of similar cases – we could investigate old cases for comparison. We could compare support costs for software products where there were previous findings of missing architecture documents. We could find out what the customer escalation ratio (probability of an escalation in such a situation) is and figure out typical escalation costs.

We already see, calculating risk exposure by extrapolation can be useful, but is complicated. It can be used, when a high or very high risk is assumed. Then such research is helpful to validate the assumption and to convince with figures and facts.

In most cases, a heuristic approach is more efficient and most of the time equally effective. Still, experience and similar cases in the past are used for weighing the risk. This time, in the heuristic approach, we simply skip the concrete calculation of the risk exposure. Yes a concrete impact figure would be helpful to agree on taking actions. In the end, the risk classification is still important in deciding how to treat the audit finding. Finally, you must decide who should be aware of the finding. This depends on the magnitude of the risk exposure, and less on the concrete value. The heuristic approach takes the definition of the risk classification into account and assigns the risk classification according to the classification impact.

Example 10.2.7 (10.2.1 continued and using Example 10.2.4)
We still have the finding: "An architecture document does not exist." We look at the risk classifications. High means report to top management. From the architecture experience we know that architectural work is usually not addressed by top management. So, we choose either medium or low risk. The difference, according to the definition in Example 10.2.4., is the company impact and the level of management needed to treat it appropriately. If we talk about a software development, which is comparable to other software development projects, we certainly can leave the finding to lower management responsibility: Risk classification is low. If, however, we audited a strategic development project using new and unknown technologies, the finding could be worth being monitored by mid management as well: Risk classification is medium.

These descriptions of defining the business impact, to evaluate the risk exposure are certainly not complete. In this book we can only scratch the surface of possible risk measuring methods. However, we selected those aspects, which can be used as a fair foundation to treat risks in audits reports appropriately.

10.2.4 The Risk Response

A proper risk based audit report contains three risk-related elements. Two of them have been already touched: The facts, which we report as findings, and the risk, which we judge based on the finding and our experience. The third and still missing element is the risk response. The risk response is the way in which a known risk is treated. A manager can respond to risks in different ways.

- A risk can be accepted and potential damage can be managed
- A risk can be watched or monitored; a decision for further risk response is taken later, depending on changes of the risk situation
- A risk can be mitigated to limit the potential damage (risk impact)
- A risk can be mitigated to limit the risk probability
- A risk can be remedied by resolving the issue (respond to the finding)

The type of risk response depends on the severity of the risk on the magnitude of the risk exposure or the level of the risk classification. A low risk can be accepted. Medium and high risks deserve other means of treatment. Hence, the risk impact (or risk classification) is a natural input parameter for a decision on an appropriate risk response.

A Software Sustainability Auditor should have these options of risk responses in mind. "IS [information system] auditors should also understand the concept of materiality. i.e., the relative importance of findings based on business impact" [2]. The types of risk responses become important in the audit report. Stating the findings and judging the related risks provides the responsible managers

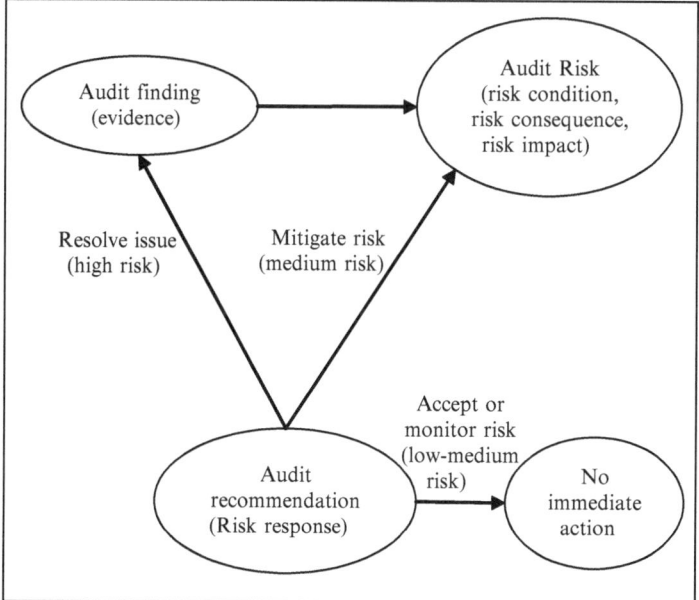

Fig. 10.8 Recommendation as risk response

transparency about the risk. The recommendation to the finding is the risk response, where the auditor provides advice. The recommendation on actions should consider materiality. It could be more efficient to accept a low risk and it could be hazardous to not resolve the issue for a high risk. The audit recommendations should balance the severity of the finding related risk with an appropriate risk response type. Figure 10.8 gives an overview of risk responses depending on the risk categories.

10.3   Summary

In this chapter you have learned, how risk assessment can steer both your audit portfolio and your audit reporting. You encountered a proposal, how you can combine several dimensions like software development processes, products and also stakeholders, who are involved in making risk based Software Sustainability Audit proposals. You can use the proposed approach to properly address your risks and get transparency on the most relevant parts of your software development.

The second section explained how you can use the element "risk" to shape your audit report to a business relevant reporting.

References

1. Ramamurthy, A.B., Gil, E.G., Laube, M., & Yshinari, T. (2010). Assessment of architecture audit in a large enterprise software company. MBA thesis.
2. Certification Information System Auditor (CISA), Review Manual 2010, KS1.8, ISBN 978-1-60420-092-8.

Think About It!: Effective Governance

What's in It for Me?

In this chapter we look at the effectiveness of different control mechanisms. These controls should ensure the achievement of objectives subject to governance. For a look at these controls based on your IT role, see the following sections.

CIO/CTO

From an executive point of view, it is important that strategic objectives are effectively achieved. This is not quite easy when it comes to software development. You need mechanisms that provide assurance about the status and progress of a software solution. We discuss the relation to traditional governance of IT processes in Sect. 11.2. It is essential to understand why the traditional approach is less effective for software development. For this purpose, we give some relevant examples in Sect. 11.3. You can limit your reading to these sections. The remainder of the chapter is an in-depth discussion of the problem space. Give this chapter to the person responsible for defining your software development processes.

Software Architect

The topic of internal controls from a theoretical perspective is probably new to you. In a development organization, such controls are things like quality gates, review meetings, or spread sheets you have to fill out. You might have a negative association with such controls. The reason could be an impression that the taken measures are ineffective and do not add value. This is annoying, especially as development projects are under constant pressure to deliver results.

We have based the discussion in this chapter on relevant examples from software development. The first part outlines the core issue. In Sect. 11.4 we

(continued)

R. Gutbrod and C. Wiele, *The Software Dilemma*, Management for Professionals,
DOI 10.1007/978-3-642-27236-3_11, © Springer-Verlag Berlin Heidelberg 2012

provide the theoretical background of internal controls. Although outside your classical territory, we recommend reading it for better understanding of the mechanisms.

Auditor
As an auditor, you are – most likely – familiar with assessing the effectiveness of internal controls. This is a standard audit procedure. Nevertheless, software development is somehow different. Strict processes and formal controls do not apply in many cases. This chapter provides the chance for better understanding these specific aspects. If you have already audited development projects, take the examples from this chapter and compare them with your experience. When asked to shape or re-shape a development process this chapter (and Chap. 12) can be consulted for making the process effective.

11.1   Sustainable Software: Not Without Effective Governance

In the course of this book we tried bringing across the importance of sustainable software. Different influencing factors were discussed as well. We promoted the ideas of governance and Software Sustainability Audits. Audits are a very specific means of governance, only applicable to a limited extent. The limitation is induced by the required effort. Assuring sustainable software requires governance approaches with a higher scalability and reach. Besides scalability and reach, the applied governance means have to fulfill two additional requirements. They have to be effective and they have to fit to an empowered environment. Empowerment is a necessary prerequisite for successful software development.

In this chapter, we analyze the different aspects of governance measures in depth. The discussion is intended to foster the understanding that sustainable software requires effective governance.

11.2   The Standard: The Traditional Governance Approach

Let us briefly outline at what we call the traditional approach of governance. Governance – whether IT or corporate governance – is established to align processes and products with a defined strategy. It should reduce the risk of failure. Ensuring legal compliance is a frequent driver for governance activities. The business and IT strategies – or to be more precise, the derived goals and objectives – build the center of the governance universe. It is all about achieving these goals.

So, why do processes exist? The main purpose of processes is ensuring the achievement of our goals and objectives. This should be done in a reliable, repeatable, and maybe even predictable way. Processes that do not effectively and efficiently support the defined goals should be changed (or eliminated). Yes, it might sound strange to some people, but processes *can* be changed.

Without going into too much theory, we still need to understand what a process is. A process is a set of rules and procedures that people executing the process have to follow. If you follow the rules and procedures, in the best case, you achieve the intended result.

For IT-related processes there are great frameworks like COBIT (*Control Objectives for Information and Related Technology*) or ITIL (*IT Infrastructure Library*) that help when implementing best practices. You want 99,999% availability of your production system? You need an authorization concept with corresponding processes for granting system access? No problem, there are good and best practices available. Surely, it takes effort, resources, and expertise to get sound processes. For many objectives there are corresponding blueprints for processes, rules, and procedures. These will help enable you when achieving the related objectives. Unfortunately, this can give the misleading impression that all objectives are covered by corresponding best practices. We will come to it in a moment.

What role does auditing play? From the traditional perspective, auditing is applied to check for compliance. Do people follow the rules, or do they deviate (including fraudulent behavior)? Compliance can be checked against internal rules, as well as external rules like legal requirements. Besides this traditional understanding, audits increasingly focus on the optimization of processes. For instance, the assessment of a process can be based on one of the existing process maturity models like CMMI (*Capability Maturity Model Integration*) or PEMM (*Process and Enterprise Maturity Model*). Industry standards or other known best practices can also act as a reference.

This is all well known, especially to (IT-) auditors. CIOs and CTOs should also be familiar with it. For architects, it might be a little different. They are exposed to the rules without explanation of the ideas behind.

Nevertheless, this traditional approach of setting up rules – no question valid and valuable – turns out to be ineffective and inefficient in some cases. Let us look at this.

11.3   Lost?: Where Is My Best Practice?

No surprise, we are looking at the software development process. This book is about *software development*. To be more precise, this book is about developing sustainable software. Keep this in mind. With all the discussion about governance and auditing, this can easily get lost along the way. Software development differs from other IT-related processes. This has an impact on the way it has to be governed.

You might wonder why we think software development differs from other standard IT processes. Hasn't software been developed since decades? Aren't there best practices already established? Yes, software has been developed since decades. And yes, there are models for the development lifecycle. Different accepted approaches like the waterfall model, or agile methodologies exist. Still, there is something to remember. Software development is a *creative* process. It is more like an art than engineering. This can be understood easily. If software development would be predictable, there would be no competition on best products. Anyone with the intention to provide software would come to the same solution. There could be competition on the price, time, or additional services, but there would be no competition on the product itself. However, this is not the case. Software companies do compete on the best products. You can perform better or worse with software development. There is not the one best practice for software development. If this were not the case, there would not be so much unsustainable software developed and delivered. Today's results highly depend on the skills and the experience of the people developing the software, and success is not so much a result from effective development processes.

This is the difference as compared to many other IT processes. Outsourcing IT operations can only work because the corresponding processes can be standardized. Software development cannot; at least not the creative – and thus differentiating – part. This is best understood by looking at some examples. We look at some areas where software development projects often struggle. The examples comprise business objectives that are essential for making software successful and sustainable. Some examples have already been discussed in the context of Software Sustainability Audits. We will go beyond the previous discussion, trying to understand the issues in more depth.

11.3.1 What Do My Customers Want?: Go Ask Them!

Imagine you want to develop a new piece of software. This software will be used by somebody. Either you intend to sell the software (maybe bundled with some kind of hardware), or it is intended for internal usage. In any case, you should know what is expected by your customers and users. This is one of the key success factors. Sure, a software development project can be messed up at different stages, but failing in the identification of customer requirements and expectations is one of the most promising ways to end up in a disaster. Why? Any subsequent decision depends on the customer and market requirements. What technology is the software built on? What is the right architecture to serve the needs of the customers? Which features are developed in different releases of the software? What kind of service and support do I have to provide for the software? The answers to all these questions depend on the customers' expectations. This sounds trivial, but doing a great job here is anything but trivial.

So, how do I know what my customers want? How do I ensure development meets my customers' expectations? Well, this is not what we are going to tell you in this book. Instead we take a different perspective – the governance perspective. From this point of view, the central question is phrased differently.

We put it this way: What kind of boundary conditions do I have to establish to ensure my development teams will (at least most likely) develop software products that meet customer expectations?

There is a fine but important difference in this question. If you ask how to know what your customers expect, you have to look at the concrete project and customer environments. However, the right approach for identifying customer requirements highly depends on this context. Trying to give answers for any of the possible circumstances and contexts is a hopeless endeavor. Taking the governance perspective, we will help you finding the best approach suited for your situation.

This will take some time to develop. Let us slowly explore the terrain. Software development requires different roles. For example, product managers, software architects, software developers, quality managers, and technical writers. These roles come in different flavors, and can be named differently in each organization. Sometimes product management is called marketing, and architects are called engineers. Smaller organizations might not have dedicated product managers. This is not important for the purpose of our discussion. It is sufficient to stick to this set of roles. Surely, there are other roles surrounding the core development process like administrators running the technical infrastructure, but they are not involved in the actual development process. We will not take them into our consideration.

11.3.1.1 Whom We Need: Roles in the Development Process

All people involved in the core development process – no matter which role they have – require a certain understanding of the customer environment and expectations. This is essential making the project successful. Let us look at some aspects for the different roles.

Product managers are responsible for rolling in requirements from customers. They need to understand the addressed markets, customers, and other boundary conditions. They define the target market, and prioritize requirements accordingly.

Architects need a good understanding of the customer and market requirements. Of special interest are the non-functional requirements like performance, scalability, or supportability. A sustainable architecture can only be defined based on a good understanding of these kinds of requirements. We will look at this specific aspect in detail below.

Developers have to implement the functional requirements and the architecture defined by product management and architects. It is quite a challenge to define requirements in such a way that there is no room for interpretation. If you have experience with off-shore development, you know what we mean. If the process does not ensure developers having the correct understanding, the whole software product is at jeopardy. Whatever it takes, you should ensure your developers know what is expected by the customers.

Quality managers and engineers are testing the software according to the specification and defined test cases. The tests have to reflect the way the software will be used by customers. Without a clear understanding of what customers expect, and how they will use the software, such a task will be of limited success.

Technical writers have to document the product in a way making it easy for customers to consume. Think for a moment. Can you recall a (technical) documentation that could have been improved by focusing on the user? Okay, customer focus is also important for technical writers.

11.3.1.2 Before We Start: The Boundary Conditions

In brief, all the different roles in software development require understanding the targeted customers. What's next? Before we start, we have to be clear about the boundary conditions under which the software will be developed. The boundary conditions can be very different across different software development projects. Finding the best way of customer engagement we need clarity. For instance:

- *Relation*: The targeted customers and consumers can be internal or external to your company. The software product might be intended for selling to customers, or you develop software for in-house usage.
- *Layering*: You might have different software layers where lower-level components are consumed by higher layers. In this case the "customers" of the lower levels are the consumers on the higher levels. You need to take all stakeholders for the final product into account. This includes stakeholders from the different layers.
- *Reach*: The software might be for a single customer only, or it could be intended as standard software package for many customers.
- *Lifecycle*: The software project might be a complete new development or an enhancement of an existing product (for instance a feature pack).
- *Customers*: You might have existing customers willing to cooperate on the development project. Or you might have to start from scratch without customers.

The list is by far not exhaustive. It is intended to give a good idea of the variety of influencing factors for a software development project. Now, remember what we are looking for. We need a setup or process that best ensures meeting our customer's expectations. As an initial step, this includes correctly identifying our customer's expectation.

11.3.1.3 The Key: Governing Customer Engagement

What is the right way to interact with your customers? Which governance model do we have to embrace from an executive perspective? How do we best ensure that development projects effectively take customer requirements into account?

Software products developed with insufficient incorporation of customer requirements risk a complete failure. They might end up as long-tail products. Even worse, we might have to re-implement them at a later time. This risk of failure needs to be minimized. In other words, the chance of success needs to be increased. Let us look at some options.

As a first option, we can try formal rules. The advantage of formal rules is the ability of a formal compliance check (maybe even performed automatically). If a formal rule is effective, it is sufficient to check for compliance to ensure the corresponding objective is achieved. The important term is *effective*. What about formal rules for gathering customer and market requirements? Let us try to use "Software development projects have to involve ten customers in the project to gather requirements". A formal check of this rule is possible. At some quality gate during development the project would have to provide a list with ten customers on it. What would happen? 100% guarantee, the project would provide a list with ten names on it. Would the software reflect the requirements of the customers? Maybe it would, but surely not because of this rule. Getting a list with ten names is easy, getting the right requirements not. Are there any other formal rules that would work better? Not that we know of. The right approach of interacting with customers highly depends on the boundary conditions. Is it a new product, or an extension to an existing one? Are we talking about 10, 1,000, or 10,000 person days of development? Is it a radical new approach, or a safe harbor? Is there an active user group, willing to cooperate for new developments? Trying to put all these aspects into formal rules is a hopeless endeavor. And even you think you succeeded – try it out. You will see projects failing with all formal rules perfectly met.

Okay, if formal rules don't apply here, what else? What about empowerment? We empower our development teams to do whatever they think is required to do. If formal rules don't apply, let's try the other extreme (which by the way seems to be a typical pattern of human behavior). Big and successful software companies have been built by bright and empowered people. Their freedom probably was not limited by any governance and formal rules. These people had been empowered to make great things happen. So, why not completely empower the development teams, leaving governance and control out? Just let them do what they think needs to be done. Hmm, for small start-ups this might be the right approach. For any larger corporation, unfortunately it is not. This is easily understood by looking at all the start-ups failing along their way (surely for different reasons). These start-ups had been empowered doing the right things – and failed. This is the point. The essence of governance is mitigating the risk of failure. Leaving customer interaction completely up to the teams *can* result in great products. There are product managers, architects, and developers that will surely do the right thing. However, you will also see the opposite. Without any *effective* control activity, the risk of failure is not mitigated.

We provide a possible solution to this issue in Chap. 12, but before this we do two things. First, we will give two similar examples of business objectives facing the same dilemma. Secondly, we will give some more theoretical background from the governance perspective.

11.3.2 Center of Sustainability: Non-functional Requirements

A specific subset of the customer requirements are the non-functional requirements. Non-functional requirements cover qualities like performance, scalability, supportability, internationalization, upgrade paths, etc. Non-functional requirements build the backbone of sustainable software. Note that there is one issue with non-functional requirements – they lack attention. Functional requirements often receive the main attention during product development. Non-functional requirements, on the contrary, are an endangered species. The discussion around software development is often extremely functional-oriented. Functions and features are much more tangible than non-functional qualities. It is obvious that a system providing all kinds of non-functional features but lacking functionality required by customers is doomed. The reverse is equally true, but less obvious. The nature of non-functional requirements makes them hard to grasp. The absence of non-functional qualities often surfaces only late in software implementation projects. It could even become only evident when the software is deployed and used at the customer site. Judging the effective performance and scalability might require deployment and configuration in the dedicated customer environment. Issues with the ability of upgrading a system to new version might even occur years later.

Understanding the relevance of non-functional requirements for the definition of a sustainable architecture is essential. What if performance requirements have not sufficiently been taken into account during development? How could the chosen architecture and design ensure meeting the performance expectations of the customers? The fundamental architecture cannot easily be changed. A complete re-implementation might become necessary to meet customer expectations.

We are facing the same challenge as before: Ensuring that non-functional requirements are effectively taken into account during development projects. Once again, the two extremes – formal controls and full empowerment – are rather bad candidates.

11.3.3 Make Them Clear: Product-Specific Business Objectives

Honestly, who developed software products in the past and was 100% sure what they were good for? When auditing a software project, which auditor was always convinced that the project team knew what it was doing? Has it always been clear for what reason the product was built? Which market was addressed? Who were the targeted users? How did the central theme of the product fit to customer expectations and requirements?

Software projects can fail for many reasons – bad project management, technical difficulties not foreseen upfront, and changing markets, to name just a few. One major reason for failure is the lack of clear objectives for the project. Only clearly defined objectives allow projects to have a direction and stay on track. These business objectives define the targeted market, intended market share, customer segment, and required key functionality. Furthermore, the priorities of the different – often competing – objectives have to be clear. This is required to ensure the most important objectives are kept in focus whenever decisions have to be taken. Most software projects face the challenge of reducing the scope to meet the timeline. Lack of priorities between the different objectives could lead to random scope reductions. The result could be a useless product.

The same pattern emerges. The definition of clear objectives for a specific product cannot be controlled formally. Our experience with governance and Software Sustainability Audits verified the risk of unclear objectives. The activities showed that often objectives are not defined appropriately to guide development. Take the example where the target market for a product was defined too broadly. In this case, the functional requirements could not be covered by the development team with the given time and resources. This could result in the product not meeting the expectations of any customer in the target market. Or take the example where the objectives have been defined as very marketing-oriented, leaving too much room for interpretation. This would bear the risk of not meeting the intended objectives. What do you think about "Develop a superior product that will revolutionize the way people work"? Yes, anyone wants to build such a product, but is it enough to guide development along its path? Probably not. What does superior mean? And what is the revolutionary way people will work? Nobody will know what to do based on such an objective.

Project-specific objectives have to be understood by all people involved in the development process. This is similar to understanding customer requirements. A developer, as well as the technical writer, has to have an understanding of the objective. Everyone has to make decisions here and there. Who will be the user of the software? How many customers will use it? Where do my customers reside that I have to support? All of these are important aspects that a developer (or anyone else in the development team) has to take into account when implementing certain features.

The development process has to ensure that all involved parties have a common understanding of the business objectives set for the project, not only a few.

11.3.4 Recap: What Have We Learned?

Let us briefly recap what we learned from these examples. The common pattern shared by these examples comprises the following aspects:

- *Lack of Process*: For the specific examples, it is not possible to define a detailed process upfront that would assure achieving the respective business objectives at the end of the development process.
- *Ineffective Formal Rules*: Formal rules (checklist, existence check, etc.) are not effective for the given examples. This does not mean formal rules do not apply in general, but there is a certain set of objectives that cannot be achieved by setting up formal rules.
- *Beyond Empowerment*: Pure empowerment without control might be successful but does not fulfill the requirements of corporate governance. Corporate governance requires a certain level of control to limit the risk of failure.
- *Common Understanding*: The development process has to ensure that all involved parties have a common understanding of the business objectives and requirements to be achieved or implemented.

We introduce the concept of Control Self-Assessment (CSA) in Chap. 12 as a response to this problem space. First, we will put some more effort in understanding and generalizing the class of problems we address here. To do this, we have to get a bit more formal.

11.4 Internal Controls: The Essence of Governance

Unfortunately, the world of governance and auditing comes with its own terminology, and this terminology is usually not familiar to people working in software development, so we have to find a way to address the gap between the two. We could invent our own terminology or using terms familiar to developers, but this would make life for auditors harder, and one goal of this book is to foster mutual understanding. This sometimes requires getting used to each other's terminology. We – the authors – have a development background and ourselves, we had to pave the way to the world of governance and auditing.

The main term to get used to is called *internal control*. There are different but similar definitions of this term. In the text box below we provide the definitions given by ISACA and COSO (see [1, 2]).

ISACA Definition of Internal Control

The policies, procedures, practices and organizational structures designed to provide reasonable assurance that business objectives will be achieved and that undesired events will be prevented or detected and corrected.

COSO Definition of Internal Control

Internal control is broadly defined as a process, affected by an entity's board of directors, management and other personnel, designed to provide reasonable assurance regarding the achievement of objectives in the following categories:

- Effectiveness and efficiency of operations.
- Reliability of financial reporting.
- Compliance with applicable laws and regulations.

These two definitions are quite general and broad. We can see that internal controls comprise all measures taken by a company assuring the achievement of business objectives. What does this mean for the software development process? Basically, all measures taken to ensure the success of a software development project can be seen as internal controls. The requirement to write and review specifications, quality gates, sprint reviews, and code scans are all examples of internal controls. It is just unusual terminology for people working in software development.

Now, remember what we learned about corporate governance in Chap. 3. One of the requirements imposed by corporate governance is monitoring the effectiveness of the implemented controls. If a control appears to be ineffective, corresponding corrective measures have to be taken. This makes sense. Ineffective controls cause effort but do not help achieve your goals. People might be annoyed by the burden imposed by the control – even more if it does not add value.

It is not always easily understood that a certain measure (or internal control as we learned) is ineffective. To this end, we have to dig a little deeper. We will look at different types of controls to understand how effective they are in the context of software development.

11.4.1 Prevent, Detect, Correct: Internal Control Types

Let us start with the different types of internal controls. Internal controls can be classified in different ways. We adopt the common classification of preventive, detective, and corrective controls. We have a dedicated focus on the software development process. So we limit the discussion to this specific context.

11.4.1.1 It Shall Not happen!: Preventive Controls

As the name suggests, preventive controls comprise a class of measures intended to prevent something from happening. Preventive controls should avoid situations that put important business objectives at jeopardy. This is best understood by looking at some examples. Here are examples of preventive controls applied in software development.

- *Employ Only Qualified Developers and Train Them According to the Needs*: This should not only be good practice but also obvious as being a preventive control. If you want to be successful with a software development project, you should run it with qualified people. Your business objective is to deliver high-quality software. By employing only qualified people, the risk of failure is mitigated.
- *Development Policies and Programming Guidelines*: Most development policies and programming guidelines can be seen as preventive controls. These documents describe how development has to be performed. For example, programming guidelines might define a naming convention or require a certain component structure that developers have to adhere to. The business objective would be the delivery of maintainable and supportable code.
- *The Technology Strategy for Software Development*: The technology strategy comprises aspects like allowed programming languages, supported operating systems, or the user interface technology. The strategy prevents the proliferation of technologies beyond accepted boundaries. The corresponding business objective could be the harmonization of the software landscape. The result would be operational cost and better supportability.
- *Process Flow Definitions*: The definition of a process flow can be regarded as a preventive control. Here we have to be careful, we are only talking about the process flow, not the complete process. The flow defines the different steps of the process. This flow has to assure the achievement of corresponding business objectives.

11.4.1.2 Little Brother of Sherlock: Detective Controls

As seen from the examples above, preventive controls define the direction. But not all controls effectively ensure that this direction is taken. Take a real life example. The speed limit on a motorway is a preventive control. It is intended to prevent severe accidents, excessive noise emission, or maybe environmental pollution. Is this control effective by itself? Apparently, not. Otherwise there would be no need for speed traps. They remind us of the rule. Speed traps are detective controls.

We require some measures capable of detecting deviations from the intended direction or status. A deviation exposes the risk of missing our business objective. A programming language not permitted by the technology strategy might put the support concepts at jeopardy. This would negatively impact the operational costs.

Detective controls comprise any measure to detect deviations from an intended status. Only the detection allows responding to the implied risk. As before, we will explain the concept of detective controls by examples. We make a small but significant addition here. For our upcoming discussion we distinguish two sub-classes of detective controls – formal and qualitative controls.

Formal Detective Controls: You Can Count on Me!

Formal controls can be applied without human interaction and judgment. This does not mean that they are always applied without human interaction. It means that theoretically the control could be implemented without the requirement of human interaction. These controls can be automated. Let us look at some examples.

- *Automated Code Checks (e.g. Syntax Checks)*: Automated code checks are a very popular and often very effective control. Syntax checks in an integrated development environment (IDE) compare written code with defined syntax structures. In case of deviations the syntax is highlighted and an error message is issued. This does not have to take place while the developer is online. Often, these kinds of checks are applied offline during nightly builds. The concept of code scanning is also applied to detect security flaws, open source snippets, or similar code-related checks.

- *Checksums and Hash Algorithms*: To protect your code from unintended or unauthorized changes, checksums or hash algorithms can be applied. The automated check detects deviations. In case of changes, the computed value does not match the original one.

- *Existence Checks*: Not unusual, your development process might require the creation of specification or design documents. The existence of these documents could be formally (and automatically) checked. These kinds of documents have to be uploaded to a specific repository where it is accessible for an automated check. But is this check effective? Think about the intention for the rule. Has the rule been defined to ensure the pure existence of the document? Probably not. Nevertheless, the existence check is very popular in some audit scenarios as it is very easy to apply.

- *Checklists*: Imagine your development process requires fulfilling certain requirements of similar type. For instance, think about guidelines to develop accessible user interfaces, or secure code. Each of these guidelines might contain a set of requirements that have to be complied with. This set of requirements (or deliverables) can be combined into a checklist. This checklist has to be filled by the development team to prove compliance. The checklist itself is a formal control. It could be automatically processed.

Formal controls have the charm of being highly scalable through automation. Formal controls should be applied whenever possible if they are effective. This approach is most efficient with a high scalability – if effective.

Qualitative Detective Controls: Quality Counts!

Besides formal controls, there is a set of detective controls that explicitly require human action and judgment. We call this class of measures qualitative controls. This again is best understood by looking at some concrete examples from software development.

- *Reviews*: Reviews are a very common type of qualitative controls. They are applied at different stages of the software development lifecycle. During planning and design of a solution, specification and design reviews are applied. If an agile methodology is applied, something like sprint reviews are conducted to monitor the progress of development. At the final stage of development, we have an acceptance test to review the achievement of defined and agreed functional and non-functional qualities. All reviews have the common goal of identifying issues or deviations from a planned status. Reviews cannot be formalized and automated. Successful reviews require skilled people with an understanding of the topic at hand. We will take a closer look at reviews as qualitative controls when analyzing their effectiveness.
- *Product Audits*: From a content perspective, audits – and especially product audits – have much in common with reviews. They are much more formal, and often with a stronger focus on detecting issues than reviews. On the other hand, audits have a very limited scalability. Auditing requires dedicated resources. Only samples can be analyzed. A broad application is not feasible in the context of software development.
- *Quality Gates*: Specific milestones during the development process, called quality gates, focus on the assessment of the overall status of the project. Certain deliverables are defined for each of the quality gates. These deliverables could be the provisioning of project plans, compliance reports, or proof of certain software qualities. Some deliverables might have the character of formal controls. The overall quality gate requires human assessment to decide on passing or failing.

Most qualitative controls lack scalability. Skilled people are required to implement qualitative controls. Qualitative controls often cannot be applied across the board. They are limited to samples. Also qualitative controls depend on the judgment of humans. This can never be as accurate and independent as formal controls. Nevertheless, qualitative controls are essential for any development process.

11.4.1.3 Oops, It Happened!: Corrective Controls

Okay, the speed limit has been set, and we were caught by a speed trap. What's next? We feel guilty and promise to do better in the future. To support the process of becoming better citizens, we will receive a friendly reminder – a ticket for speeding. This is an example of a corrective control. More drastic corrective controls apply if we are not caught in a speed trap, but instead cause an accident. Things like ambulance and towing services, as well as the overhauling of the guardrails are corrective controls in this case. There are corresponding corrective controls available for software development. Corrective controls are always intended to limit the impact of an unfavorable situation. You try to prevent such situations by implementing preventive controls, or to detect them early in the process by detective controls. Still, situations occur that require a dedicated response limiting the impact. Here are some examples.

- *Mitigation Plans*: One of your detective controls might have revealed an issue somewhere in the software. If the issue cannot be resolved immediately, a mitigation plan is often put in place. This mitigation plan defines a mutually agreed roadmap to resolve the issue.
- *Postponing Shipments*: You developed according to your plans. You did your best to achieve the objectives set for the software product. Still, at the final stage of the project, you have not reached the defined quality criteria. Delivering the software at that stage might not be a good idea. Instead a controlled postponement of the delivery is a possible corrective control ensuring sufficient time to resolve the remaining issues.
- *Customer Escalation Management*: You did your best to deliver a high quality product to the market. Nevertheless, you face customer escalations at some point in time. This might not be your fault. Software can be used by customers in unforeseeable or unintended ways (yes, customers do this). Whatever the reason for an escalation might be, you are better prepared by implementing an escalation management team. This team can react to an escalation, limiting the impact on all sides.

Understanding the concept of corrective controls is important to grasp the overall concept of internal controls. Nevertheless, our intention is to reduce the need for corrective controls. The approach is to improve the development process and the corresponding preventive and detective controls. We will not dig further into the area of corrective controls, but rather focus on the other two types.

11.4.2 Are They Worth It?: Effectiveness of Internal Controls

Internal controls are intended to support or ensure the achievement of business objectives. Consequently, we have to ensure that the applied controls are indeed effective, but there is an additional aspect we have to take into account. The implementation of internal controls requires effort. Controls also put a certain burden on the process, or to be more precise, on the people executing the process. For instance, the requirement of a design review during the software development process imposes additional effort on the development team. If the affected people consider the control as ineffective, the acceptance of the control will suffer. In the worst case, the acceptance of effective controls suffers as well. What is an *ineffective* control from the acting peoples' perspective? It is effort that does not add value – or more drastically phrased – waste.

One more aspect has to be taken into account. If an ineffective control is actually considered effective, the control might provide a false level of security. You think you applied sufficient internal controls to safeguard your business. A detective control is ineffective and thus does not provide any warning about a deviation from the intended status. This might hit you much later because you expect that deviations would be detected. Let's look at an example. You are developing software for a given market segment. You have setup internal controls that intended to support the correct identification of customer requirements. If these controls are ineffective, your team will develop software that is at high risk to not meet customer expectations. You are not alerted of this situation by the ineffective controls. The issue might not be discovered during the development process. Maybe it is only discovered at the time of delivery to the customer. This is when it is hard to fix.

Having seen the implications, it is of essential importance to understand which control types are effective. After briefly looking at the effectiveness of preventive controls, we will focus the discussion on detective controls.

11.4.2.1 Effectiveness of Preventive Controls

Through the example of speeding we have learned that preventive controls alone might not be as effective as required. You need to complement the set of controls by detective and corrective controls. In the context of developing sustainable software, one main type of preventive controls is relevant. These are the definitions of development processes, procedures, and guidelines. The intention of defining processes and procedures in standard software development is the repeated execution by different groups. The intention is a constant level of quality. Strict processes only make sense if they ensure the effective achievement of business objectives. There is a prerequisite to make strict rules effective: The business objectives can be achieved independent of the acting people. In other words, there is no need for a specific expertise required. We have seen by our initial examples that strict rules can be inappropriate and thus ineffective.

Guidelines and procedures have a more dedicated focus than a complete process. They can be made more effective. For instance, development guidelines for developing secure software can be made quite effective. This has to be understood in the sense that by following the guidelines, secure software – up to the current state of the art – can be achieved.

Another important preventive control is the training of developers. Here we have a specific case. Having the right development skills is only a prerequisite for successful software development. While it will not ensure good software products, the absence of skills will definitely lead to failure.

We have to keep in mind that effective *preventive* controls are not sufficient to achieve business objectives. These controls have to be enforced and complemented by means of effective *detective* controls.

11.4.2.2 Effectiveness of Detective Controls

We now turn to detective controls. These controls are implemented to discover deviations from an intended status of a process or product. Judging the effectiveness of detective controls requires understanding the intended state. If you don't know the intended state, it is hard to detect a deviation from it. Simple as that. However, do we always know the intended state? Is it always possible to know the intended state? This cannot be answered in general. We use our examples to shed some light on this important topic.

We introduced two types of detective controls above – formal and qualitative ones. Again, we treat these two types separately.

Formal Detective Controls

Formal detective controls can only be effective if one prerequisite is fulfilled: The state of the corresponding business objective can be assessed formally. This sounds trivial, but it is not always obvious. We discussed the example of customer requirements management. The business objective is to ensure the right level of customer engagement. The development teams are required to provide a list of ten customers. It is expected that they have interacted with these customers during the requirements engineering process. A list of ten customers is something that can be formally checked. If there are fewer customers on the list, an automatic alert could be triggered. Is this control effective? No, it cannot. The reason is that the right level of customer interaction cannot be assessed formally. It requires human judgment. Any mapping to a formal number is highly misleading. So, let us look at the other examples given above.

- *Automated Code Checks (e.g. Syntax Checks)*: Code checks can be highly effective if the relevant patterns are known. The patterns are the limiting factor. Virus scanners are the best example. For known viruses, the detection is highly effective. However, the scanning approach is only effective in general if the patterns are kept up to date. Syntax patterns of a programming language are stable so that the check is very effective. Security checks on the source code on the other side are harder to conduct. Patterns are not as simple as for syntax checks. Often security scans can be effective, but they are not efficient. Many false positive messages are generated to cover potential security vulnerabilities. We do not want to dig deeper here, but we hope you get an impression about what can be achieved by code checks. The context of the scan has to be included in the assessment of its effectiveness.
- *Checksums and Hash Algorithms*: Checksums and hash algorithms are highly effective. These controls are hard to compromise. However, there are not many use cases in the software development process itself where they can be used, except for the identification of unauthorized code modifications.
- *Existence Checks*: We touched the effectiveness when introducing the example of an existence check. Is it really possible to check the achievement or status of a business objective by existence checks. This is not the case for required documents that have to be provided during the development process. This control is highly questionable for the process of software development.
- *Checklists*: Although checklists are a kind of formal control, the effectiveness highly depends on the way answers in the checklists have been generated. For instance, the answers could be based on other effective measures like code scans

or automated tests. In this case, the checklist would represent the actual state of the software. On the other hand, the answers might be based on the individual assessment and judgment of a person. The effectiveness in this case depends on the knowledge, expertise, and even the opinion of that single person. The result might even depend on the willingness of that person to provide the correct answer. This could be the case if the answers would not be independently double-checked. An internal control based on the provisioning of a checklist requires careful consideration of the way the data is collected for the checklist.

Qualitative Detective Controls

Looking at the prerequisite for the effectiveness of formal controls, it becomes clear that formal controls are ineffective for anything requiring a qualitative assessment.

- *Reviews*: When you have worked in software development for some time, the following might sound familiar to you. You are invited to some review session, for instance a design review. The document under review has been sent out prior to the review (okay, you are lucky, seems to be a serious one). The invited architects, developers, and product manager meet in a room for the review. Now, what happens first? Exactly, all laptops are opened up (if not, smart phones and tablets are fine as well). People start working on their emails, or whatsoever. The poor guy in front walks you through the document under review and hopes to get some feedback. Some colleagues have actually read the document upfront and give comments every here and there. Other colleagues (having not read the document upfront) might start some unmotivated discussion. Once in a while they pick something out of context … Admittedly, this might be not a typical example. Definitely not all reviews are performed in this way, but the fact that reviews like this one actually happen shows that reviews are not effective per se. Much more often, we have to look at the boundary conditions under which reviews are conducted. So let us shed some light on these boundary conditions. Reviews are intended to assess the status of an object, project, or something else by a peer group. The first prerequisite – even if it sounds trivial – is the existence of the object under review. For instance, if the document under review – think of a design or architecture document – is not complete, the review cannot be effective. The missing parts cannot be reviewed. Secondly, the object under review has to be understood by the reviewers. Besides the obvious use of appropriate language and terminology, this mainly applies to the expertise and knowledge of the reviewers. If a reviewer is not equipped to understand the object under review, he or she will not be able to effectively provide feedback. Lastly, there has to be some reference to which the reviewers have to refer to. On the one hand, there are business objectives that have to be achieved – for instance, a sustainable architecture or a secure product. On the other hand, there have to be some good or best practices which can act as benchmark. In the case of software development, this can be certain patterns, programming paradigms, guidelines, or proven existing solutions. From the operational perspective, reviews lead to action items to resolve identified issues. If these action items are not executed and tracked, the review remains ineffective. The above aspects are the prerequisites of a successful and effective review. Then there is one additional thing we want to take a look at. What about the motivation of the reviewers? Are they willing to give honest feedback? What could be impediments to an effective review from that perspective? The reviewer might be shy or afraid to offend someone by giving feedback. Does the reviewer really have a personal interest in giving honest feedback? There might be no direct consequence for the reviewer if the project under review fails. Even worse, the reviewer's project could benefit more if the reviewed project failed. This should not suggest that this is a regular issue with reviews. It is more important to emphasize the point that effective reviews require reviewers having a vital interest in the success of the review, or better said, the object under review. All in all, reviews can be made very effective, but this requires careful consideration of the boundary conditions – as just seen.

- *Product Audits*: The success factors of audits have been discussed in much detail throughout this book and we will not repeat everything here. Similar to reviews, the effectiveness of audits heavily depends on the boundary conditions. The audit framework, the top management support, as well as the expertise of the auditors are just a few to mention here. The quality and effectiveness of – centrally-organized – audits can be controlled better than reviews, but they have one major disadvantage – they do not scale. The need for highly qualified auditors only allows a sparse coverage, taking some samples of processes, or products.
- *Quality Gates*: Quality gates can be seen as a specific form of review, usually more formalized. A development project has to provide a set of deliverables for the quality gate. These deliverables are checked or reviewed by the quality team. The effectiveness is influenced by similar factors as for reviews and we do not repeat them here.

11.4.2.3 Assembling: The Role of the Development Process

So far we have looked at individual internal controls and their respective effectiveness. We did not touch the broader scope of the complete development process or the different sub-processes. This was our starting point. We brought up the examples of ensuring the right level of customer interaction and handling of non-functional requirements. We now briefly return to this question to see where we are.

Development processes and sub-processes are a set of different but interconnected and interrelated internal controls. The definition of the process flow can be seen as a preventive control. It gives direction to the development teams and thus is intended to prevent them from inventing other process flows. This definition reflects how the flow is intended to assure the achievement of underlying business objectives. The process flow is complemented by additional preventive controls like specific development guidelines, architecture concepts, etc. Furthermore, detective controls like reviews, audits, quality gates or others complete the core process definition. Whether corrective controls are regarded as part of the process definition is probably a matter of choice.

11.4.3 More Freedom!: The Role of Empowerment

Looking back on the broad definition of internal controls, it covers any measure taken to assure the achievement of business objectives. We discussed situations where strict process definitions or guidelines are not appropriate or feasible to provide sufficient assurance. Nevertheless, a company has to respond to this situation. Instead of strict process flows, other preventive controls have to be established. These have to be better suited to cover such situations. We are looking for alternative boundary conditions that support the achievement of business objectives. One possible option is the approach of empowerment. This term can be understood in the following way:

- *Freedom of Path*: Instead of defining strict process flows, a single person or a team is allowed to choose the appropriate approach for achieving a specific business objective. For instance, a team can decide on its own what the right measures are to gather customer requirements. They are responsible to ensure that the team gains a common understanding of these requirements.
- *Creativity*: The boundary conditions provide sufficient room for the required creativity to unfold. Software development – as any other development process – is at least partly a creative process. If processes are too strict, they will not allow for that kind of creative freedom.
- *Accountability*: An individual is made accountable for the achievement of the specific business objectives. Although this should be self-evident, it is of special importance in the context of empowerment. A strict process flow does not leave much room for deviation. An empowered environment puts more responsibility on the accountable to ensure the objectives are actually kept in focus and are achieved.

Taking these different aspects into account, empowerment can be understood as a preventive control. Empowerment prevents in a sense strict process flows from impeding the achievement of business objectives. Understanding empowerment in this way, two important consequences become obvious:

1. *Empowerment Does Not Replace the Need for Detective and Corrective Controls*: As empowerment only provides certain boundary conditions and thus enables the achievement of certain business objectives, it does not actually ensure the achievement. Corresponding (effective) detective and corrective controls are still required to assess the status of achievement and assure required changes. This is depicted in Fig. 11.1.
2. *Empowerment Does Not Affect the Requirement for a Valid Information Basis*: From the corporate governance perspective, we have learned that the board is required to act on a valid basis of information. This requirement is neither ensured nor otherwise affected by the concept of empowerment. Although a single (empowered) person might be accountable for the achievement of the business objective, this individual is not suited as the sole source of information about the status.

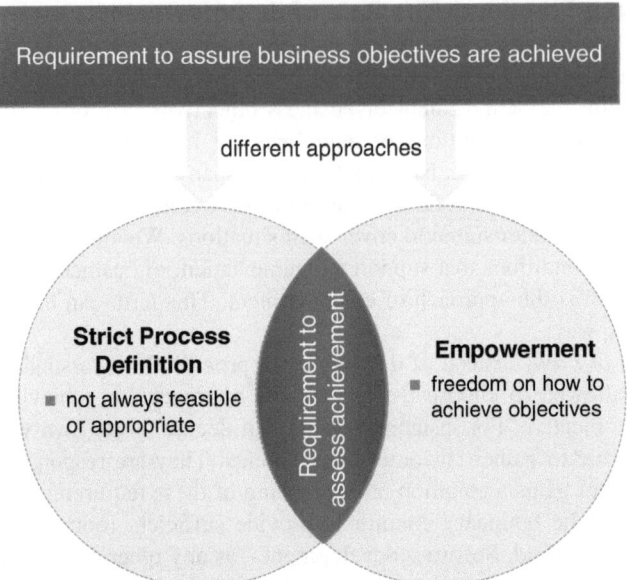

Fig. 11.1 Different approaches for achieving business objectives

11.5   The Gap: Scalable and Effective Qualitative Controls

11.5.1 Where Are We?

After all this discussion, we are finally at the stage to take a look at where we are and what is left. Why did we are go through this – maybe a little abstract and painful – discussion? We started with the observation of missing best practices for dealing with customers for gathering requirements. We also looked at other examples. The driving question was and still is – from a governance perspective – how can we assure sustainable software? This brought us to the underlying theory of internal controls and some considerations regarding their respective effectiveness.

In the course of the discussion, we saw different options on how business objectives can be ensured by defining preventive controls. The traditional option is the one of defining strict process flows and rules. The alternative – better suited for some aspects of software development – is the approach of empowerment. In any case, the boundary conditions – or preventive controls from a governance perspective – need to be complemented by effective detective controls. This is required to identify situations that put the achievement of business objectives at jeopardy. Deviations from strict process flows and rules can often be detected by formal controls. On the other hand, areas of empowerment more likely require qualitative controls.

In Fig. 11.2 we have outlined the different approaches that we discussed as options for the qualitative assessment of business objectives. Each approach has its advantages, but also clear draw backs:

- *Individual Assessment*: In this case, a single person assesses the status. An example is filling a checklist, or providing the status of a complete process or sub-process. This approach is very efficient, and the source of the information is known. The draw backs are that the correctness of the result depends on the individual's expertise. The bias, individual goals or interests could prevent correct or honest answers.

- *Independent Assessment*: An independent assessment targets towards an objective, or almost objective assessment of the situation. The optimal case is the one of an effective formal control. The business objective allows for a formal assessment and a corresponding formal control exists. An example is the syntactical correctness of code. Unfortunately, formal controls are not always feasible. Important business objective require a qualitative assessment. An (highly) objective alternative for these cases is an audit approach. This requires adhering to common audit standards ensuring an independent assessment. The drawback of this approach clearly is the lack of scalability. Audits cannot be applied across the board. Audits are rather intended assessing a set of samples to focus on individual cases, or to validate the effectiveness and efficiency of development processes.

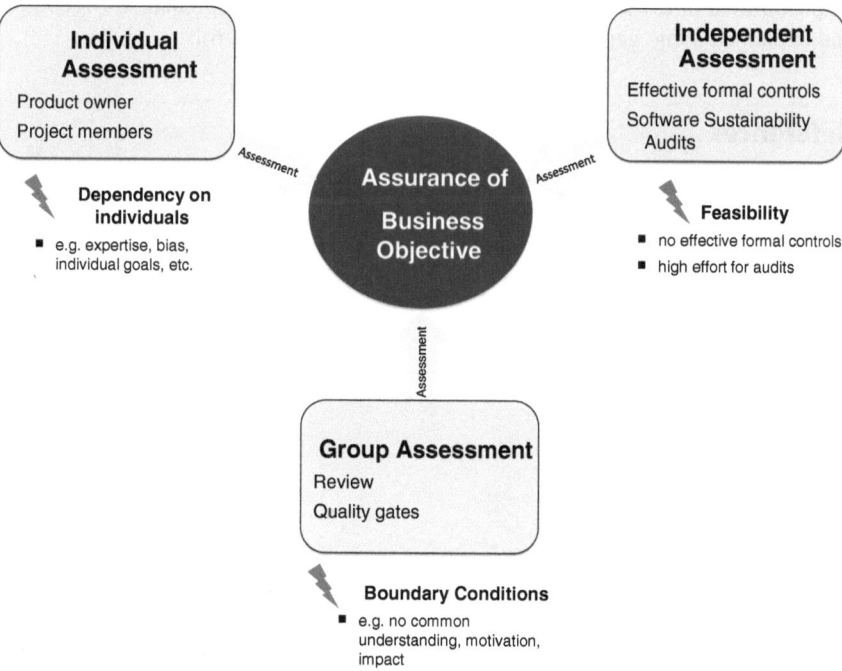

Fig.11.2 Different assessment approaches

- *Group Assessment*: A common alternative to individual or independent assessments is the approach of a group assessment. Reviews are an example. The advantage is obvious. By involving several people in the assessment the dependence on individuals is mitigated. Compared to an audit approach, the group assessment is much more scalable. But the usual approach for reviews has several draw backs, or at least risks that need to be taken into account. For instance, the concept of review does not enforce a common understanding of the business objective to be achieved or assessed. Reviewers might not have a vital interest to critically assess the object under review, making the whole approach ineffective. At the point of review it is not transparent whether it is effective or not. A performed review can give a false impression of security if no major issues have been identified.

11.6 Summary

Developing sustainable software requires effective governance. Mechanisms need to be implemented that assure the achievement of relevant product qualities. We discussed the problem space and the traditional governance approaches and controls. They have been analyzed and assessed with regard to their effectiveness in the context of software development. Some classical controls lack effectiveness in the given context as software development requires room for creativity and the empowerment of teams to decide on the best development approach. We identified and explained some gaps that exist in the current set of controls.

References

1. Certification Information System Auditor (CISA) (2010). Review Manual 2010, ISBN 978-1-60420-092-8.
2. COSO. Definition on web site http://www.coso.org/resources.htm; retrieved October 2011.

Governance Where It Belongs: Control Self-Assessment

What's in It for Me?

We explained in the previous chapter that software development processes face a specific challenge. They have to bridge the gap between creativity and empowerment on the one hand and required governance on the other hand. Governance is required to effectively align development with strategic guidance and other business objectives. We introduce a new concept – control self-assessment (CSA) – that can help in this regard. CSA is a well-known concept from auditing. We have adapted it to the specifics of software development.

CIO/CTO

From an executive perspective you should understand the core idea of control self-assessment. Your interest is the strategic alignment of your software development. CSA is an option that can help better achieving of these goals and objectives. Focus on Sects. 12.1 and 12.2 covering this basic idea. We leave it up to you to read the remainder of the chapter. There we focus on the CSA process in detail.

Software Architect

As architect you are familiar with reviews and also with handling non-functional requirements. You might have experienced that both can be ineffective. CSA can help you improving your work. For instance, CSA can help to ensure that non-functional requirements are effectively defined and understood by the development team. The approach can help you implementing software according to strategic guidance. CSA can be applied even without a central governance entity. It can even be applied on a project level. We recommend that as a software architect you read this chapter completely.

(continued)

R. Gutbrod and C. Wiele, *The Software Dilemma*, Management for Professionals, DOI 10.1007/978-3-642-27236-3_12, © Springer-Verlag Berlin Heidelberg 2012

Try adapting the ideas from CSA. For instance, improve your review meetings by engaging an external facilitator for the discussions.

Auditor
As an auditor you might already know the concept of CSA even though it has not yet found broad adoption in classical auditing. CSA in the context of software development can be seen as a kind of guided review. It requires a corresponding framework that can be provided by the audit department. As an auditor you can act as a facilitator for the discussions within the product teams. By going through the CSA concept you can also further strengthen your understanding of how software development actually works.

12.1   Decentralized Governance: The Missing Piece

Let us review what we have learned so far. At the end of the day we want to ensure that our development teams deliver sustainable software. The concrete technological and architectural requirements might depend on the product at hand and the respective context. Sustainability is more generic and requires adherence to a set of common principles and objectives. There are dedicated product qualities determining the sustainability of the software. Especially a customer- and user-centric development paradigm and the consideration of non-functional aspects foster sustainable software. We learned in the Chap. 11 that particularly the objectives related to these product qualities lack effective governance. Classical controls like checklists, reviews, and other formal compliance assessments do not apply here. The related development processes can hardly be formalized. They require empowered teams to drive the achievement of sustainability related objectives. Nevertheless, from an executive point of view we need effective governance. In other words, we have to find a mechanism that balances the need for freedom and flexibility of the development teams with the need for effective governance. To be more succinct, we are looking for a mechanism with the following qualities:

- *Empowerment*: The mechanism has to support an empowered environment. An empowered environment allows development teams choosing the appropriate approach for solving development related issues whenever there is no best practice available. The choice of the best approach is highly dependent on the specific situation of the project or product. Empowerment is a key element in successful software development as it provides the required freedom for unfolding creativity.
- *Effectiveness*: Without a doubt, the mechanism needs to be effective. If the achievement of the sustainability-related business objectives cannot be reliably supported, it is not worth taking the effort for implementing it. From the view

point of the traditional approaches, the new mechanism has to be at least more
effective than the existing ones.

- *Scalability*: Lastly, the mechanism has to be scalable across the organization.
As explained in Chap. 11, an audit approach – even highly effective – cannot be
applied on a broad scale. Audits are not intended as such. They can only cover
some samples to assess whether measures taken to achieve a business objective
are effective. To put this requirement into context, the mechanism might not
scale indefinitely. Still it has to scale better than an audit approach.

12.2 All You Need: The Basic Idea

12.2.1 Take the Best of Both Worlds

The above requirements impose quite a challenge. But fortunately there is hope.
Let us outline a possible approach. It might not be the only one, but at least a very
promising one. Bear in mind, new solutions are often derived by combining existing
ones. There is no difference here. Not everything with the existing mechanisms – or
controls – is bad. Take the good parts and compensate the bad ones. So let's try.

Our approach is based on the Control Self- Assessment (CSA). The concept of
CSA has long been known in the area of audits (see for example [1]). But so far it
has not been actively applied or promoted as a solution to our sketched problem
space. Very likely most people in software development have never heard of this
concept. Sometimes it is applied in the IT world as part of IT governance for
operating software systems. But it is definitely not a mainstream topic.

So, let's have a brief look at the CSA concept. We start by digesting the term
Control Self-Assessment. It tells us that something – a control – is assessed.
A control assessment – a typical task of an audit team – analyses the effectiveness
and efficiency of a specific control. For example, an audit could focus on a guideline
for secure programming. The auditors would analyze whether by following the
guideline, secure code would really be ensured (to the level that could be ensured by
a guideline). There could be different outcomes from such an assessment. For
instance, in the best case, the guideline could be regarded sufficient. But there
could also be the need to update or improve the guidelines. Moreover, the auditors
could recommend complementing the guideline by other controls making it more
effective. This could be security training for developers, code scans, or code
reviews. Any other control could be in the scope of an audit and so subject to a
control assessment. Now, let us turn to the little word *self* in Control Self-Assessment. Obviously, the control is not meant to assess itself. No, a control will always
affect individuals or groups of people. For instance the secure programming
guideline will affect the project team developing software. Not only do developers
have to follow the guideline. Product managers have to plan for certain security
features, and architects have to design security into the architecture. Instead of

having an independent audit team assessing the secure programming guideline (and related measures) it could be assessed by an affected project team. This team would *self*-assess whether the measures in the project are sufficient and effective to assure the objective of secure code. Similar to an audit, there could be different outcomes. Maybe the project develops code in a programming language not covered by the guideline. Product managers might not have taken into account all relevant security features. Or, the need for training is identified.

Briefly summarizing what we just explained, the basic idea of CSA is based on the concept of a group assessment. This group assesses the status of an objective, or mechanisms (controls) to assure the achievement of an objective. To make this assessment more effective the approach has to compensate for the draw backs of classical reviews. This compensation is achieved through four main measures:

1. The objective under assessment and the group performing the assessment have to fulfill certain prerequisites.
2. The assessment is performed within a framework ensuring a standardized level of quality.
3. The process takes feedback from the group members into account effectively.
4. The process is facilitated by a person external to the group performing the assessment (for instance an auditor).

By applying these measures some audit principles are established, and thus the strength of reviews and audits are combined. In the following we will explain these aspects in more detail. Afterwards we look at the CSA process to see how they are embedded into a formal framework.

12.2.2 Prerequisites: When to Apply CSA?

Now, let's start by looking at the prerequisites. The prerequisites can be split into two separate sets. The first set of prerequisites has to be fulfilled upfront, i.e. before starting the assessment:

- *There Is No Best Practice to Achieve the Business Objective*: Why? If there would be one you better implement it. Any other approach probably is less effective or less efficient – or in worst case both.
- *The Group Has an Inherent Interest in Achieving the Business Objective*: What does this mean and what is the assumption behind this prerequisite? Remember, when we looked at the effectiveness of reviews. We discovered that the effectiveness could be impeded by reviewers not fully committed to seriously assess the review topic. Only if your personal success is connected to the achievement of the business objective, will you fully engage. For instance, as a developer in a team you want to make the project a success. Looking at the software development process, the natural choice for such a group is the product team developing the product. The product team comprises not only the developers and architects, but also product management, quality engineers, and information developers. The product team has an inherent interest making the product successful (and thus to achieve the business objectives).

- *The Group Has the Ability and Empowerment to Drive the Achievement of the Business Objective*: This is an obvious prerequisite. If you neither can make changes nor have influence on the direction, how could you achieve something? This does not only include the right to make decisions, but also time and resources. In other words, the approach of CSA has to be accepted and supported by upper management.

The second set of prerequisites is a little different. These prerequisites have to be achieved and established as a result of the initial phase of the CSA process:

- *The Group Has the Required Expertise, Background, and Business Knowledge to Perform the Assessment*: Let's look at an example. If your task is to assess the architecture of a software product you will need to understand the context in which the software will be used. Otherwise you will not be able to determine whether the architecture is appropriate for this environment. This is not a necessary prerequisite to start with the CSA approach. The initial step in this process could be providing the required background information to the group.
- *The Group Has a Common Understanding of the Business Objective*: This is an essential prerequisite for success. How can you assess something if you do not understand what this *something* is actually about? Take the example of non-functional requirements. From a business perspective the objective is to drive the architecture by non-functional requirements. The group has to have a common understanding why this business objective is relevant. The relevance is best seen by looking at the impact on the success of a software development project if the objective is not achieved. What will happen if non-functional aspects like supportability, performance, or accessibility are not ensured? If there is no common understanding of the objective to be achieved there cannot be an alignment on the measures required to achieve the objective. As before, if the common understanding is not given up front, it has to be established during the initial phase of the CSA process.

These are the central prerequisites. They are essential for making this approach a success. Compare them to what you know from classical reviews. The difference should be obvious.

12.2.3 Feeding the Loop

As just seen the CSA process requires alignment of different aspects. Alignment requires transparency on different viewpoints or levels of understanding. How can I know whether we reached a common understanding of the required product qualities? Is there still a need for discussion? Which aspects need further explanation? If something is missed here the whole process is at jeopardy. In other words the opinion and needs of all parties have to be taken into account and an effective feedback loop is required.

One very effective way of a feedback channel is an anonymous survey. Participants can openly give feedback in this way and make deficiencies on the alignment transparent. From the software development process point of view a feedback cycle – and thus a survey – is required at four occasions:

- *At the Beginning*: The initial survey assesses whether the business objectives and the measures defined to achieve them have been understood and agreed by the team members.
- *In the Course of the Project*: During software development, the project team members have to assess whether the defined measures are actually implemented and applied. They assess whether the measures are effective, or whether need for corrections and change is seen.
- *At the End of the Project*: After the software has been developed, the team assess whether the corresponding objectives have been achieved.
- *After the Project*: As a follow-up it is recommended to survey the team about the success of the CSA approach and about possible improvements.

12.2.4 Help Your Teams: Facilitate!

Software development teams are comprised of people with different skills, backgrounds, tasks, interests, and responsibilities. Alignment of a development team along certain – maybe complex – aspects, requires discussion and the consideration of different opinions and understandings. This is not always an easy task. For that reason the CSA concept embraces the idea of an external facilitator. Facilitation can be helpful in fostering open discussions and balancing arguments and contributions of the involved parties.

The product team can request a facilitator to be provided by the organization owning the CSA process. This could be for instance a central governance entity. Facilitated discussions are required as follow-up to a survey that signals missing alignment. In contrast to the surveys, facilitated discussions are rather optional. Nevertheless, team members – and not only the product owner – have to be aware of the option to request facilitation.

Besides the facilitation which helps the team as a whole, further dedicated help for the product owner has to be foreseen by the CSA process. We have briefly outlined above, that the product team decides on the most appropriate way of achieving certain business objectives. To this end the product owner proposes a plan with associated measures. But the product owner might need support for this task to adapt available practices or to get an understanding of different options. To this end the product owner can request consulting services. The scope of this consulting is the implementation of available practices or on defining and selecting appropriate measures. This consulting service has to come from a corresponding topic owner. Example topics are customer engagement, security, or other non-functional requirements.

12.2.5 Standardize!

The last aspect to take into account is the one of a framework standardizing the CSA approach. We have seen that some prerequisite are not given upfront but have to be established by the process itself. Furthermore, we need a feedback loop and some facilitation of discussions during the CSA process. Lastly, you may want to apply CSA on a broader scale – maybe for all development projects. This only makes sense if the results of assessments are comparable across projects.

To fulfill these different requirements a more formal framework with a clear definition of the CSA process is required. This framework needs to be owned and controlled by someone. This owner also has to continuously improve the framework or adapt it to changing business environments. Also other roles are required which we look at later on.

12.2.6 Remember Your Goals!

Before we explain the CSA process in more detail we have to remember once more where we are heading. We need to keep our goals in mind. This will allow us at any time to check whether we are still on track. Once you use a CSA approach, go back and review this section. If you see deviations, stop and think what went wrong. Apply corrections if necessary. CSA requires more effort than a classical review. This is only justified if the added value is higher. When the goals of CSA are not achieved the additional effort is wasted, and will not help you in better achieving a specific product quality.

Let us start with the two central goals of the CSA approach:

- *The Group Has an Aligned Understanding of How to Achieve a Specific Product Quality*: Remember we started off from the assumption that no best practice exists. Consequently, some other means is required to determine how the respective product quality is achieved. Let us continue with the example of non-functional requirements. What is it we have to align on? First we need to identify the non-functional requirements relevant for the specific software project. A lot of questions have to be answered. How are requirements gathered, aligned, and validated? How is the architecture defined, reviewed, and validated? How do we ensure that the design reflects the requirements, and that developers actually implement the design accordingly? What are effective test cases to ensure the goal has really been achieved? All these questions need to be answered and aligned in the course of the CSA process.
- *The Respective Product Quality Is Actually Achieved*: This is the obvious goal. CSA is intended as a control to ensure a specific product quality is achieved to foster the sustainability of the software. If this is not the case, only part of the approach has been fully effective.

12.3   Making it Happen: The CSA Process

So far we looked at *what* we want to achieve. Now we turn to the idea *how* to achieve it. As explained we need some formal framework that allows a standardized implementation of CSA across different projects. This framework comprises the definition of roles, content required for a CSA, process flow, and some technical boundary conditions.

12.3.1 Who Owns What?: Roles in CSA

Before we look at the content and flow of the CSA process we have to understand the different affected roles.

12.3.1.1 CSA Process Owner

The CSA process owner is a person responsible for providing the CSA framework. The framework allows conducting CSA within product development teams. If a central governance organization exists, the CSA process owner is probably part of that group. But a central governance organization is not a prerequisite. For instance, a lead architect might want to implement a CSA approach for a limited number of projects without central governance. In that case the lead architect could take the role of the CSA owner.

The framework comprises the process flow and its description, the topic-related content for CSA, and for instance, a survey infrastructure. Furthermore, the owner is responsible to monitor the effectiveness and efficiency of the CSA approach and to take corrective measures if required.

12.3.1.2 Product Quality Owner

Our main consideration for adopting CSA for the software development process is ensuring product qualities are achieved. Especially qualities that could not be reliably ensured otherwise are relevant for CSA. Most of the non-functional requirements having an impact on the product architecture and the sustainability of the software, like performance or supportability, fall into this category. To be effective and efficient, we need a clear definition of the corresponding qualities. But the focus should not only be on the definition itself. Especially the impact for the product, company, and stakeholders (like customers) has to be explained if the quality is not achieved. Or in other words, the impact of lacking sustainability.

To this end we require an owner for each of the qualities subject to CSA. Surely we also need them if no CSA is applied, but this is not discussed here. These topic or product quality owners have to provide roll-out material to be used during the CSA process. But the owners also have to offer corresponding consulting services. This is required to help the product owners define the corresponding plans and measures for a specific software development project.

12.3.1.3 Product Owner

The product owner is overall accountable for the success of a specific product. In the CSA process, the product owner takes on a very important role. A central element of CSA in the context of software development is aligning the approach on how to achieve a certain product quality. The product owner's responsibility is to define, roll-out, and align the approach to achieve the respective quality. The product owner has the operational lead for CSA which comprises organizing workshops, discussions, and conducting surveys.

12.3.1.4 Team Members

Team members are the ones having to implement the measures defined and rolled-out by the product owner. This requires an aligned understanding of the product qualities and corresponding measures. Team members have to actively participate in the discussions, and surveys. CSA is nothing that is intended for pure consumption, but requires effort and active participations from all team members.

12.3.1.5 Auditors and Facilitators

CSA originates from the classical governance and auditing business. It was intended to complement audits having a control that could be applied on a broader scale. CSA approaches might be driven from an internal audit organization. From this perspective, an auditor might act as the CSA process owner, or act either as consultants or facilitators in the CSA process. Auditors can also provide an independent assessment of the effectiveness and efficiency of the CSA approach through implementing corresponding audits.

Nevertheless, the role of a facilitator or consultant in the CSA process does not necessarily require an auditor. The role could be taken by anyone with the relevant skills.

12.3.2 Cold Water?: The CSA Process Flow

Now that we have understood the different roles, we turn to the CSA process itself. We have talked about the product qualities, but have not been too specific about the selection process so far. We assume the product quality to be assessed by CSA has already been selected. Later we will give some criteria for the selection, but won't focus on the selection process itself. Furthermore, for the time being we assume that the relevant content for the CSA, like presentations, survey questionnaires, etc. exists. We will also take a more detailed look at the content later on.

Surely, we need a development project implementing a new product to which we want to apply the CSA approach. Try thinking of a specific project you have been involved in or that is currently running. Imagine how CSA could be applied to that project. At each step think about what you would have presented, discussed, or decided.

The basic process flow of CSA is depicted in Fig. 12.1. Actual implementations might differ in some details, but the core concept remains. CSA is implemented in

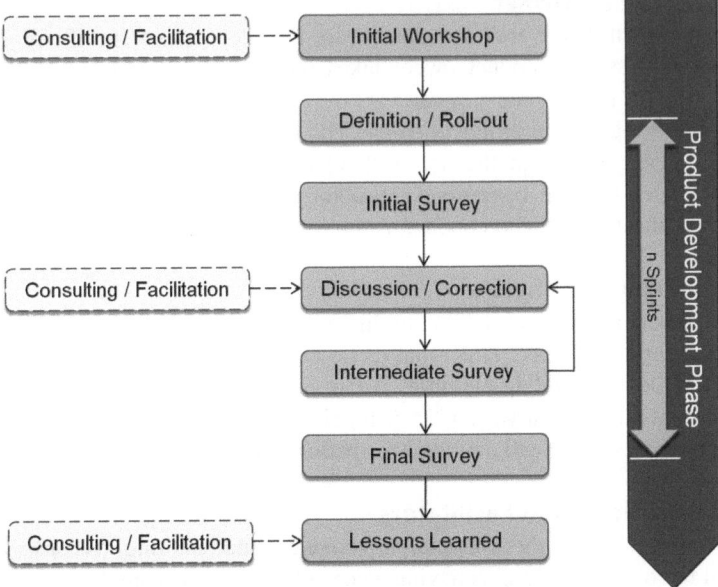

Fig. 12.1 The CSA process

parallel to the actual software development process. The context of a specific software project is required as otherwise there could be no impact on the product.

12.3.3 Step by Step: The CSA Process Steps

To get a detailed understanding of the CSA process we will now walk you through the individual process steps.

12.3.3.1 Kick-It Off!: The Initial Workshop

Consider a development team comprising all the different roles like developers, product managers, architects, and so on. They probably have never heard of CSA (as probably most people have not). Consequently, the first vital task is getting them involved. Their buy-in is needed for making the approach a success. Remember, all team members need to actively participate. Only this participation can ensure the required alignment on different levels. During the initial workshop the concept of CSA is explained, as well as the roles within the CSA process. What is expected from whom? How is the alignment driven? What effort will it take from me? Especially the latter point is important. As software development projects are constantly under time pressure, additional effort has to be justified. Only if the added value is understood will people buy into this concept, and are willing to invest the time.

In addition to the CSA concept itself the corresponding product quality is introduced in the initial workshop. One of the prerequisites of CSA is a common understanding of the product quality to be assessed. The initial workshop lays the foundation for this alignment, but is not necessarily the last step.

It is obvious that all team members should participate in the initial workshop to ensure an efficient implementation. The workshop is organized by the product owner before the actual development phase starts. The introduction to CSA is provided by an external facilitator. This could be the CSA process owner, an auditor, or anyone familiar with the CSA concept. The goal of the initial workshop is getting to a common understanding about the CSA process, the corresponding roles, and the expectations and deliverables.

12.3.3.2 Get It Rollin': The Definition and Roll-Out

The actual work starts after the initial workshop. It has been clarified which product quality has to be achieved. Still it is open how the product quality is best achieved. To this end the product owner creates a proposal for the approach and selects corresponding measures. This should happen in a standardized format. To support the product owner in this task, a collection of available practices could be provided. These practices should have proven to work in a certain context. The product owner could then select accordingly.

After the proposal has been created by the product owner, the information has to be rolled out to the product team. The appropriate roll-out approach (email, workshops, conference calls, etc.) is up to the product owner and depends on the practice and habits of the organization. The roll-out should happen prior to the beginning of the development phase, or latest early in the development phase. This is required to ensure product team members have the required information available early in the development process. This is important to take the information into consideration during product architecture definition and design. Otherwise corrections could be required later on.

12.3.3.3 Did They Hear the Message?: The Initial Survey

Transparency is essential to achieving a common understanding across the product team. The survey helps revealing different understandings or areas requiring action. The initial survey covers the product quality, and the understanding of proposed measures to achieve the quality. Furthermore, it is surveyed whether the measures are perceived as appropriate. To ensure a constant level of quality, the questionnaire used for the survey should be standardized. The results are only provided to the product team for subsequent discussion. The initial survey is conducted shortly after the roll-out of the intended approach.

12.3.3.4 Ready For Change: Discussion and Correction

The product owner rolls out the survey result to the product team and ensures the project team can openly discuss the results. The survey might reveal major deficiencies in understanding, or a lack of agreement with the intended approach. In this case, corrective measures have to be discussed and implemented within the product team. To help in resolving possible issues, it is recommended to request support from a facilitator (e.g. an auditor). This is especially important to ensure all different viewpoints are discussed and taken into account and consideration.

This kind of discussion and correction round is always conducted after a survey. This will ensure an alignment within the product team. The discussions are a central element of CSA. Together with the surveys they are the key measures for an effective assessment.

12.3.3.5 Where Are We?: The Intermediate Surveys

During the development phase intermediate surveys have to be conducted. The main focus is the progress of achieving the corresponding product quality and the effective implementation of corresponding measures. If the survey reveals issues, corrections can be applied. To have sufficient time for corrections, intermediate surveys should be conducted not later than at 50–60% of the development phase. An intermediate survey is also required if the initial survey can lead to some corrective measures. In this case an intermediate survey should focus on whether the alignment after the discussion and correction has improved.

Similar to the initial survey a discussion might be required to align on corrective measures. So, the survey and discussion concept together build an effective feedback loop. This is one of the main differences when compared to classical reviews.

12.3.3.6 Done!: The Final Survey

After the development project is finalized, a final survey is conducted. The final survey provides the basis for the lessons learned session and focuses on the overall achievement of the corresponding product quality. Furthermore, the questionnaire should focus on the approach taken to achieve the product quality, possible corrections, and possible improvements to the CSA process.

12.3.3.7 Can We Do Better?: The Lessons Learned Workshop

At the end of the development phase a lessons learned workshop has to be conducted. During this session the experience with CSA is discussed. Focus is the identification of possible improvements for the next development cycle. As for the initial workshop and the discussion sessions it is recommended to request a facilitator (e.g. an auditor) to support the lessons learned.

12.4   What Remains?: Additional Aspects

The core concept of CSA should be clear by now. In this section we discuss some additional aspects of CSA that might be important for you when considering the implementation of CSA in your company.

12.4.1 Selection Criteria for Product Qualities

We introduced CSA as new control or mechanism better assuring the achievement of dedicated product qualities. In other words the assumption is that CSA is more effective than existing mechanisms like reviews, etc. On the other hand CSA requires additional effort compared to classical controls. This requires a careful selection of product qualities that should be subject to CSA. To be most effective, CSA should be limited to important product qualities that cannot be controlled otherwise. For instance, implementing CSA instead of an effective code scanner would make no sense. Consequently, we need some selection criteria to help making decisions which product qualities to cover by CSA. Here are some aspects to guide you through the decision process:

1. *The Respective Product Quality Impacts the Sustainability of the Product*: The primary criterion is the relevance for the sustainability of the software product. In other words the long term impact of the respective quality has to be considered. This includes development, support, or operational cost, as well as potential impact on the reputation of the software company.
2. *The Respective Product Quality Cannot Be Achieved by Following a Strict Process Flow*: Some product qualities cannot be achieved by strictly following a defined process. Instead, only certain boundary conditions can be defined. It is up to the empowered development team to decide on the appropriate approach to achieve the product quality.
3. *Formal Detective Controls Are Not Effective or Feasible*: Formal controls like checklists, code scans, etc. do not effectively assure the achievement of the product quality.
4. *Buy-in and Good Understanding of the Respective Product Quality is Required from Development Teams*: The product quality can only be achieved if at least the major part of a development team has a good understanding of it. Furthermore, the team is required to actively support the achievement of the product quality.
5. *Cumulative Risk Exposure*: The risk associated with the product quality is not specific to a certain product, but affects all products. This results in a very high risk exposure through cumulating risk exposures across all products. For instance, if the appropriate customer engagement cannot be assured in general, the risk affects all products, not only a single product.

12.4.2 CSA Everywhere: Embedding Into Standard Development

There are several ways of embedding CSA into the standard development process. While the CSA process itself remains fixed, it has to be decided which projects have to run CSA and for which product qualities. The decision about the projects and product qualities should be based on the risk exposure. CSA means additional effort. This effort needs to be justified by the added value, or the mitigation of the risk exposure. CSA might be a good choice for a complete new development, or some strategic projects. However for smaller extensions of existing products – not subject to extensive risk – could be overkill.

From a standard development perspective there are three basic options:

1. *CSA Is Mandatory for All Projects*: All projects have to conduct CSA for selected product qualities. For instance, secure programming or customer engagement could be required to be covered by CSA. The implementation of CSA could be enforced through corresponding deliverables (e.g. proof of conduction during a quality gate).

2. *CSA Is Mandatory for Selected Projects*: Projects are selected based on defined criteria like project size, projected revenue, or others. Projects matching the criteria have to conduct CSA. As before, CSA can be limited to dedicated product qualities. Similarly, the implementation is enforced through corresponding deliverables (e.g. proof of conduction during quality gates).

3. *Projects Can Volunteer for CSA*: In this case projects are not required to implement CSA. Instead the implementation is done on a voluntary basis. This could be the case if the product owner or the product team see added value in conducting CSA to better assure dedicated product qualities.

If CSA is embedded into a standard development process a central owner and corresponding central organization is required to ensure the standardization of the process.

12.4.3 Here and There: CSA On An Ad-Hoc Basis

Besides integrating CSA into the standard software development process, it is always possible to apply CSA on an ad-hoc basis. This might be an option to address issues specific to individual software products. While there is more flexibility with regard to the affected product quality and content, the CSA process itself should be conducted in the standardized fashion.

An ad-hoc CSA could be a response to the result of a Software Sustainability Audit. This audit might have revealed short comings in a product or corresponding development process which could be addressed by a dedicated and tailor-made CSA.

12.4.4 Integrate!: CSA as Part of the Control Framework

If CSA is applied as part of the standard development process, it becomes part of the internal control framework. CSA complements other existing internal controls by closing gaps in the framework, and partially replace ineffective controls. Let us look at some aspects of how CSA fits into the control framework and how it can be understood in terms of the different control types. This is a more formal consideration targeted towards auditors and audit organizations. Architects and others are free taking a look at it.

1. *CSA Acts as a Preventive Control*: CSA acts as a preventive control in the way that it forces the product owner defining a clear approach towards achieving a respective product quality. Although there is no best practice or general standard on how to achieve the quality, it ensures that a product/project-specific approach is defined, documented, and communicated within the product team.

2. *CSA Acts as a Detective Control*: CSA acts as a detective control in the way that product team members are surveyed. The surveys focus on the understanding of the product quality, the approach taken to achieve it, and whether the approach is considered appropriate. The surveys are intended to detect misalignment within the product team. It addresses the risk of not achieving the respective product quality.

3. *CSA Acts as a Corrective Control*: CSA acts as a corrective control in the way that it forces the product team aligning on appropriate measures to achieve the respective product quality. If a survey has revealed misalignment across the product team, the product owner has to correct the approach or to better communicate the plans.

4. *CSA Implementation is Enforced Centrally*: CSA as an internal control is enforced centrally. If CSA is mandatory for all or a selected set of standard development projects, the proof of implementation could be a deliverable for a corresponding quality gate. In case of a risk-based selection of projects, the implementation could also be enforced by a central governance body.

5. *The CSA Concept Has a Central Owner*: The CSA concept and process is required to have a central owner to ensure the process is conducted in a standardized fashion. The owner also has to ensure the continuous improvement of the process.

6. *The Product Qualities Under CSA Have Central Owners*: Each product quality that is covered by CSA requires a central owner. The owner ensures that the product teams implementing CSA receive the required information about the respective product quality. The owner is also required to update the documentation on a regular basis.

7. *Survey Content Is Standardized*: The content of the survey questionnaire has to be standardized to ensure a high level of quality and comparable CSA implementations. The content of the survey can be specific to the product quality subject to CSA. The content is owned by the product quality owner.

8. *CSA Is Not a Replacement for Audits*: as a means of an independent assessment of products, projects, and development-related processes. Rather audits are required to assess the effectiveness of the CSA approach to assure the goals of the CSA approach are met.

12.4.4.1 Does It Add Value?: Assessing CSA

As CSA is intended to extend the inventory of existing controls it needs to be ensured that CSA is as effective as assumed. To assess the effectiveness, clear goals and objectives have to be defined that allow assessing the success of CSA as an additional control.

The overarching goal of CSA is to effectively assure the achievement of qualitative business objectives in a scalable manner.

- *CSA Provides a Significant Better Assurance of the Achievement of Business Objectives*: The achievement of business objectives in projects applying CSA must be significantly higher than for projects not applying CSA.
- *CSA Fosters the Common Understanding of Business Objectives and Its Importance*: Compared to peer groups (i.e. product teams not applying CSA) the understanding of the objectives is significantly increased.
- *CSA Can Be Applied on a Much Broader Scale than Audits*: As the limiting factor of audits is the high effort, CSA needs to require much less (central) effort to allow for an application across the board, or at least in the majority of product teams.
- *CSA Has a Significant Higher Acceptance Than Other Controls Applied in the Past*: The effectiveness of CSA highly depends on the acceptance as a control and the buy-in of development teams. Other controls like checklists have a limited acceptance in development. This results from their limited effectiveness.

When integrating CSA into the standard control framework the concept needs to be carefully assessed according to these objectives.

12.4.5 Yes, There Is Some!: Risk of CSA

We introduced CSA as an alternative to other control mechanisms. The reason was to better assure the achievement of certain product qualities. Other controls have some drawbacks and might not be effective as expected. Similarly, we have to consider the effectiveness of CSA. In other words we have to analyze the associated risk that CSA remains ineffective. The impact would be a failure to achieve the corresponding product qualities. Let us look at the different conditions which would render CSA ineffective. For instance:

- *Behavior*: Team members do not insist on understanding the product quality and an appropriate approach to achieve it. This might not be an intentional behavior but could be a response to a high work load and the attempt to minimize additional load.
- *Measures Not Implemented*: The team conducts CSA, and aligns on corresponding measures. But in the course of the project effective measures are not implemented.
- *Malicious Behavior*: A conscious decision by the team to only formally conduct CSA but not to invest in effective measures to achieve the product quality. Whether this is a realistic scenario cannot be answered upfront. It would come close to a fraudulent behavior.

The probability of the above examples cannot be defined a priori. The appropriate response to the overall risk is monitoring the CSA approach with regard to its effectiveness. Auditing or spot checking the CSA process would for instance be a reasonable measure. As for any other control, corporate governance rules apply to CSA.

12.4.6 What's Left?: Guiding Principles for CSA

In order to be effective and to meet the intended goals and objectives, the CSA-framework and implementation have to follow certain guiding principles. These principles also provide the basis for understanding what can be achieved with CSA and what cannot be achieved. Some of the principles have already mentioned before, but we give a comprehensive overview here.

1. *CSA Is Conducted Within a Group that Has a Vital Interest in Achieving the Business Objectives*: An essential success factor for CSA is that the participants have a vital interest in achieving the corresponding business objectives. This group should also have the empowerment to align on an approach and implement it accordingly. In this sense, the product teams can be seen as natural candidates for CSA as they have clear boundaries and the required empowerment. As long as not stated otherwise, the assumption for the following discussion is that CSA is conducted by product teams. A counter example would be a group of architects conducting a classical architecture review. Architects from areas outside the development team usually do not have a vital interest in the achievement of the business objectives as they are not directly impacted by a failure of the product. Furthermore, this group of architects is not empowered to change the approach or direction.

2. *CSA Supports the Idea of Empowerment*: Empowerment of development teams is required to effectively and efficiently drive development, i.e. development teams need to be able to decide on the best approach to provide a solution to a business problem. At the same time, the company has a vital interest in ensuring defined business objectives are met which requires a certain level of control.

3. *CSA Provides a New Approach that Can Help Balance the Requirement of Empowerment and Control*: There are three aspects supporting this balance.
   (a) *CSA Establishes a Right for Team Members to Understand Business Objectives and How They Will be Achieved*: If all team members have the clearly communicated right to understand the business objective covered by CSA and the approach of how to achieve them, they will force the product owner to take corresponding measures. In this way a controlling force within the product team is established that balances the power of the product owner.
   (b) *CSA Establishes a Duty for the Product Owner to Explain Business Objectives, Achieve Alignment Across the Team, and Take Corrective Measure*: As CSA establishes a right for the product team members to understand the business objectives and the approach to achieve them, at the same time it establishes a duty for the product owner to drive the team-internal alignment.
   (c) *Survey Results Are Not Disclosed*: A key point to foster acceptance of the CSA approach is that survey results and the internal discussions within a product team are not disclosed to the outside. Especially MBOs must not depend on the result of surveys to ensure an open communication style within the product teams.

12.5   Summary

Sustainable software development has to reconcile the need for empowered teams and the requirement of effective governance. A concept known from auditing – Control Self-Assessment (CSA) – has been adapted to the specific context of software development. CSA is an effective control mechanism in cases where classical controls are not effective and no best practice is available. CSA is the proper approach for empowered teams. We outlined the core concept and basic idea of CSA. But we also looked at the relevant prerequisites, the affected roles, as well as the CSA process itself.

Reference

1. Dani Saad El-Dine, Control Self-Assessment: Concepts and Applications, Thomson South-Western, Mason, Ohio, ISBN 0-324-22601-2

It's Not Only About the Facts: Communication Matters

13

What's in It for Me?

Beyond the Software Sustainability Audit framework itself, there is one more essential element we need to consider: communication. Ultimately, your communication style can determine whether an audit succeeds or fails. This chapter offers some fundamental advice on communication. We start with the different roles you can assume ("police" or "advisor"), and explain why communication matters. We then outline some key communication principles. Based on our own experience with Software Sustainability Audits, we look at how these principles apply in an auditing context, and share some typical examples. The chapter also includes useful references for further reading.

CIO/CTO

Do you have the right people for Software Sustainability Audits? Do your auditors have the right skills? In this chapter, we are not talking about technical and architectural skills. We are talking about how essential it is to communicate effectively. We recommend that you read two sections: Sect. 13.1 discusses the different communication styles your auditors can adopt and how these styles can impact an audit. In the end, you are the one who decides which approach your auditors follow. Section 13.2 underlines why communication matters in Software Sustainability Audits. This section also covers communication training that you might want to offer to your auditors.

Software Architect

In this chapter you can put your technology know-how aside. Section 13.1 outlines the two communication approaches you can adopt, assuming either a policing or advisory role. Section 13.2 explains why choosing the right

(continued)

R. Gutbrod and C. Wiele, *The Software Dilemma*, Management for Professionals, DOI 10.1007/978-3-642-27236-3_13, © Springer-Verlag Berlin Heidelberg 2012

communication strategy can make you more effective. In Sect. 13.3, we try to summarize some key communication theories in just a few pages, and look at how they apply in practice when we conduct Software Sustainability Audits. In Sect. 13.4, you can learn more about communicating effectively in your audits.

Auditor

As an auditor, you have probably already chosen your communication approach. Nevertheless, Sect. 13.1 might help you step back from your role and reflect on your decision. You can skip Sect. 13.2, since you experience the power of communication in your day-to-day professional life. Section 13.3 offers a helpful refresher on communication theory. If you are inspired by one of the topics, you can learn more by reading a book from our reference list. You can use Sect. 13.4 to reflect on where you might be able communicate more effectively during your own audits.

13.1   Police or Advisor?

When you embark on an audit, you need to decide on your fundamental communication approach: Should the auditor assume a policing role, or offer advisory services like a consultant? This approach defines your communication style throughout a Software Sustainability Audit. But how does the communication style differ in each case? And what communication aspects do we need to take into account?

Let us start at the end, with the result you achieve using each method. Consider this dialog between a software architect and an auditor:

After learning a great deal during the architecture reviews and the entire preparation phase, Greg was keen to start his first official Software Sustainability Audit. However, one question still hung in the air, and Greg was unsure how to proceed. In all his previous architecture reviews, he hadn't really given too much thought to communication. He just invited the experts he thought he needed for clarification, and jumped right into the interrogation. To get to the bottom of an issue, he usually persisted until he had squeezed out every last morsel of information. After each interview session, Greg always wondered how his colleagues perceived him. Yes, he wanted to be friendly. But at the same time, it was his job to ask all these questions, and he was expected to provide reliable answers himself. Nevertheless, when he thought about all these meetings, he wasn't quite sure. He felt uncomfortable. Was this really the best way to get the information he was looking for? He had certainly damaged some good relationships in the process. Were these relationships worth sacrificing? He felt like a police officer. But was this his role? And if not, what was the alternative?

A good friend of his, Sam Tamies, works for the internal audit team. Since Sam's job is similar to that of a Software Sustainability Auditor, Greg met up with him and asked the burning question.

"Sam, how do you behave in internal audits? How do you live with being the police officer?" Greg had already decided how the job has to be done, so Sam's answer took him by surprise.

"It's your decision. It's up to you whether or not you act as a police officer!"

"What do you mean?" Greg was puzzled.

Sam continued, "In our internal audit team, everybody can choose whether to adopt a policing or advisory role. Either way, you need to evaluate the situation first. If opt for a policing stance, you feel the power of execution. You give orders on what to do. But as in real life, individuals may disagree with police decisions, and it is left to judges to decide. In a company, the judges are the managers, mostly from top management. But that's just one way of doing it. Some of us – and I am proud to be one of them – feel more like an advisor or consultant. We consult on recommendations. It is then up to management to follow the recommendations."

Now Gregory was really confused. "But ..?" Greg struggled for words. "But don't you give up all your authority if you just act as a consultant?" He could not believe how this attitude could succeed.

"Both approaches have advantages and disadvantages", Sam agreed. "And overall, you can succeed with both attitudes. There are different views on which approach is more appropriate. As I said, it's your decision."

You can approach Software Sustainability Audits in both ways: You can act as the police. And you can act as an advisor. But the communication style will be totally different, which in turn has a tremendous impact on the process. As Sam mentioned, if you take the policing approach, you will eventually need a judge, somebody who decides about the tickets you hand out. This is a thorny, tough road, where the default procedure for resolving an issue is to escalate. Yes, people will respect you next time you approach them. Or, put differently, they will be afraid of you. And as a consequence, they will be much more reluctant to share what they know. They will think twice about what they say. They will choose their words carefully. You will have to expend a lot more energy to get to the bottom of an issue. You will get more excuses for postponing meetings. You will receive more politically-motivated answers. In other words, you will find yourself as a police officer would; people will try to avoid you. This is one option, and there are auditors who like this kind of respect. However, we don't subscribe to this approach. If you want to act as a police officer, you are free to do so. But bear in mind that you may find yourself alone at the end of your audit journey.

We think the other option is much more promising. We are firmly convinced that an advisory role is more successful in the long run. The key benefit of an operating in an advisory capacity is that it encourages openness. Openness is a precious property. You will gain a better understanding of a situation if people meet you with an open mind. If you know people who just talk freely, you will know what we mean. Open people say what is weighing on their mind. You don't have to squeeze it out of them. They just will tell you.

There is a long list of other reasons. Ultimately though, Software Sustainability Audits depend on two success factors: How comprehensive are your findings? And how well will your recommendations be executed? This second factor is another good reason for acting as an advisor; whenever people are convinced, they will follow your recommendations. If they are given orders, they will carry them out only begrudgingly, and you will need to invest more time in controlling execution and quality.

Another good reason for choosing an advisory role is people. We care about people. We do not just analyze things. We do not just weigh a brick, and measure its length, width, and height. We talk to, and with, people. We meet individuals, who have feelings, who work under certain constraints, and who have their own needs. Treat people with respect. They deserve it. Moreover, the police come round when people have done something wrong, something forbidden. Our assumption is that people want to do the right thing. Individuals have good reasons for acting as they act. If we are able to understand why they act as they do, we can even provide better advice. And we might help the people at the same time.

13.1.1 Advisor from the Outset

"Okay, I understand the difference in the attitude." Sam has aroused Greg's curiosity. "But what is the difference in the process? What do I need to do differently?"

"Let's start where you introduce the Software Sustainability Audit." Sam begins to explain the two different roles step by step. "How are you used to introducing a Software Sustainability Audit?"

"Well, the beginning is always easy. I just refer to my sponsor. 'I have been asked by Mr. X to review your architecture.'", Greg answered promptly. "And since my sponsor is always an important person, like our CIO, there is usually no discussion about my mandate. From there, I move on to explain the scope, the project structure, and so on." Greg likes to kick off his projects efficiently.

But Sam wants to know the details. "How do your colleagues react? How is the mood in the room? What do their faces tell you?"

Greg was irritated. Has he ever watched people's faces while introducing a Software Sustainability Audit? He always needed to concentrate on the meeting structure.

"Greg, look. To me, that sounds like a police officer's approach. 'By law I have to give you a ticket.' Your law is the CIO. I often notice that people are nervous when they are invited to audits for the first time. They are thinking 'What did I do wrong?' I notice stern faces. People sit rigidly, wondering what will happen to them. How would you feel? An advisor starts with explanations to take away the fear. Explain why people have been selected. They are important contributors to an important product. What is the reason for the audit? It could be a standard review, and the product might have been selected because of its strategic importance. And sense the emotions in the room. Appreciate that the participants feel uncertain and uncomfortable. It is a new situation for them. Give them time to feel good. If you spend some time addressing these soft factors at the beginning, it will pay off throughout the audit."

Police officers command, advisors advise. This basic difference counts right from the beginning of a Software Sustainability Audit. An advisor has three tools that are more important than the audit structure. These are: "explain", "appreciate" and "allow time".

Explain whatever is new to the participant. You want the participants to listen. And they will listen, as soon as they have been heard. They are saying to themselves "I can't be assertive, because I don't know ..." Hear them by explaining. Explain what an audit is. Explain why this audit topic has been chosen. Explain why they have been selected. Explain the procedure and the next steps. Explain what you expect from them.

Appreciate the participants' feelings. They have a right to feel uncertain in a new situation. You want the participants to listen. And they will listen as soon as they have calmed down. Help them calm down by sensing their emotions. Talk about how they might feel. Try to understand what they need to feel at ease. Appreciate the importance of their work and their role.

Allow time to make them feel comfortable with the process. You want the participants to listen. And they will listen as soon as they have had enough time to adapt to the situation. Their priorities should be your priorities. What they need to know is more important than what you need to say.

13.1.2 Advisor in Interviews

"Okay", said Greg. "That sounds reasonable. Now I understand. I often found that colleagues would ask questions quite late on in the audit process about something I had already explained. That made me furious. 'Why didn't they listen the first time?' If I understand you correctly, their minds were initially blocked by all their questions about the Software Sustainability Audit, and by their feelings. That prevented them from taking in what I told them."

"Correct!" Sam said. "It is like an electronic network, like a handshake protocol. You cannot send messages unless the recipients are ready. And they will be ready if you have addressed their needs and appreciated them."

Greg liked this architectural pattern. It explained many strange events in the past.

"Now, what about the interviews?" Greg continued. "How can you act as an advisor there? Isn't it your job to ask questions, to interrogate? That sounds more like a policing function, doesn't it?"

Again, Sam sees a big difference. "Assume that you are at a police station to report damage to your car. How will the police treat you?"

"No idea." Greg is bemused.

Sam answered his own question. "Look, the police will almost certainly ask you a set of fixed questions. 'What is your name, your address, your telephone number, your date of birth? When did the event take place?' They might not even know what actually happened, and what damage has been incurred. They don't want to hear about anything else until they are satisfied that you have answered all their questions in full."

Sam seems to have had experience with the police. Greg thought. Or he watches a lot of crime movies.

Sam continued to explain. "In audits you can follow the same approach, or handle it differently. It's your decision. Of course you have a list of questions you need to address. However, that doesn't necessarily mean that you need to ask them in a fixed sequence. Nor does it mean that no other information can be provided in-between. In fact, it doesn't even mean that you have to ask all the questions. If people give you information freely, you might not need to ask for it. You could get the answers for nothing."

"Ah, I understand." says Greg. "I assume that the colleagues have priority again. First, let them talk, and then ask the remaining questions. Is that what you are telling me?"

"Exactly!" Sam is delighted with how quickly Greg has grasped this communication principle. "Approach the interviewees in an open manner, and make sure that you leave with all the necessary information."

From this dialog, we can take some principles for interviews. As Sam stated, openness is the most important one. An open atmosphere has several flavors.

Firstly, try to ask open questions, questions starting with "what, why, how, which, and so on." People tell stories when you ask open questions. Most of the time, you will receive more information than you expected, often with surprising details. Closed questions that require only a yes/no answer are appropriate for confirmations. Otherwise, favor open questions, which also help to create a relaxed atmosphere, and make interviewees feel more comfortable.

Secondly, don't stick rigidly to a set of questions in a given order. Let the interviewee provide information as it comes to him, even if the corresponding question is lower down on your list, or perhaps not even on your list at all. Let people talk, at least as long as the content is valuable. With this strategy, you get the information you need, and the interviewees feel good. Most of the time, they want to tell their story. Let them tell it.

Thirdly, check if your questions have been answered. Take a brief list of questions into the interview, and at the end of the discussion, make sure you are fully satisfied with the answers you have been given. If important questions remain unanswered, this is the time to continue with the open questions from your questionnaire.

Finally, motivate the interviewees to share their burning issues. During the interview session, you will have covered a lot of facts, and might have had intense discussions – all relating to the audit topics. When you reach the end of the session, take the opportunity to ask about entirely different issues. "Besides what we have discussed, are there any other issues that could I help you to address?" Don't hurry. Give the interviewees time to think about it. It is surprising how often essential facts come to light when you give people a moment to reflect after an exhausting discussion.

13.1.3 Advising on the Results

Greg was excited. He was starting to understand the difference between a policing and an advisory role. "I can already imagine what you are going to tell me about the audit reports. In a policing role, you would just send a final report, which would have to be accepted as given – with all its statements and recommendations. Sure, somebody could object, but that would mean starting an escalation process. I assume that in an advisory role you involve the participants when you provide guidance. But how do you balance the advice that is based on your own expertise and experience with the input from the other stakeholders?"

"Almost", Sam replied with a smile on his face. Sam noticed that Greg now thinks too cautiously. "This time, you need some strength to act as consultant. You are expected to bring in your expertise and offer an independent view. So you need to provide clear recommendations. At the same time, it is still a good idea to convince the managers responsible that your recommendations make sense for them as well."

Now Greg was puzzled again. "How can I convince people to follow my recommendations? How can I succeed if I do not have executive power? How can I enforce things without acting as a police officer?"

Sam smiled and answered. "How do good managers succeed, even though they can never have absolute control over the individuals who work for them? That's when communication really matters ..."

Audit sponsors want clear guidance on how to resolve the issues you have identified in Software Sustainability Audits. In parallel, it is important that you align with those managers who will be responsible for carrying out the actions you are proposing. In a policing role, you would just throw the actions over the fence; you would present the required measures, and then order their execution. As an advisor, you explain the situation to the managers responsible. You explain why you are recommending certain actions. You convince them that your suggestions are crucial for their success. And you document their acceptance of the proposed measures.

13.2 Where Communication Matters

"Effective and clear communication can significantly improve the quality of audits and maximize their results. Audit findings should be reported and communicated to stakeholders with appropriate buy-in from the auditees for the audit process to be successful. Auditors should also take into account the motivations and perspectives of recipients of the audit report so that their concerns may be properly addressed. Communication skills (both written and verbal) determine the effectiveness of the audit reporting process. Communication and negotiation skills are required throughout the audit activity." [3]

The Information Systems Audit and Control Association (ISACA®), an organization that educates information systems auditors on auditing principles, also emphasizes the relevance of effective and clear communication. In its book for certification of information systems auditors, it highlights five areas where communication counts.

First, communication matters throughout the audit process. To make the audit successful, you need to communicate clearly at all times. Secondly, good communication is a prerequisite for ensuring that all the events and meetings for the audit run smoothly. The third area is conflict resolution; as effective as your communication may be, there will always be difficult situations. Fourthly, findings need to be reported in such a manner that they will be accepted. Lastly, the findings and recommendations need to be explained. Negotiations may be needed to convince others about the necessary activities.

But what is clear and effective communication? There are situations where clear communication can be everything but effective. It seems that clear communication can ignite the emotions of participants. They feel ashamed or just irritated by the reported findings. And as a consequence, they are reluctant to implement the recommended measures. Convincing people can be difficult when emotions run high. Does this mean that clear communication and effective communication are opposing goals that we need to balance?

Greg had invited all interviewees to a final meeting. After several interviews and other audit activities he had realized that the situation was critical. They would need to act immediately. Clear communication is important now, thought Greg.

"Good afternoon colleagues. I've analyzed the facts and come to the conclusion that we need to take urgent action. Given the limited time we have, I will summarize my observations: Number one, architecture results are not being communicated clearly. I recommend . . ."

"What do you mean by 'not being communicated clearly'? We report all major decisions in our project newsletter." The project manager was very agitated.

"That might be the case, but I read your architecture document. In the interviews, architects talked about an abstraction layer that has been rejected . . ." Greg tried to answer the question he had understood.

"That was just an irrelevant discussion we had in the project" the project lead contested.

"It is absolutely relevant . . ." Greg tried to explain.

"Do you have any experience in project management?" The project manager was about to explode.

Greg didn't understand what was going on. What was wrong with his summary of the findings?

Clear communication can be difficult. There are obstacles like summaries, which stand in the way of clarity. A summary is a generalization of a concrete observation. And generalizations hide the facts. Generalizations involve assumptions that are not stated explicitly. By contrast, clear communication states the pure facts first. Clear communication leads to effective communication. That just leaves one question: What is clear communication?

There are other situations where appropriate communication strategies can help. Consider an interview with an over-talkative colleague. How do you best interrupt and steer the conversation back to the relevant topics? Or what about silent individuals? How can you get them to share what they know? And how do you deal with people who are politically motivated?

It matters how you communicate. But what is appropriate communication? What is clear?

13.3   Communication Principles

Most of the communication principles we will be introducing here can be found in pertinent literature. So why are we citing literature on communication? We want to highlight communication principles that we feel are relevant and important in the context of Software Sustainability Audits. We will explain these principles using examples from Software Sustainability Audits to make them more tangible. The topics we have selected are issues that we come across over and over again in Software Sustainability Audits.

13.3.1 Four Sides of a Statement

If we talk about communication principles, we cannot afford to ignore the German communication psychologist Friedemann Schulz von Thun. It would be rather unfair to reduce Schulz von Thun's achievements to his model depicting the four sides of a statement [10]. There is much more in his books about communication psychology that is worth exploring (e.g. [10–13]). Here, we can only introduce the essence of his theory. Figure 13.1 illustrates the main idea of the four sides of a statement (also known as the four beaks and four ears model).

> *Greg started to explain the main result of his Software Sustainability Audit. "There is evidence that the documentation of the architecture is incomplete."*
>
> *The responsible architect replied: "Oh, you want us to add a graphic with all the building blocks. This is incredible! . . ."*
>
> *"No, no", answered Greg. "You got me wrong. I don't mean it personally. It is just, you know, it is not that I am judging your architectural expertise. I know and value your skills. . ."*
>
> *"Now I am irritated", interrupted the architect. "I am disappointed with your judgment in this case."*

It's easy to talk at cross purposes. And the best way of doing so it is to use a different side of the message. Schulz von Thun calls them four ears and four beaks. There are four ears you can use to understand a message, and four beaks you can use to send one. The example above moves around these four sides using different beaks and ears. Greg intended to send a message with factual information. *"The documentation is incomplete"*. For some (good) reason, this was understood as an appeal. *"I have to complete my architecture documentation."* thought the architect. In turn, the remark thrown in by the architect ("This is incredible!") made Greg nervous. He took this to be an indicator that their good working relationship was in danger. Greg tried to kit this relationship again, but the architect responded by saying how he feels ("I am disappointed . . .") – a typical self statement in the four-sides model.

You cannot avoid sending messages other than those you intended to send. Nor can you prevent someone from hearing a bundle of different messages in a single

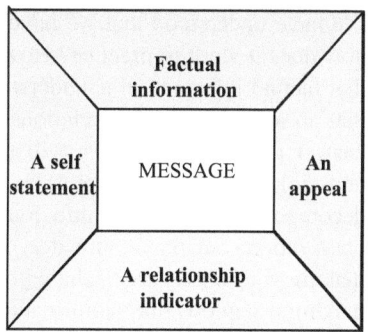

Fig. 13.1 Schulz von Thun's
four sides of a statement

statement. There are ways to emphasize the side of the message you want to send, and we will introduce those techniques later. First though, it is important to realize that you always send and receive different messages. Be aware of this communication dilemma, and try to understand what kind of message has been received. In complicated communications, it can be a good idea to take one step back and repeat the intended message, rather moving to another side of the message – like Greg and the architect did in the example above.

13.3.2 Perception Is Reality

Greg asked, "Why are you not listening? I just started to explain the root cause of one main result. The architecture documentation is not complete."
"Why are you not listening?" replied the architect, now becoming even angrier. . . .

A typical pattern is to take the intended message as reality. "I have said what I have said. Period!" But the words spoken are not reality. The listener perceived something differently, and perception is the one and only reality. In other words, something that is not perceived has not been (effectively) communicated. Don't try to blame the recipient of your message. If a message is not perceived correctly, start to correct the way you are sending of the message. Schulz von Thun's four ears four beaks model can help you see what is happening. When you feel that your message has not been heard, try to identify which side of your message has actually been received. And be careful. You might already be hearing another side of a message yourself.

Ultimately, perception is reality. As long as the person you are talking to doesn't hear the message you want to send, reality is distorted. Work on the perception and you will change the reality.

13.3.3 Non-violent Communication (NVC)

We have understood that we have to take care in sending the right message. But, how does it work in practice? How can we send factual information in such a way that factual information is understood? How can we send an appeal in such a way that an appeal and not a relationship message is received by the other party? To answer these questions, we will borrow from Marshal B Rosenberg's theory on non-violent communication [5]. Like Schulz von Thun, Rosenberg suggests decomposing a message into four parts. His theory is simple: Start with your observation, but make sure it is impartial, and leave out any evaluations. After making your observation, share your true feelings, and outline your needs. End by making a request, but avoid making a demand. Figure 13.2 gives an overview of these four message components.

Fig. 13.2 The four
components of a message
according to Rosenberg's
NVC model

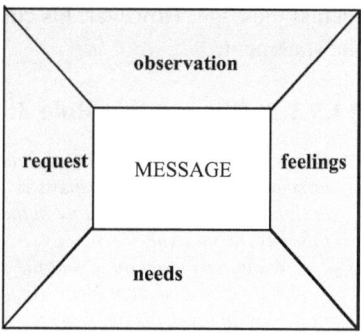

That sounds simple enough, and this communication style is also very effective. But it is incredibly difficult to practice. We are just not used to it. We talk differently in our everyday life. And the difficulties start with the observation.

13.3.3.1 Observation Rule 1: Avoid Generalizations

Greg started to explain his results again. "All the architects in this department lack an understanding of the business requirements."

"Well, maybe this is true for others, but not for me ..." is a common response, regardless of whether it is actually spoken out loud.

Generalization already involves a judgment, and violates objective observation. How can Greg know all the architects? Has he interviewed every single architect in the department?

13.3.3.2 Observation Rule 2: Avoid Adverbs and Adjectives

"Okay, let's try to phrase it differently," Greg tried to correct his statement. "I have interviewed two architects, Tom and Tim. They told me that they were introduced to the business requirements only briefly."

"When you say 'briefly', what do you mean exactly? What information were they missing?" Alex, the architect, now wants to understand the issue in detail.

"The business requirements outlined to them were very vague." Greg tried to remember.

Typically, adjectives and adverbs carry an implicit evaluation. While we use these little words to adorn our statements and to excite others, adjectives and adverbs can be communication killers. They are yet another form of abstraction. What does "briefly" mean? Furthermore, adding the word "only" conveys a judgment: if the explanation is brief, it won't be understood. So Greg actually stumbled over two communication hurdles by saying "only briefly". First, he did not describe the concrete observation. Second, he added his evaluation of the situation to the observation. The impact of failing to make clear observations can be explained using the four-sides model by Schulz von Thun. Greg wanted to communicate a factual message. However, his counterpart receives one of the three other sides of the statement.

13.3.3.3 Observation Rule 3: Do Not Mix Your Opinion with the Truth

Greg is exhausted. Explaining the pure observation is difficult, he thought. He made a third attempt. "Without clear business requirements, the architects won't be able to deliver an architecture that will be stable in the business environment." Let's try to explain the facts this way, he thought.
"What makes you think that the architects will fail?"
The response made it clear. Again, Greg had not succeeded in expressing an observation. He had given his opinion on a possible impact, and made it sound like a fact. But it is not. It is merely his assessment of a possible consequence.

It is okay to talk about consequences. As an advisor, you are expected to bring up risks and potential consequences. But a different format would be more appropriate. And consequences should be addressed at a later stage, not to replace an observation. Separating opinions and facts is not always a trivial task, but if you fail to do so, the impact on communication is destructive. Some people might take your opinions as given, as statements of fact. This can lead to a sequence of misunderstandings, which typically cause confusion and conflicts. Others will just be irritated by the discrepancy between what they perceive and what they have just been told. It irritates them. They either express their discomfort with an outburst of emotion, or just sit in silence. However they react, the communication channel is broken and needs to be restored.

13.3.3.4 Observation Rule 4: Avoid Comparisons

"A picture is worth a thousand words", thought Greg. "So, why not use a comparison to illustrate the observation?"
"In other departments, more documentation is available on the architecture", Greg started to explain again.
"Yes, I know. But the other departments need much more time to do the same as we do. We are much more efficient because we don't waste time producing documents that don't add value." The principal architect responded with another comparison, a very emotional comparison.

Comparisons are always false friends when you want to communicate pure facts. You might think you can describe a situation better by contrasting it with other, well-known situations. You assume that the difference will be obvious, and that your message will be implicit in the comparison. A picture can say more than a 1,000 words, and can shed light on the facts. But, taken personally, a picture can also provoke emotions. In terms of the four-sides communication model, you want to use the comparison to send factual information. However, the person receiving the message often hears an appeal; "The other team is better. You have to behave like the other team." Continuing to mention this other team will just cause resentment.

Greg decides to apply what he has learned. When making observations, he takes care to avoid generalizations, adverbs and adjectives. He separates his opinion from the facts, and expresses his opinion as a risk. He replaces the comparison with the missing facts, and recommends additional documentation.

"I have interviewed two architects, Tom and Tim. They told me that they have been introduced to the business requirements, and confirmed that they have understood the business processes. However, some important information was missing, such as the expected number of concurrent users in the system, and the expected user response times. According to Tom and Tim, the business owner was unable to specify the load on the system, so Tom and Tim had to make their own assumptions. Since these are only assumptions, and not figures they were given, they did not document them as non-functional requirements in the architecture document. I agree with Tim and Tom that we have a potential risk here; if the assumptions turn out to be wrong, the current architecture will have to be rebuilt. I would also recommend documenting the assumptions in the architecture document. In addition, I recommend specifying which part of the architecture diagram could break if the assumptions are wrong."

13.3.3.5 Attend to Emotions to Resolve Conflicts

Dealing with emotions professionally is also an important aspect in non-violent communication. However, these topics extend beyond the scope of this book. They would lead us into the territory of conflict resolution methods, which justifies a book in its own right. Our reference list includes a number of excellent books about conflict resolution, which we can highly recommend.

13.3.3.6 The Company's Needs as the Foundation for Recommendations

We want to pause for a moment at the third component of non-violent communication, the needs. Rosenberg talks about addressing individual needs. This can involve revealing your own needs, or mentioning the needs of others. Addressing needs is also an essential part of conflict resolution. For Software Sustainability Audits, we would like to introduce another kind of need: The needs of the company, the department, or the product that is going to be developed and shipped. As with individual needs, it is very powerful to identify and address these needs. By combining the facts you have observed and the needs you have identified, you can make powerful recommendations. If the fact is agreed as a fact, and the need is a real and recognized need, how can anybody object your recommendation? On the contrary; your recommendation will be seen as professional, business-driven advice.

This brings us to the last component of non-violent communication, requests. Requests should be formulated such that they are not perceived as demands. What is the difference between requests and demands? Rosenberg has many answers to this question, but with respect to Software Sustainability Audit, we would reduce them to two crucial statements:

13.3.3.7 Request Rule 1: Be Precise and Concrete

First, like observations, requests need to be clear. They should not be formulated vaguely, allowing several interpretations. Requests should include all the information that is needed to actually carry them out.

13.3.3.8 Request Rule 2: Give an Option to Agree or Disagree

Secondly, requests should be suggestions that the other party is free to take on board. Demands have to be followed. They are instructions. Period! By contrast, requests are proposals that can be accepted or rejected. You still have the option to decide.

These two rules may sound contradictory at a first glance. Why not listen to Gregory and his CIO Kai again to understand them better?

> Greg summarized the most important result of his investigations. "The two projects I have assessed have had numerous customer contacts in the past three months." Greg started with his observation on customer interactions. "These projects had failed on customer acceptance in the two previous releases, which forced them to intensify the customer relationship. They have reached out to at least four customers to gain a better understanding of their needs and business requirements."
>
> "I understand" said Kai. "That sounds very impressive. So what is the issue?"
>
> Greg continued. "Actually, there are no more issues with these two projects, since they now talk to their customers. But before they did, they failed. The issue is more about ensuring that other projects also involve customers. The interviews and the process assessment revealed that there is no control mechanism to ensure that project teams involve customers to understand their product requirements."
>
> "You've lost me", said Kai. "Haven't all the development teams been advised – strongly advised – to integrate customers in their scrum meetings?" Kai was irritated.
>
> Greg noticed Kai's confusion and moved on. "Yes, development teams are asked to invite customers. However, even though customer interaction has been preached as a success factor, the teams are empowered to handle these interactions as they see fit. There is no control over how customer requirements are considered. While we have seen good progress in the two projects I mentioned, there is a high risk of other projects failing."
>
> "I understand," Kai nodded. "The two projects you assessed have learned from their problems in the past. But you are worried about all the other, new projects. What would you recommend?"
>
> Greg felt that the observation and the risk had been communicated clearly. He could now move on and request actions. "It's vital that we have a clear understanding of customer requirements to build successful products. While I respect the empowerment of the individual development organizations, I recommend installing controls to verify customer interactions before products are released. There is a method called "control self assessment", which respects the autonomy of teams and still provides controls in the team. This could be an option, though there are also other methods. If you would like to know more about this method, I would be happy to elaborate."

Greg split his recommendation into two parts. First, he made a clear recommendation to install controls. He defined the control objective (verify customer interaction) and was also precise about the timing (before the product release). But he left the method open. In the second part of his recommendation, he mentioned one method (control self assessment), and pointed out that other methods also exist. It was clear that Greg favored the control self assessment method, but he offered it as an option, and Kai could easily opt for another one. Greg made a strong recommendation for a control mechanism, but left it to Kai to decide on the method.

13.3.4 Getting to Yes: The Harvard Concept

In many Software Sustainable Audits, negotiation is paramount to success. While findings are often easy to consume, the acceptance of recommended actions can be difficult. Roger Fisher, William Ury and Bruce Patton [5, 6] propose a package of methods that can help in conducting successful negotiations. Two of these methods are particularly relevant for Software Sustainability Audits.

13.3.4.1 Each Perspective Has a Subjective Truth

Greg has audited a recently-developed product in the area run by development manager Macdonald. In the closing meeting, Greg explained that he found security awareness lacking in the audited development teams. As a result, he sees a risk of security gaps in the finished solution. The manager Macdonald disagreed, and they scheduled a follow-up meeting to discuss the finding further.

It is the third time that this development area has been involved in a Software Sustainability Audit. Greg was always annoyed by the arrogant behavior of the manager, who always ignored Greg's audit findings when they were presented in the closing meeting. However, Greg found out through his architect's network that all his recommendations were implemented almost immediately. "Why can't the manager respect me?" Greg thought.

In this particular audit, Greg had found evidence that no security threat model has been designed, even though the architect and other experts in the development team agreed that they were developing a sensitive component with a high risk of being hacked. Due to pressure from the market, however, the product owner prioritized full functional coverage over performing security tests and resolving potential security issues. Greg even identified a potential security weakness in an architecture document. This risk needs to be assessed further and then handled properly, depending on the outcome. For Greg, all of this was evidence that there was a lack of security awareness in the team!

"The manager probably doesn't want to know all the details" Greg anticipated. "So, I'll just summarize. But he should at least accept that the lack of security awareness poses a risk. Let's stick to that finding," thought Greg. "The negotiation will be difficult and lengthy enough. I wonder why Macdonald couldn't accept the finding in the first place."

Some negotiations fail because each party sticks to his own priority and trusts only his own perception. But every perception is based on a perspective and has its own truth. Respecting perspectives can be helpful during two audit phases.

Firstly, trying to figure out the other's perspective during an audit can help to identify the root cause of a problem in interviews. Learning more about the others' perspectives gives you insight into why something has been done or omitted. This can reveal the true issue underlying the initial finding.

Secondly, putting yourself in the other person's shoes when you compile the audit report can invite you to consider other arguments; arguments which are easier to accept at closing meetings, and which can help you to achieve a consensus on the required actions.

Greg feels hurt by the manager's reaction in all three audits. It is very likely that he will react emotionally in the upcoming meeting. But Greg has an option. He can ask "What prevents Macdonald from accepting the finding? What is the rationale behind his objection? What is his view?" Greg would find it easier to reach a consensus if he were to stop insisting on the finding for a moment, and try to understand the manager's perspective first.

> *The development manager Macdonald was in a bad mood when he went to the closing meeting. This was already the third audit in his department. "The audit team must have some secret reason for running audit upon audit in my area" Macdonald felt. "I think that I know how to manage my department. And I don't think that I need audits to do a better job."*
>
> *Macdonald had in fact spoken to his teams several times, encouraging them to take security seriously. He had also monitored whether everybody had attended the security awareness training course – his department had a 100% participation rate. "Security awareness isn't an issue in my department" Macdonald was sure.*
>
> *However, he was curious about the details of what Greg had identified. He respects him as experienced architect. "Greg might have noticed something that neither I nor my software architects have picked up on so far – as he did in the last two audits. But I will not allow him to behave as the manager of my department!"*

These two perspectives are worlds apart. Greg believes that his results are ignored by the manager, while Macdonald actually respects his architectural expertise. As such, Macdonald is curious about details, while Greg assumes that he only expects a management summary. At the same time, the summary deviates from the objective findings, and incorporates Greg's personal conclusion that the team members are not sufficiently aware of security. In reality, the manager Macdonald had made a considerable effort to raise the level of security awareness.

Different perspectives led to different conclusions and different perceptions. The result was a major misunderstanding. However, it is easy to escape this vicious circle. Greg just needs to park his own perspective and try to put himself into Macdonald's shoes.

13.3.4.2 Focus on Interests, Not on Positions

The story above also brings another truth to light. Both the manager and the auditor focus on their own positions. Greg's position is that the manager should admit the lack of security awareness. Macdonald's position is that he has invested enough in educating the team on security awareness. Again, the simple question "why?" would have helped them overcome the mutual misunderstandings. What are their true interests? It is likely that both Greg and Macdonald have a vested interest in delivering a successful software product. And alongside these common business interests, basic human needs hidden beneath the surface may in fact be the most powerful interests.

Both parties are seeking respect for their roles. They are people and want to be treated with respect. Both of them want to save face, and they react accordingly.

As an auditor, Greg insists on the abstract finding, because he believes his findings are accurate. However, he never asked if the manager wants to learn about the details. He assumed that a management summary was sufficient.

As a manager, Macdonald wants people to respect his authority. He had taken the necessary steps to bring security awareness to the teams. In the closing meeting, he cannot accept a finding that questions his authority.

As soon as Greg starts to understand Macdonald's view and needs, instead of concentrating on his own, he will succeed.

13.3.5 Neuro-linguistic Programming (NLP)

You are probably wondering why we have included a section on NLP [1, 2, 7]. We are a long way from introducing instruments that can re-program the brains of other people. Nor are we interested in providing guidance for hypnosis in Software Sustainability Audits. Nevertheless, we admit that this could improve the quality of the information we get. Someone under hypnosis would certainly talk more. We would find out about interesting details, which nobody would have told us about otherwise. And re-programming brains could help us to plant our recommendations directly in the brains of the colleagues who have to support and execute them. So we can't deny that the idea of using such methods bears some fascination. However, this is not an approach we will ever subscribe to. Not only because we are not NLP experts, but primarily because of the stance we have taken in the section "Police or Advisor". An approach based on control and intervention would not tally with our understanding of dealing with and respecting other people.

So why are we interested in NLP? The reason is that NLP also covers linguistic analytics, which can be very helpful in explaining what happens to a message when we communicate it to someone else. It is this linguistic theory we want to introduce.

When we looked at non-violent communication and how to define observations, we came across a challenge. To relate the facts precisely means that we have to dig for "hidden" information and make it more explicit. In natural language we like to cloud information. A story is more entertaining if we leave certain aspects open. We invite the brain to think about what we have said. The brain feeds on puzzles, and we provide this "brain food" by hiding facts. Our brains immediately start to eat these hidden facts. They perceive them as puzzles and start to solve them. However, in non-violent communication, our aim is to make precise observations. Any unclear, hidden information can block the communication. We have to do the opposite. In observations we unveil hidden information, we delete the holes. The question that remains is: How do we hide information in the first place? And how can we add these pieces of information back in again? O'Connor and Seymour [8] talk about a deep structure and a surface structure. The deep structure contains the exact details. On the surface you only see fragments of the original information set.

Figure 13.3 below gives an example of linguistic transformation. The word "specific thoughts" is first generalized to just "thoughts". This word is then deformed again; the characters of the word "thoughts" are shuffled to "toushhgt". Later, some of the characters are deleted, leaving us with "tgt". In the end, the character "g" is even replaced by an "x".

We can transfer this linguistic concept to communication. The sections below look at how the different transformation operations can affect our communications in a Software Sustainability Audit.

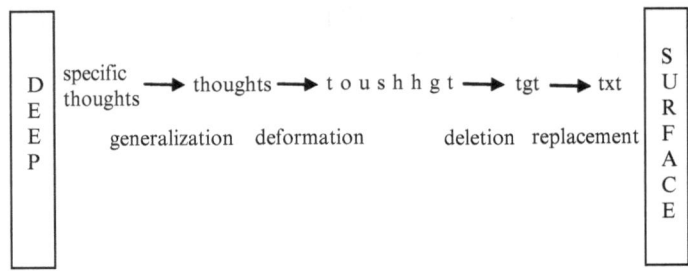

Fig. 13.3 Linguistic transformation according to NLP by O'Connor and Seymour [8]

13.3.5.1 Generalization

Generalization is one of the most prominent operations that lead from the deeper, detailed level to the surface. We have already encountered generalization in non-violent communication. The basic observation seems too simple, so the brain tries to combine two steps: capturing what we have observed, and concluding what it means. And this often leads to a generalization of the facts. The specific observation Greg made was that "*he got information from two architects, Tim and Tom.*" While formulating the observation he was already thinking of the next step: What does this mean? He generalized the pure fact and transformed this observation into "*all architects*".

13.3.5.2 Deformation

Deformation is another transforming operation. Changing the order of information can impact communication. Let's look again at non-violent communication. This approach strictly separates four communication elements: observation, feeling, need, and request. If we deform statements by mixing these elements, we are likely to end up with a statement that will be misunderstood by the listener. For example, if we mix our feelings with the observation, our statement will be judgmental.

Another common example of deformation is when the summary comes before the actual finding:

> "*The architecture is not robust. The architects Tim and Tom did not consider non-functional requirements.*"

This statement combines an observation "Tim and Tom did not consider non-functional requirements" with Greg's conclusion that "there is a risk that the architecture is not robust". Note that even the observation is distorted; Greg states that Tim and Tom did not consider non-functional requirements. In reality, these requirements were not explained to them.

13.3.5.3 Replacements

Deformation often goes hand in hand with replacements. Consider the following statement made by Greg:

> "*The architecture documentation is incomplete.*"

But what was missing? If the architecture documentation is incomplete, then for whom or with respect to what is it not complete? Somebody must have decided that certain information, which Greg hasn't found, is essential. Who made this decision, and for what reason? There may not be an answer to this compliance question, because it might not be a compliance issue at all.

Greg could have simply said:

> *"I feel uncomfortable when I see that the architecture documentation does not include a statement on performance and scalability requirements. I think that performance and scalability are important for this solution. If we are not clear on these non-functional requirements, we risk implementing the solution without taking these factors into account. And when the solution is used productively, we might find that the architecture should have allowed for greater throughput."*

This analysis would have clearly separated the observation, Greg's opinion, and the risks Greg sees.

Initially, Greg not only mixed up the observation with his opinion. The "missing performance statements" and Greg's opinion on "the risk of an instable architecture" were simply replaced by "the architecture documentation is incomplete."

13.3.5.4 Deletion

The last transforming operation we would like to discuss is the deletion operation. Architects know that they have to provide concise statements. Managers are short on time and expect to be briefed efficiently. This is a good reason to leave out any irrelevant information.

All these transforming operations remind us of grammar. Okay, it is nice to understand what can happen to statements. But what is it good for? The benefit is that if we can recognize the transformations, we can react properly. What "properly" means depends on the situation. This will become clear when we apply these communication principles to Software Sustainability Audits later on in this chapter.

But before we start to look into Software Sustainability Audits and how to use these communication principles, we would like to touch on a few more aspects of communication.

13.3.6 Further Aspects of Communication

There are a few other simple communication rules that we encounter almost daily in Software Sustainability Audits (and in other circumstances). Even though these aspects may seem trivial, we think they are important enough to be mentioned. If something is simple to understand, it does not mean that we apply it in reality. We see the opposite in our daily life. As such, these communication aspects may also be relevant for you.

13.3.6.1 Communicating Effectively Means Communicating Frequently

Kai sent out his monthly CIO newsletter, which included an article about the company's new security guidelines. When he realized that the guidelines were being ignored completely, he was shocked.

"Insubordination!" Kai cried.

He called Gregory to discuss the consequences. Greg noticed that his CIO was in a very bad mood.

"What security guidelines?" Greg asked innocently.

The CIO exploded.

This story sounds ridiculous. A topic like security is important enough to warrant a comprehensive rollout strategy. In this case, the new security guideline would not just be mentioned in a newsletter. There would be posters on all the walls. A video would be posted in the company portal. And all managers would be instructed to brief their teams. We would automatically send updates on the topic. The message has to be heard, read and understood. In other words, the statement has to be broadcast repeatedly.

The way we consume messages is no different for other topics. If you want information to reach your audience, you need to send the message frequently. We all suffer from information overload. We receive dozens of monthly newsletters and countless emails. We attend team meetings, departmental meetings, and all-hands meetings held by upper management. We use our breaks to read blogs. And even as we walk from one meeting to another, we continue to gather information. Welcome to the information age!

However, when it we communicate ourselves, we often fail to acknowledge this new reality. We communicate our message only once. Sometimes we add an importance flag. Yet we are irritated when we notice that our message has not been understood, or perhaps not even been registered.

The same fundamental truth applies to both important and less important news. We have to communicate it frequently. In the end, perception is reality. A message that is not perceived has not been sent successfully.

13.3.6.2 Not Being Heard Blocks Communication

Kai has been asked by his CEO to conduct an infrastructure audit. Daily news about hackers is making the CEO nervous. He is seeking greater clarity about the security status of the company's infrastructure. Kai has invited Gregory to discuss the upcoming audit.

Greg was glad to receive the meeting invitation. He is currently running a Software Sustainability Audit, and has encountered some difficulties. One manager keeps rejecting his meeting requests, even though this manager's input is crucial for the success of the audit. Greg hopes to get support from his CIO. The meeting, Greg thought, is a good opportunity to address this challenge.

Kai started the meeting: "We need to audit our infrastructure. I think we should start to interview the managers responsible."

"Well, that might be difficult", Greg replied. "It's not easy to get hold of the managers." Gregory had his issue in mind.

> *Kai responded, "I'm confident that you'll be able to handle that. What I'd like to do is ..." Kai wanted to continue with the new audit.*
>
> *But Greg interrupted. "How can you support me if managers decline interviews?"*
>
> *"That won't happen," Kai was sure. "The security topic is too important. And we have support from the top. It's a request from your CEO."*
>
> *Greg was not convinced. He persisted. "But what can I do if they remain reluctant? What support can I expect from you?"*
>
> *Greg actually had his recent case in mind. He was talking about a current problem with one manager in the ongoing audit, rather than about the new audit Kai was proposing. And Kai had no clue why Greg was so reluctant. He seemed to be different this time. But why?*

Obviously, Kai and Gregory are talking about different things. Greg has an issue that, for him, is a real burden. He wants his issue to be heard, and until he feels this is the case, he will not be able to listen. His problem does not need to be solved immediately, but Kai has to acknowledge it. Until Kai signals that he has heard Greg's problem, he himself will not be heard. Communication is blocked.

There can be several reasons why somebody is not heard. But they all have one thing in common: communication is blocked. If you notice obstacles in your communication, check whether somebody needs to be heard first.

13.3.6.3 Don't Ask Why

"Don't ask why!" – Now that sounds silly at a first glance. You are more likely to have heard of a contrary rule: Ask "why" five times. If you want to identify the root cause, ask "why" five times.

> *"There is no architecture documentation."*
>
> *"Why?" – "There was no time to write the document."*
>
> *"Why was there no time?" – "The development team had other priorities."*
>
> *"Why did the team have other priorities?" – "Management has assigned new tasks to the team."*
>
> *"Why?" – "The new tasks were more important"*
>
> *"Why were the new tasks more important?" – "Well, the previous project had been stopped and a new project has been started."*

"Why" can indeed shed some light onto the situation. So, why not ask why? There is a psychological aspect we need to consider whenever we ask questions starting with "why" [4]. By the time you are an adult, you will have used this word many, many times. As a child, busy exploring the world, you asked, and asked. You will have pestered your parents with questions like "Why is the earth round?" But there will also have been other situations, where your parents were the ones asking why. "Why have you broken the glass?" "Why have you come in with dirty shoes?" "Why" has been misused as an accusation. Your parents did not expect to find out the rationale for your behavior. And this "why" still rests in your subconscious. Sometimes, more often than you would think, your question "why" will not lead you to the underlying rationale, but instead activate these parked feelings from childhood. And that can trigger an emotional discussion.

> *"There is no architecture document."*
>
> *"Why?"*
>
> *"Why do you ask?"*

"Sorry? It was a simple question. I just want do understand why there is no architecture documentation."
"Is there a particular reason why you are asking for the architecture documentation? Is anything wrong?"
"Could you please just explain to me why there is no architecture document?"
"Yes, I can. But first I need to understand why you are asking me."

So what can you do if you need to find the root cause and "why" is such a dangerous word? There are other words you can use instead that do not carry this connotation. For example, you can ask: "What caused . . .?", or "Who ..?". These other words have an additional advantage. You can get a more qualified explanation of the root cause. It is not always the rationale or the "why" that you are interested in. Sometimes you actually want to know who triggered something, what has happened, or where you can find something. Why is just much easier. You don't need to think about your real question. But it could lead you into a lengthy discussion. Our recommendation here: Avoid why, wherever possible. Think about what your actual question is.

13.3.6.4 What to Do If All Else Fails?

We could continue with many other communication tips. And communication psychologists have written books containing much more about successful communication. However, no matter however much you read, and however much of this you manage to put into practice, there will always be communication situations where you feel you might fail.

Whenever you feel trapped in such a situation, we have a final recommendation: Take people seriously. Take people seriously with all their emotions and needs. When you feel that you are going to fail in your communication, and you do not know what led you into such an uncomfortable debate, take a break. Stop to think. Anything else you say could make the communication even worse. Break off your current line of thought and ask yourself why the discussion could have derailed? What might the person you are talking to be feeling that could have steered the conversation in this direction? What need has to be met before you can turn it into a constructive conversation again? Take people with their feelings and needs seriously. And address both before you push on with your own agenda.

13.4 Communication in Software Sustainability Audits

While the communication theory we discussed in the last section is helpful in a variety of situations, some aspects are particularly relevant for the different steps in a Software Sustainability Audit. In this section, we want to present some important use cases.

13.4.1 Throughout the Process

13.4.1.1 Continuous Communication Provides a Comfort Zone

Emotions are your constant companion throughout the process. You are confronted with feelings from the moment you begin a Software Sustainability Audit. You send an announcement that a Software Sustainability Audit will take place. And you ask the affected managers and their teams for support. Typically, they will get back to you straight away. People tend to get nervous. Why this audit? Why will they be interviewed? And most importantly, what does the process look like? What will happen? Who will receive what information? Everything is unknown. And because everything is unknown, individuals feel uncomfortable. They need security, and to get it they need information.

As we have learned, we start Software Sustainability Audits with an opening meeting. There, we meet these needs, and address the discomfort of the people who have been invited. To put them at ease, we explain the process, what will happen, and what they can expect from the interviews and reports. We can see the effect immediately. The participants calm down and are ready for the next steps of the audit. As the audit gets underway, remember that day-to-day business will push the details from the opening meeting into the back of their minds. The next steps need to be communicated frequently throughout the audit process. We recommend informing the audit participants regularly about the status, about ongoing activities, and about when they can expect the results. Providing information on a recurring basis demonstrates transparency. People can see how the audit is being run, and are not kept in the dark about how the information they have provided is being used. To keep people on board, keep them up to date.

13.4.1.2 What Comes Next?

You know the Software Sustainability Audit process inside out. However, the participants will not memorize all the details you provided in the opening meeting. They will usually keep asking "and what comes next". This just shows their uncertainty. As for other aspects of the audit, communicate the next steps frequently.

For example, when you hold a closing meeting to present your draft results, explain what will follow. Explain what you expect from the participants (namely agreement or disagreement with your findings and recommendations; comments on findings and recommendations, and so forth). And explain what they can expect from you (namely the draft report in timely manner). Reiterate this information by sending an e-mail shortly after the closing meeting. Repeat the expectations and next steps.

We're nearly done, thought Greg. He had presented his draft results in the closing meeting. There had been almost no discussion. Everybody had seemed to accept what he had figured out. His recommendations had also been well received. The day after the closing meeting, he sent the draft report. He thanked everybody for the constructive audit, and asked them to reply to the report as he had explained in the meeting the day before.

Right after sending the e-mail, he received the first responses. "What exactly are we supposed to do?" some people asked. Others wanted to know what will happen with the report. "Can I distribute the report already?"

Greg did not understand these replies. Hadn't he explained all these questions already in the closing meeting? Why did he bother holding a closing meeting if nobody was listening? For a moment, Greg became pretty angry. But after a while he noticed his own mistake. He should have explained the next steps and his expectations to the participants again in his e-mail. He had wasted the opportunity!

13.4.2 During Interviews

13.4.2.1 Establish a Comfort Zone at the Beginning

When people first have contact with Software Sustainability Audits, they are nervous. You will notice this in the interviews. They are very careful about what they say. Nobody wants to give away too much. Everybody is curious about what will happen in the next 60 or 90 min. Creating a safe territory is always a good starting point. Why not recap on the process that you described in the opening meeting? The interviewees remember the context and warm up quickly.

13.4.2.2 Create an Open Atmosphere

The usual interview techniques also apply to Software Sustainability Audit interviews. Keep the number of closed questions to a minimum, and only use them to verify observations, where a yes/no answer can be helpful. In all other cases, lead the discussion with "why", "who", "what", "where", "how", and so on. You will be amazed by how much information you receive without asking for it specifically. If you leave your questionnaire on your desk and let the discussion flow, you will usually get a much better understanding of the situation. When people are given the freedom to talk, they will talk. Acknowledge this, and don't put too much pressure on interviewees to answer the question you have in mind. It's better to let the conversation flow for a while, and let the interviewees choose the direction. As we saw earlier, others' priorities are your priorities. Allow this open atmosphere. Allow the interviewees to set their own priorities – for a while.

Nevertheless, keep your scope in mind. When you notice that the conversation has veered too far away from the boundaries of the audit, you need to bring it back into focus. The best recipe for interrupting a monolog is to rephrase what you have understood so far. Ask for confirmation, and then add a question that brings you back to your scope.

A good open interview is a balance of letting people talk and getting them back on track. Whenever you sense your scope is at risk, remember the questionnaire you have prepared.

13.4.2.3 Identify Anchors for Root Causes

When Gregory conducted his first Software Sustainability Audit, he was unsure that he was getting the relevant information. The colleagues talked and talked, and he made a lot of notes during the interviews. After each interview, he tried to summarize what he had understood. And he felt even more uncomfortable when he put all the pieces together.

What did the developer Jim mean when he said that his manager supported the architecture? How did his manager support the architecture? Was this a polite phrase showing loyalty? It would be interesting to hear what the manager was doing to support the architecture.

And when Jim mentioned that their architecture team was better than the architecture teams in other areas, which areas did he have in mind? And what was this comparison based on? I should have asked him, thought Greg.

In many Software Sustainability Audits, you will still have some questions at the end when you prepare your final report. Sometimes you will still have time to arrange a meeting. In most cases, though, it is just too late. You have to make the most of the information you have.

However, the lessons from NLP offer some hints on how you can improve the quality of the information you get during interviews. You can train you mind to be alert whenever you notice "surface" information instead of depth. The linguistic theory from NLP can give you valuable guidance on how to dig deeper.

13.4.2.4 Step 1: Acknowledge Surface

We know that generalization, deformation, replacement, and deletion are operations that transform a "deep" statement into a more superficial "surface" statement. But how can you spot these linguistic operations? One way is to watch out for typical phrases that indicate the transformations:

- Non specific nouns: *All* projects ...
- Non-specific verbs: Help, support, ...
- Comparisons: Compared to the other project ...
- Evaluating adjectives and adverbs: Obviously, incorrectly, unclear ...

13.4.2.5 Step 2: Dig Deeper

Once you have identified a statement that lies on the surface, interrupt and ask further questions.

1. *Non-specific Nouns*: "An architect" or "all architects" are good examples. Another common formulation is something like "The architect's job is ..."? Does this mean all architects, or does the interviewee have a specific group of colleagues in mind? Is there a formal job description for architects? Or are certain expectations associated with the architect's role? Expected by whom?
2. *Non-specific Verbs*: "She helped me", or "the manager supported us". Do you know what kind of help or support was given? What does the interviewee consider as help or support?
3. *Comparisons*: "Our team is better than the other team." "The quality of our architecture is better." Compared to what? How is quality measured? Who compared the quality?
4. *Evaluations*: "Obviously ..." For whom is it obvious? What facts make it obvious?

13.4.3 When Reporting

We call our reporting style "non-violent communication of our findings". Rosenberg's NVC helps us to structure communication and avoid communication blocks, or even to resolve conflicts. It is an answer to Schulz-von-Thun's analysis about the four sides of a statement, and improves the quality of communication by helping us to articulate clear messages.

We propose adapting the non-violent communication model (NVC [9]) to Software Sustainability Audits. Rather than "observations", we talk about "findings", which stand for all the essential information we have learned from a Software Sustainability Audit. We combine these findings with consulting services, which we call "recommendations", and communicate them using the NVC principles. We clearly separate the finding as a non-evaluative observation. We replace the original "feeling" segment with the "risk" for the company or department. In our context, the "needs" are represented by the potential "business impact", which reflects the company's needs. And we conclude with clear but open "recommendations", similar to NVC's "requests". Figure 13.4 shows our proposed adaptation of Rosenberg's non-violent communication model.

Finding: A finding describes what we have observed. We explain what we have understood in interviews, or what we have found out by reading relevant documents. This is a critical entry point, where the non-judgmental format is crucial. We can fully follow NVC guidance on how to formulate non-evaluative observations. In Software Sustainability Audits, we are particularly vulnerable to generalization. As architects, we always tend to present the big picture. In Software Sustainability Audits, it is also helpful to describe the context, not only to explain individual parts of the picture, but also how they fit in. However, our first attempts often lead to generalizations of the pure observation. While straight observations are rarely disputed, generalizations can trigger emotions and lead to heated arguments.

Risk: Having shared our observation, we look at the risk to the company. In the end, management needs to decide whether to take the risk or to mitigate the risk. Typically, the risks that auditors consider to be critical are evidenced in a Software

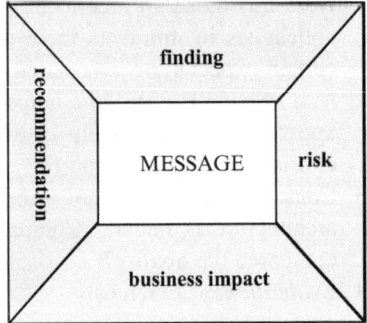

Fig. 13.4 Rosenberg's non-violent communication model, adapted to software sustainability audit reporting

Sustainability Audit report. This means that the auditor strongly advises mitigating the risk.

Impact: While the risk describes what can happen, the impact refers to the business impact. The impact depends on the business case for proposed activities in the future. As such, the impact addresses the potential situation the company will face if the risk event actually occurs. It is like a threat to a "need" the company has.

Recommendation: Risks and impacts are straightforward. Recommendations, however, carry communication risks. Recommendations are seen as consulting services. As such, they have two opposing objectives. On the one hand, the advice should be clear. It is most valuable when it is specific, rather than just a vague pointer. By giving additional advice on how to resolve the situation, you can give the audit the flavor of a professional consulting service. On the other hand, managers like to make their own decisions. In the end, they are the best judge of their situation, and can balance the issues with other aspects they have in mind. Hence, recommendations should offer clear guidance, but at the same time leave open alternative paths of action, giving managers the freedom to choose the most suitable approach themselves. Getting back to non-violent communication, recommendations should be structured and phrased like requests. You should request clear actions, but not make demands.

13.4.4 In Closing Meetings

> *"It is done." Gregory thought as he prepared for the closing meeting. Most of the work is done. The draft report has been written. He just has to present the results. And once the others have agreed, he can send the final report.*
> *"Almost finished" Greg said to himself, and opened his final meeting. He started to introduce his first finding.*
> *"This is incredible!" cried one of the managers. "You are completely wrong!"*
> *"Something must have gone wrong." Greg thought.*

13.4.4.1 No Surprises, Please!

Managers do not like surprises. And even less so if they are confronted with surprises at a meeting with a broader audience. If you want a smooth closing meeting, then anticipate the managers' feelings. Don't overwhelm them with new facts. Before you invite everybody to an official closing meeting, get hold of the managers affected, and explain your findings to them individually. This makes it much easier to deal with any emotions and clarify all potential questions and concerns. Try to get an unofficial agreement upfront.

13.4.4.2 And the Next Steps Are ...

It will take some time to get agreement from all the colleagues who are assigned to recommended activities. And everybody will be curious during this period. "What happens now? I haven't heard anything for a long time." The people involved will get nervous. "Are there any covert activities?" It is helpful to keep the participants in the loop. Make them aware of whatever will happen, and what response you will expect from them. Your first opportunity is the closing meeting. Tell the participants clearly what the next steps are. Explain what you expect. It might be trivial for the auditors. The Software Sustainability Auditors know the process inside out. But the participants are not used to it. Make it clear that you expect them to comment on and agree to the findings. Explain that the final report might take some time, because you need acceptance from everybody for all the findings. It's better to explain the next steps at least twice.

13.4.4.3 Give Me Advice and Respect My Authority!
The final report should make clear recommendations for all the findings. However, at the closing meeting, business owners and managers might be overwhelmed by strict guidance. We propose a two-step approach: In the closing meeting, focus on the findings. Hint at the recommended activities, but allow room for feedback. Later on, when you add clear recommendations to the draft report, incorporate any feedback you received during the closing meeting or afterwards.

13.5   Summary

In this chapter, we left the procedures and frameworks of Software Sustainability Audits, and paused to talk about effective communication. You have learned the two approaches an auditor can take, acting as the police, or as an advisor. You now understand why communication is a vital component of effective Software Sustainability Audits. You have refreshed or learned important communication principles and how to adopt them in Software Sustainability Audits. We hope that we have inspired you to learn more about communication theory.

References

1. Andreas, S., Faulkner, C., & Praxiskurs, N. L. P. (2007). *Ängste überwinden und neue Überzeugungen entwickeln.* Paderborn: Junfermann Verlag. ISBN 978-3-87387-335-3.
2. Bandler, R., & Grinder, J. (2001). *Metasprache und Psychotherapie, Die Struktur der Magie I.* Paderborn: Junfermann Verlag. ISBN 3-87387-186-6.
3. Certification Information System Auditor (CISA) (2010). Review Manual, KS1.8.
4. Chong, D. K., & Smith-Chong, J. K. (1995). *Frag nicht warum …, Zur Struktur der Wirklichkeit und der Erweiterung unserer Fähigkeit.* Paderborn: Junfermann Verlag. ISBN 3-87387-145-9.
5. Fisher, R., Ury, W., & Patton, B. (2009). *Das Harvard Konzept.* Frankfurt/New York: Campus Verlag. ISBN 978-3-593-38982-0.
6. Fisher, R., Ury, W., & Patton, B. (2011). *Getting to Yes, Negotiating agreement without giving in.* Boston/New York: Penguin. ISBN 978-0-14-311875-6.
7. Jochims, I. (2010). *NLP für Profis, Glaubensätze & Sprachmodelle.* Norderstedt: Books on Demand GmbH. ISBN 978-3-8391-9874-2.

8. Joseph O'Connor, John Seymour (2009). Neurolinguistisches Programmieren: Gelungene Kommunikation und persönliche Entfaltung, VAK Verlags GmbH Kirchzarten bei Freiburg, ISBN 978-3-924077-66-2.

9. Marshall B. Rosenberg, Gewaltfreie Kommunikation, Eine Sprache des Lebens, Junfermann Verlag Paderborn, ISBN 978-387387-454-1

10. Friedemann Schulz von Thun (2009). Miteinander Reden 2, Werte und Persönlichkeitsentwicklung, Rowohlt Taschenbuch Verlag, Reinbek bei Hamburg, ISBN 978-3-499-18496-3.

11. Friedemann Schulz von Thun (2009). Miteinander Reden 1, Das "innere Team" und situationsgerechte Kommunikation, Rowohlt Taschenbuch Verlag, Reinbek bei Hamburg, ISBN 978-3-499-60545-1.

12. Friedemann Schulz von Thun (2009). Miteinander Reden, Kommunikationspsychologie für Führungskräfte, Rowohlt Taschenbuch Verlag, Reinbek bei Hamburg, ISBN 978-3-499-61531-3.

13. Friedemann Schulz von Thun (2009). Miteinander Reden 1, Störungen und Klärungen, Rowohlt Taschenbuch Verlag, Reinbek bei Hamburg, ISBN 978-3-499-17489-6.

The Authors

Dr. Roger Gutbrod is *Ombudsman for Development* and *Vice President* for SAP Architecture Audits at SAP AG in Walldorf, Germany, roger.gutbrod@t-online.de.

Dr. Roger Gutbrod studied Mathematics and Computer Science at University Würzburg. He joined SAP in 1991 as developer for financial applications. He has held various positions as a software developer, project lead, people manager, and chief architect. He has contributed to many customer projects and was responsible for many activities in industry tailored solutions, which gave him many insights in different aspects of software architecture.

R. Gutbrod and C. Wiele, *The Software Dilemma,* Management for Professionals,
DOI 10.1007/978-3-642-27236-3, © Springer-Verlag Berlin Heidelberg 2012

Dr. Christian Wiele is *Chief Development Architect* for SAP Architecture Audits at SAP AG in Walldorf, Germany, christian@expectrain.com, http://expectrain.com.

Dr. Christian Wiele studied Physics at the University of Kiel and Marburg, and received a Ph.D. from the University of Essen. He joined SAP in 1999 as technology consultant. His various positions in pre-sales support and as chief architect in development provided the basis and the experience to help establishing the new concept of SAP Architecture Audits. He enjoys thinking about difficult problems, and is interested in physics, complexity theory, and music.

Index

R. Gutbrod and C. Wiele, *The Software Dilemma*, Management for Professionals,
DOI 10.1007/978-3-642-27236-3, © Springer-Verlag Berlin Heidelberg 2012